GW00322485

Why this book was written

Soon after the publication of my first book, *Gliding*, it became obvious that, although it was a valuable reference book, it gave the beginner very little real assistance with his personal problems in learning to glide. Knowing what has to be done is far from being able to do it, particularly in flying.

Most of this book has been written to help the beginner and his instructor to see how to make learning to glide easier.

I expect that some readers will be disappointed to find so little about soaring techniques. However, the basic principles of soaring are in my previous book and there have been few improvements over the years except for better gliders and glider instruments.

I hope that this book will help many pilots to fly more efficiently and safely, and that they will enjoy reading it.

Derek Piggott

By the same author
Gliding: A Handbook on Soaring Flight

Beginning Gliding

The Fundamentals of Soaring Flight

Derek Piggott

ADAM AND CHARLES BLACK
LONDON

First published 1975
A & C Black Limited
4, 5 & 6 Soho Square, London W1V 6AD

ISBN 0 7136 1578 8

Printed and bound in Great Britain by
Morrison & Gibb Ltd., London and Edinburgh

Contents

List of illustrations   6

Introduction   9

 1   Is Gliding for You?   11
 2   The Glider and Your First Flights   23
 3   Learning to Glide   34
 4   Help with the Landings   54
 5   Spoiling the Gliding Angle   77
 6   Using the Airbrakes   89
 7   Planning the Approach and Landing   102
 8   Stalling and Spinning   135
 9   The Effects of the Wind   147
10   Aerotowing   173
11   Advice for Power Pilots Converting to Glider Flying   190

Appendixes

A   The Yates Effect   198
B   Gliding Awards and Records   200
C   Conversion Tables   203

Index   205

Photographs

between pages 88–89

Typical cockpit layouts of an ASK 13 two-seater training glider and a Kestrel high-performance sailplane

ASK 13 two-seater training glider and Caproni Calif high-performance two-seater sailplane

19 metre all glass fibre construction Kestrel sailplane and a Kestrel with tail parachute deployed

Typical two-drum winch and preparations for an aerotow at the launch point

Figures

1	Parts of a glider	14
2	Handling on the ground	18
3	Danger areas on a gliding site	21
4	Flying attitudes	24
5	Pitching	24
6	Banking	26
7	Yawing	27
8	Big Dipper	28
9	Chair-o-plane	29
10	Sensation of sideslipping	33
11	Aileron drag	39
12	Slipping and skidding in a turn	40
13	Control movements for a turn	42
14	Limitations on the circuit	47
15	Circuit planning	50
16	Styles of landing	55
17	Variations in landing characteristics	57
18	Aids to judging height	61
19	Changing perspective views	62
20	Perfect landing	67
21	Round out	69
22	Directional control when wheel is ahead of C of G	74
23	Directional control when wheel is behind C of G	75
24	Sideslipping	78
25	Spoilers	79
26	Airbrakes and geometric lock	81
27	Types of airbrakes and flaps	83
28	Comparison between effect of airbrakes and flaps	84
29	Various uses of airbrakes	90
30	Stretching the glide	94
31	Closing airbrakes to prevent a heavy landing	97
32	Controlling the approach and landing	104
33	Effects of changing the attitude	106
34	Aiming point technique	107
35	Detecting over- and undershooting	108
36	'Play it safe' method of approach	109
37	Approach angles	110

38	Judgement and the angle of approach	112
39	The 'clutching hand' effect	113
40	Height and distance method of approach	118
41	Angle method of positioning final approach	120
42	Wire frame training aid for landing	122
43a } 43b }	Running out of height on circuit	124
44	Running out of height and speed	125
45	Loss of height in sinking air	126
46	Integrated power flying and gliding	127
47	Effect of bank on height lost in a turn	132
48	Airflow in normal and stalled flight	134
49	Stalling and the centre of pressure movements in flight	136
50	Speed and angle of attack in flight	137
51	Variations of stalling speed in turns	137
52	Lateral damping	138
53	Autorotation	139
54	Full spin and spiral dive	141
55	Full spin and recovery	143
56	Spinning off an over-ruddered turn	145
57	Blocks of air	148
58	Landing into and with the wind	150
59	Track over the ground while circling in strong wind	151
60	Turning onto base leg in strong wind	151
61	Drifting across wind	153
62	Wind gradient	154
63	Veering and backing	155
64	Effect of wind gradient	156
65	Effect of wind gradient on a low turn	158
66	Lee waves and turbulent flow	160
67	Exchanging height for speed	162
68	The result of the Yates effect	163
69	Formation of thermal bubbles	164
70	Cross-section of thermal bubble	165
71	Inflow and outflow in a thermal	166
72	Circling near a hill	167
73	Dynamic soaring	169
74	Path of a model aircraft in still air and in wind	171
75	Normal aerotow position	175
76	Keeping station on aerotow using a sighting mark	176
77	Weaving on aerotow	178
78	Getting back into position on aerotow	179
79	Rope break on aerotow	184
80	Rope break procedure	185
81	The wave off	187
82	Airbrakes open on tow	188
83	The Yates effect	199

Introduction

In Britain it is customary to use the word *glider* whereas in many other countries the same aircraft are more commonly known as *sailplanes*. Both are correct.

By definition, every motorless aircraft is a glider, but a sailplane is a glider for soaring flight. Most of us visualise a sailplane as a beautifully designed modern machine but even a Primary glider or the Rogallo type of hang glider is really a sailplane since it is designed for, and is capable of, long soaring flights. Probably the only gliders which are not sailplanes are some of the flying devices which are dropped from high flying aircraft for research purposes and, of course, the heavy military troop-carrying gliders of the Second World War.

For the purposes of this book I prefer to use the word *glide* in connection with learning to fly a glider or sailplane. Soaring is only one aspect of gliding and is by no means the most important. Safe gliding is a matter of basic flying skills and an understanding of glider flying. These are the foundations of soaring flight.

Many readers will not be familiar with the use of knots (nautical miles per hour) as a unit of speed in connection with flying. A knot is almost exactly 100 feet per minute and this makes it particularly useful for glider flying where the pilot may want to estimate his gliding angle quickly. For example, a rate of descent of 2 knots at a speed of 60 knots indicates a gliding angle of 1 : 30 in no wind. The same calculation with the variometer calibrated in feet or metres a second and speeds of miles or kilometres per hour requires a mental calculation involving multiplying by 60 twice, and this is not practical for the average pilot in flight.

It seems probable that in spite of the move towards metrication, discriminating glider pilots will continue to use knots and nautical miles for measurement, at least in countries where heights are referred to in hundreds and thousands of feet. The nautical mile has the added advantage of being one minute of latitude and this enables a pilot to measure or estimate distances on any map or chart by referring to the distance between lines of latitude, instead of having to find the scale – which may be inaccessible at the time.

Conversion tables are given in Appendix C.

1 Is Gliding for You?

Age	12	Deafness	17
Nervousness	14	Height and weight	17
Intelligence	15	Day-to-day fitness	19
Health	15	Colds	20
Eyesight	16	Menstrual periods	20
Disabilities	16		

If you are interested in becoming a glider pilot, the first thing you should do is to go along to a gliding club and have at least one flight to see what it feels like. (Read about first-flight sensations beforehand so you know what to expect – see Chapter 2.) It is always possible for a prospective member to have a flight before making the decision to join as a full member or attend a course of instruction. This will involve spending most of the day at the club and will give you a chance to chat to other beginners and meet their instructors.

Gliding instruction can be a very tedious and frustrating business, especially if there are a large number of beginners and only limited facilities. You should, therefore, try to talk to the other beginners to find out how much flying they actually manage to get, and how long it takes to reach solo standard. If you ask the older and more experienced members you will probably just be told how much better the facilities are than they were when they learnt to glide. This is cold comfort if a good day's flying is only one short glider flight, especially if you have arrived before nine o'clock in the morning and stayed on pushing gliders until dusk.

If you are within reach of several gliding clubs, you should visit them all and try to get a flight at each one. Before joining one, consider carefully what each offers.

If you get a regular time off on weekdays, or intend to spend your holidays gliding, it will be worth travelling a little further to a bigger club operating on a full-time basis. Large clubs tend to be rather less personal, but have the advantage that there is usually more equipment of all kinds so that a minor mishap does not stop all flying. If the club has a motor glider for training, the whole process of learning will be speeded up, for a motor glider is capable of doing two or three times as much training as a two-seater glider and is not dependent on winches or tow cars.

If you will be doing all your flying at weekends, the nearest club will probably be the most attractive. But before you actually pay an entrance fee and a year's subscription, consider carefully. Are you prepared to spend at least one whole day every fortnight at the gliding site during the period it will take you to learn to glide? Your answer will depend on the amount of flying you can get each time you go gliding and on how valuable your spare time is to you.

Alternatively, can you afford the time and money to have several weeks' continuous training on a gliding course? This is usually a far more efficient way of learning if you can set aside the time to do it. Some clubs run concentrated training courses on both motor and ordinary gliders, whereas others run Holiday Courses, designed for pleasure rather than instruction.

If you are uncertain whether you really want to glide, a Holiday Course may be attractive as the training is usually taken less seriously. A week on a gliding site having a few flights each day makes a novel kind of holiday and gives you a chance to see if you really like flying.

An up-to-date list of gliding clubs and gliding courses can be obtained from the British Gliding Association, or, in other countries, usually from the National Gliding Association or the National Aero Club concerned. If you have never been up in a glider and have just picked up this book to see what it is all about, one of the first questions you will find yourself asking is, 'could I learn to glide?' The answer is almost certainly yes, but it is worth discussing some of the problems and doubts you may have.

Age In the United Kingdom, the minimum age for flying solo in a glider is sixteen, compared with seventeen for a motor glider or light aircraft. Personally, I would not encourage any young person to start serious flying training until they are nearly old enough to go solo. There is a real risk that they will become frustrated, as everyone else, learning at the same time and no more competent, is going off solo. Although many young people are very mature in their outlook, others are not. A small number are quite incapable of concentrating for more than a few minutes while in the air and any serious training is largely wasted on them. However, young people who are interested should be encouraged to make a start by flying a few times a year until they are nearly old enough to solo.

Probably the best age for learning to fly for most people is between eighteen and twenty-five. However, there are many students up to the age of fifty learning to fly, and really there is no definite limit.

It is possible to go on gliding to a ripe old age but this is not always wise. Most old, experienced glider pilots seem gradually to lose their critical sense and fail to realise that they are beginning to become a danger to themselves and perhaps to others. Probably because they lose their concentration, they tend to find themselves suddenly confronted with an unexpected situation which they ought to have foreseen.

Doctors seem to find difficulty in assessing this gradual slowing down process in a person who in every other way is physically fit. This poses a major embarrassment to gliding instructors who eventually have to tell someone that the time has come to stop flying solo. Not many pilots are really still 'with it' beyond the age of sixty-five and many are too old at fifty.

Learning to fly is a very different matter and, for the majority, even fifty is really too old to start gliding. At this age it is often difficult to learn to co-ordinate hands and feet in the completely new manner required for flying a glider. It also takes much longer to learn to relax and become confident in the new environment. However, the real problem is almost always inconsistencies in performance caused by concentrating on one thing at the expense of all the others.

There are many situations that can occur in a glider which if unchecked lead to serious problems. Some older people seem to have difficulty in thinking clearly and decisively when faced with a sudden, unexpected emergency. This kind of situation does not occur very often with a modern powered machine except in the very unusual event of an engine failure. At any other time, except perhaps in bad weather, the pilot can open the throttle and climb up to give himself time to sort out the difficulty. In this respect the glider pilot is far worse off as he is committed to every landing and can have no second attempt.

Unfortunately, it is not until the final stages of training that an instructor can form a proper assessment about a person's ability to make decisions. Many elderly students are often rather slow learners, so that they need a large number of flights before they master the handling well enough to make a start on the planning of each flight. It is not really enough to be able to get up and fly a rigid circuit pattern satisfactorily. To be safe, the pilot must be able to cope with every possible situation that may occur. Often, these students learn to deal with a situation on one day, only to forget completely about it on the next. This kind of problem is a greater worry to an instructor than anything else. Even when every possibility seems to have been covered by instruction and the pilot has been checked and rechecked to make sure that he is safe, the unexpected may happen and the instructor can only blame himself for not stopping the pilot earlier.

Very slow learners do eventually learn to *fly* the glider safely, but these are usually people with slow reactions who cannot give their attention to more than one or two things at a time. It is always a great disappointment to both the instructor and the student to have to give up the idea of solo flying, particularly after a long battle to master the technique. In the end it is a matter of whether the student can fly and think logically and quickly at the same time.

Usually, these slow learners are the keenest and most willing helpers on the gliding site and with luck, they will still find a special niche for themselves in their club. Once they have accepted their limitations, they can continue flying without the constant psychological pressure which may well have spoilt their enjoyment previously. It is ideal if they can join a two-seater syndicate so that they fly with a friend who can get to know their flying and act as a safety pilot.

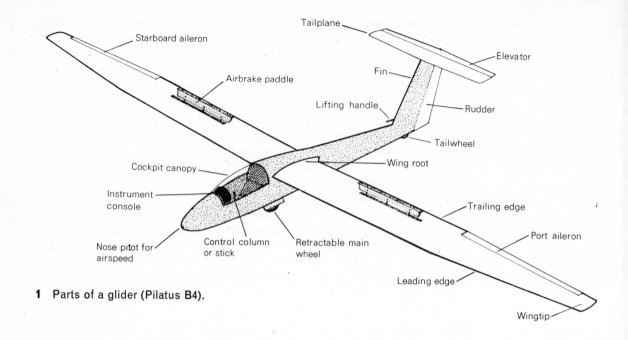

Starboard aileron

Tailplane

Elevator

Airbrake paddle

Fin

Rudder

Lifting handle

Tailwheel

Cockpit canopy

Wing root

Instrument console

Trailing edge

Nose pitot for airspeed

Control column or stick

Retractable main wheel

Port aileron

Leading edge

Wingtip

1 Parts of a glider (Pilatus B4).

The policy of gliding clubs varies considerably from place to place. At Lasham, I have always taken the view that the Centre is there to train pilots and to give enjoyment and recreation to the members. We have several pilots who continue to fly dual although they know that they will not be able to fly solo. Within reason, they are just as worthy a cause as the potential pundit. Providing that they enjoy their flying, I feel that they are always an asset rather than a liability to the gliding movement.

Nervousness   It is quite normal to be nervous at first and this will only really disappear after a number of flights. If you have a nervous temperament and, for example, have found it impossible to learn to drive a car confidently, it will take a long time for you to learn to glide and you will probably not enjoy it. People who are under any treatment for a nervous or mental problem should not start to learn to fly without both the agreement of their medical adviser and the Chief Flying Instructor (C.F.I.) of the club.

It is particularly important to ask your doctor if any medicines or drugs you are taking have side effects which could be serious when flying. You are not a fit person to fly solo if you need tranquillisers to calm your nerves before you go up! You need all your faculties for safe flying and there should be no question of flying after drinking even small amounts of alcohol.

If you are rather nervous and tend to panic, this will make your training longer. You will need to understand what you are doing in much greater detail than the average pupil so that nothing can happen which you do not understand or which has not happened before. Again, the instructor will be unable to tell you whether you will overcome this problem until near the end of the training, so do not bother to ask him after one or two flights.

Looking back over the thousands of students I have helped teach to glide, some of the most rewarding have been those with special problems, particularly nervousness.

I remember especially a middle-aged lady and her first few flights in the Falke Motor Glider. She literally clung to my leg and cried out in terror every time that we banked even slightly. I admit I was slightly surprised when she announced her intention of joining the club as a full member. However, gradually she overcame this fear, until after about five or six weeks of flying once or twice a week, we were able to start practice stalls and even incipient spins. Each new experience was a traumatic one for her and a new psychological problem for me to overcome. At last came the day when I could sit back and ask her to fly me around without any bogies left. I remember every detail of her first solo and how proud she was to have mastered the art of flying and become a really relaxed pilot at last.

However, she was probably the exception to the general rule that the very nervous person seldom makes a good pilot.

Intelligence – how bright do I need to be?

A good instructor can explain everything you need to know in order to learn to glide and become a good soaring pilot in plain language that a child of twelve could understand. No technical, and certainly no mathematical, knowledge is required. Perhaps being able to read and look things up for yourself is the only advantage any education will give you.

The main essential is to be reasonably quick-witted and to want to learn badly enough to persist until you have mastered the art. Motivation is probably more important than innate ability.

Health

Gliding will always involve a certain amount of physical work and of standing about in all weathers on a cold airfield or hilltop. It can never be just a matter of climbing into a glider, flying it, and then going away again without giving some sort of help. However, we are not all blessed with perfect health. Apart from pushing and launching gliders, there are plenty of other ways in which we can pull our weight as a club member.

Most people are fit to glide. However, you should not fly if you suffer from any kind of epilepsy, giddiness, fainting fits or sudden migraine. Diabetics and people who have suffered coronary problems *may* be fit enough but must consult their doctor and the C.F.I. of the club before learning to glide.

If you have suffered from a slipped disc, you will have to be careful. You should never carry the tail of the glider as it may only require a jerk or twist to set you back many months. It is safest to take the wingtip or push on the nose.

Hay fever is another serious problem on gliding sites. In the summer when the soaring conditions are good, the pollen count is at its highest and if you suffer from hay fever, you may find that you have to give up flying. Once in the air and above 2000 or 3000 feet, the air is much cleaner than on the ground and you may find relief from your suffering. Asthma is also helped by flying at height. Unfortunately, most of the drugs used to relieve both hay fever and asthma can seriously upset a pilot's concentration and judgement.

Eyesight The need to wear glasses is no bar to flying gliders, or in some cases, to holding a Private Pilot's Licence. It is essential for safety to be able to see well enough to spot other aircraft at a distance since you may meet them at closing speeds of several hundred miles an hour.

Poor eyesight can cause serious learning problems, particularly if you have only one eye, or have one with very poor sight. Serious muscular defects and double vision cause difficulties when learning to land and these may prove insurmountable in some cases. Normal colour vision is not necessary for gliding but is usually required for power licences. (It is sometimes possible to obtain a concession, especially if you can show that the defect has caused no problems when flying gliders.)

The minimum standard suggested by the British Gliding Association for eyesight is the minimum for driving a motor car. (Must be able to read a car number plate at 25 yards – corrective glasses may be used.) If you normally fly with your spectacles you should always carry a spare pair in case of loss or breakage during flight.

Disabilities To the disabled person, a disability is just an inconvenience which a little ingenuity will overcome. It is quite remarkable how quickly a way can be found round most difficulties.

For example, one of my beginners had lost one arm at the shoulder. To my astonishment he soon found how to hold the stick between his knees near the top of the wire launch in order to be able to use his one good arm to pull the cable release. Later he adapted his circuit planning to allow him to open the airbrakes fully at the top of the approach, again holding the stick between his legs. In this way he could make a normal landing without difficulty. Later he devised a CO_2 operated device to open and close the brakes on the K8. By means of a lever on the stick he could operate both the stick and airbrakes with one good hand. This was reasonably safe for winch or car launching but could have been highly dangerous for aerotowing if anything went wrong. A further aid would have been needed to allow him to release immediately without taking his hand off the controls. Otherwise solo aerotowing could never be really safe either for him or for the tug pilot.

A certain minimum amount of strength is needed to use the controls and this presents an insurmountable problem to people who are partially paralysed. However, with all disabilities the only thing is to try flying the glider and find out how serious your particular problem is going to be.

16

One-legged pilots *may* be able to work the rudder, but any artificial leg must be secured to the rudder pedal so that it cannot slip across and cause a jam. In flight, the leg can mostly be helped with a hand to reduce the effort, but it is important that full rudder can be applied at all normal speeds.

Many of the situations which cause difficulties can be foreseen and avoided with experience. Nevertheless, it is often better for everyone if the disabled person can accept the idea of learning to glide and of then sharing his flying with another pilot in a two-seater, rather than flying solo.

Deafness   Deafness is hardly a disability on its own, it is just another challenge to the instructor. Most completely deaf people rely to a great extent on lip-reading, so that the essential facts can still be explained provided they are combined with plenty of drawings and demonstrations with a model. The instructor has to be particularly thorough in order to make sure, by practical tests in the air, that his student has grasped all the ideas which have been talked about in the briefings.

Side-by-side seating is essential when teaching a completely deaf person and the instructor must learn that it is no good offering advice during the flight. In particular, it is vital not to talk at all during the approach and landing. If the student sees that the instructor is talking to him, he will instinctively turn round to try to lip-read. This can be disastrous on the final approach!

Both deaf people and people with very poor eyesight are a serious danger to themselves and others on the field. They may not be aware of gliders and powered aircraft coming in to land near them and they may not hear warning shouts or see the danger. If possible, they should be encouraged to wear conspicuous clothes so that pilots and club members recognise them and realise their limitations. The dangers of propellers and winch cables should be explained to them before they are left alone at the launch point.

Height and weight   The cockpits of gliders are usually designed to suit a fair range of average-sized pilots. This means that if you are either very small, very fat, or very tall, they are either fiendishly uncomfortable or impossible.

Small pilots need extra packing on the seat and behind them in order to reach the controls easily. Usually they will weigh less than the minimum permissible, normally about 150 lb (68 kilos), and will have to carry additional ballast as well as wear a parachute, which weighs about 20 lb.

The ballast can be in the form of weighted cushions fixed to the seat so that they cannot move forward onto the controls. The minimum cockpit load is critical because the glider may be unstable if there is insufficient load and it is tail-heavy. The situation is difficult if you are a small woman who weighs only 90 lb. You would need 50 lb of ballast and a parachute to fly safely! (My own advice is to make sure you find an admiring enthusiast to carry the ballast for you – you will not carry that weight far.)

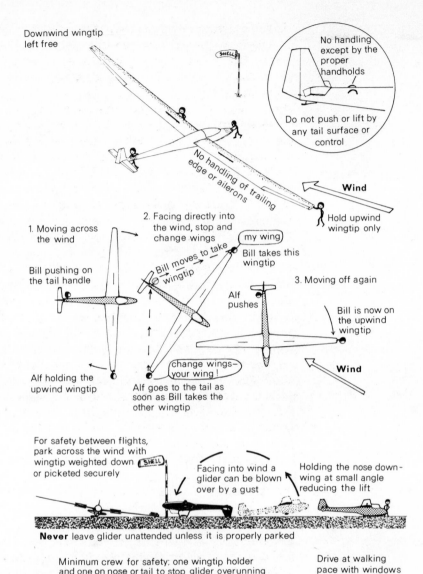

Downwind wingtip left free

No handling except by the proper handholds

Do not push or lift by any tail surface or control

SHELL

No handling of trailing edge or ailerons

Wind

Hold upwind wingtip only

1. Moving across the wind

Bill pushing on the tail handle

2. Facing directly into the wind, stop and change wings

Bill moves to take wingtip

my wing

Bill takes this wingtip

3. Moving off again

Alf pushes

Bill is now on the upwind wingtip

Alf holding the upwind wingtip

change wings— your wing!

Alf goes to the tail as soon as Bill takes the other wingtip

Wind

For safety between flights, park across the wind with wingtip weighted down or picketed securely

SHELL

Facing into wind a glider can be blown over by a gust

Holding the nose down - wing at small angle reducing the lift

Never leave glider unattended unless it is properly parked

Minimum crew for safety; one wingtip holder and one on nose or tail to stop glider overrunning into car   either   or

Drive at walking pace with windows open to listen for instructions

Tow rope at least 15 feet long

2 Gliders must be handled correctly on the ground or they can easily be damaged.

If you are very short, you may even need special thickened shoes to give you longer legs to reach the rudder pedals easily. An old pair of shoes with an extra sole of thick plywood glued onto them will do. It is essential to be able to apply full rudder in both directions without having to stretch your leg out straight.

Short fat people are the most difficult to cater for. Without blocks on their shoes they may find that although they can reach the rudder their stomach gets in the way and prevents them from getting the stick right back. If you are so endowed, make quite sure you can reach all the controls on both two-seaters and solo machines at the club you propose to join.

Many gliders are notoriously short of leg and head room. If you are over 6 feet tall you should make a special point of trying the cockpits of both the dual and solo machines to make sure that you can get into them (before joining the club)! Someone of 6 feet 2 inches is about the maximum that most gliders will accommodate.

It is generally accepted that very heavy pilots will exceed the maximum cockpit load that is stated in the cockpit (about 220 lb). This usually means that the glider will be overloaded so that it would not be wise to do aerobatics or cloud flying. In effect, exceeding this weight limitation downgrades most machines from Semi-Aerobatic (stressed to 5g) to Non-Aerobatic Category (stressed to 4g). For ordinary flying this is not a serious restriction. However, it is wise to consult a senior instructor about the effect on a particular type of machine. On a few modern types the centre of gravity moves too far forward and this causes abnormally high tailplane loads which can be dangerous.

It is wise to keep the maximum flying speed to a figure below the normal limitation in order to restrict the tail loads. (This is no handicap as the glider is not normally flown at high speeds.) The other main risk of damage due to a very heavy pilot is from a slow landing. An extra 5 knots of approach speed is needed to give extra elevator control for the round out and landing. Otherwise there is a risk that the control at lower speed may not be sufficient to overcome the extra nose-heaviness.

Day-to-day fitness   It is surprising how silly many people are when it comes to drinking and driving, or deciding when they should go to bed with a cold.

Flying is much less forgiving than car driving and it is much more a matter of survival than of whether you will lose your licence. Pilots must learn to say *no* flying if they have had even a single alcoholic drink that day. The American accident statistics for light aircraft show conclusively that any alcohol seriously reduces the ability of a pilot to cope with an emergency. In fact, the majority of the pilots involved in serious accidents showed evidence that they had been drinking recently.

The Tiger Club, a famous sport flying club in England, has a little notice in all their machines on the instrument panel. It says **All aircraft bite fools.**

Pilots who fly when they are not feeling absolutely fit are fools. Time and time again after an accident, the pilot reveals that he had not been feeling really well before he took off. Perhaps tired after a particularly heavy week's work and having promised his friends a ride, he had flown against his better judgement. A few drinks, a few aspirins, or a hangover from a party the night before, are real reasons for not flying solo that day. Flying is always simple *until* the unexpected emergency occurs. Then you need all your skill and speed of reaction to avoid an incident and prevent a serious accident.

Colds *Never* fly with a bad cold in the head. Once you are unable to relieve the changes of pressure as you climb and descend, you may do serious damage to your ears. Quite apart from not feeling well and having slower reactions, there is a real risk of either bursting an eardrum or developing a very painful inner ear infection. If you have a cold but feel fit and well, you must not fly unless you are able to clear your ears. As you climb, either in an aircraft or a car on a big hill, you feel the change in atmospheric pressure in your ears. The air pressure outside your eardrum has dropped and the air inside is belling the drum outwards. If the pressure difference becomes too great the drum will perforate or burst. This difference in pressure can be relieved by swallowing hard several times, by moving the jaw forwards and backwards, or by pinching the nose and pressurising it. The partial deafness caused by the difference in pressure bowing the drum should disappear. The inside of the eardrum is connected by the Eustachian Tubes to the back of the throat, and moving the jaw or pinching the nose and blowing helps the air to flow through the tubes to equalise the pressure. If you have a slight cold and are wondering whether you can safely fly, you should be able to clear your ears by either of these methods. There should be a distinctive 'click' from both ears if the tubes are clear. Do not fly on any account if you have even one ear blocked. Ears are delicate things and you really can damage them easily by flying with a cold. I once spent two months recovering from a flight with my ears badly blocked. It was in the war when there was, I suppose, a certain amount of malingering amongst pilots, and I had the misfortune to go sick with my ears absolutely blocked up with a cold. Perhaps rather untactfully, I said to the doctor that I could not possibly fly because my ears were completely blocked. With a typical Service-in-Wartime reaction, he scarcely examined me, gave me a bottle of medicine and ordered me off to fly. My protests only made things worse! Fortunately next day I was able to go home and see my own doctor, but the damage was done. I spent a very miserable time on sick leave, almost completely deaf, and was very lucky not to have any permanent damage.

Menstrual periods Anything which disturbs our judgement and our ability to make decisions is important where flying is concerned. It has recently been realised that some women drivers and pilots are particularly liable to have accidents when they have pre-menstrual tensions. Several women pilots have said that they can

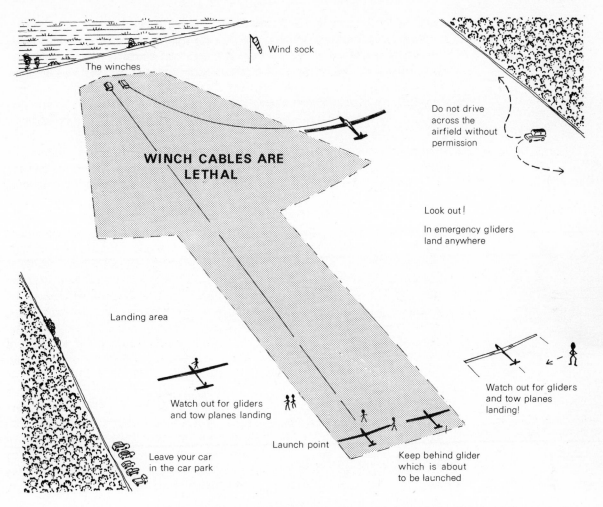

The winches

Wind sock

Do not drive
across the
airfield without
permission

**WINCH CABLES ARE
LETHAL**

Look out!

In emergency gliders
land anywhere

Landing area

Watch out for gliders
and tow planes landing

Watch out for gliders
and tow planes
landing!

Leave your car
in the car park

Launch point

Keep behind glider
which is about
to be launched

3 Danger areas on a gliding site. Always look carefully all round before crossing open spaces where gliders may choose to land in emergency. Keep away from aircraft with their engines running.

notice their flying ability deteriorate during that period, whereas others have no problems.

It is probably wise for inexperienced pilots to stop flying solo at this critical time, and for others who know that they are affected, to limit their flying to tasks which do not require the utmost concentration. It would be wise, for example, to avoid cross-country or contest flying.

Women pilots are certainly not the only ones who have their off days. For example, no one is fit to fly immediately after a flaming row, or if their business or personal problems are bad enough to prevent complete concentration on the flying. Distractions like these are the most common underlying reason for accidents and incidents with aircraft. Usually you are the only person who knows if you are fit to fly on a particular day, and if you are doubtful, fly with someone else rather than risk flying solo.

2 The Glider and Your First Flights

The glider and its controls   23   Changes in 'g' or loading   28
Sensations on your first   Sensations of sideslipping   32
    flights   25

The glider and its controls

The beginner will find it far easier to learn about the controls by going up in an aircraft and experimenting with them. The essential facts are illustrated on the following pages and should enable the reader who has no actual experience of flying to understand the rest of this book.

The controls of a glider are identical to the main controls of any powered aircraft. They consist of a control column, or stick, which moves the elevator and ailerons, and the rudder pedals which move the rudder.

In addition to the main flying controls, there is the airbrake operating lever, the elevator trim lever, the cable release knob, and, on some high performance machines, levers for retracting the main wheel and for operating the wing flaps.

A glider instrument panel has the same basic instruments as any other aircraft but, of course, has no engine instruments. The main instruments are the Airspeed Indicator (known as the A.S.I.), the Altimeter, and the Variometer. The Variometer (vario) is a very sensitive instrument which shows the rate of climb or descent of the glider so that the pilot can find upcurrents and soar. Two typical cockpit layouts are illustrated in Plate 1.

In order to fly efficiently the glider must be held in the correct attitude so that it flies at its best gliding speed. On a clear day, the attitude can be easily judged by the positions of the nose in relation to the horizon ahead. If the nose is held a little too high, the glider will fly too slowly and it will lose height more quickly than normal. A nose-down attitude will also result in a greater loss of height but this time the glider will be diving down and flying at a much higher speed (Fig. 4).

The movements of the stick which produce these changes are more or less instinctive. You always move the stick the way you want the machine to go. Move forward to put the nose down, move back to raise the nose: stick to the left will start the glider rolling over into a bank to the left: in order to bring the wings level again you just lean the stick the way you want the glider to go. Nose up and down movements (as seen from the cockpit) are known as *pitching* movements. Sideways tipping movements are known as *rolling* or banking movements.

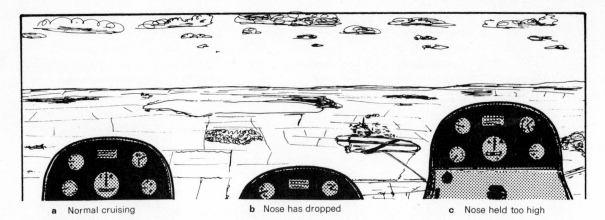

a Normal cruising   **b** Nose has dropped   **c** Nose held too high

4 Watch the position of the nose. **a** The correct position must be memorised. The exact position will depend on the pilot's eye level and will vary according to his height and seat cushions. **b** The nose has dropped. This will result in increased airspeed and rate of descent. **c** The nose is being held too high. The airspeed will be low and the glider will be mushing down losing more height.

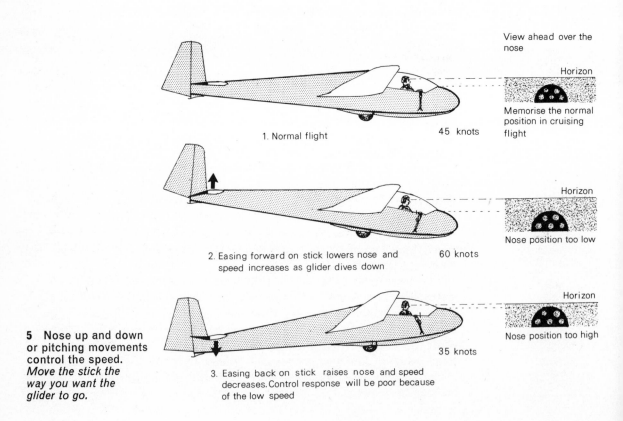

View ahead over the nose

Horizon

Memorise the normal position in cruising flight

1. Normal flight   45 knots

Horizon

Nose position too low

2. Easing forward on stick lowers nose and   60 knots
speed increases as glider dives down

Horizon

Nose position too high

5 Nose up and down or pitching movements control the speed. *Move the stick the way you want the glider to go.*

35 knots

3. Easing back on stick raises nose and speed decreases. Control response will be poor because of the low speed

24

It is important to realise that the size of the sideways movement of the stick controls the *rate* of roll and not the angle of bank. For example, a small movement to the left will start a gradual banking movement to the left which will continue to get steeper and steeper until it is stopped by a centralising movement of the stick. A larger movement to the left would produce a much higher rate of roll but again how steep the bank becomes will depend upon when the control is centralised. (In actual practice there is a tendency for the bank to become steeper during turns and, therefore, the stick has to be moved back just beyond the central position. In most gliders, because of this effect, the final position of the stick in, for example, a turn to the left, will be a little to the right of centre.)

When the rudder is applied, the nose of the glider swings, and the glider skids through the air sideways instead of turning. In fact, the rudder does very little to help the turn except to keep the fuselage of the aircraft in line with the airflow so that it presents the lowest frontal area all the time. Left rudder, that is left foot forward, makes the glider swing to the left. Centralising the rudder again will allow the nose to swing back to the original position. Movements of the aircraft like these are called *yawing* movements.

Sensations on your first flights

Unless you have already spent a considerable time flying as a passenger, you are likely to feel rather tense and nervous during your first few flights as a learner. This is perfectly normal and soon disappears.

The controls of an aeroplane are not nearly as positive as the controls of a car and may at first feel as though they are not properly connected. They vary in effectiveness according to the flying speed, and at low speed the beginner may often wonder whether the aeroplane is still under control. Also, on many days the air has invisible bumps and potholes and it is difficult to be sure at first whether the aircraft has moved because of a bump or a movement on the controls made by the pilot. If possible, choose a day with a light wind and good visibility for a first flight.

Frequently these bumps are sufficiently powerful to delay the effect of a control movement for several seconds and occasionally a bump may coincide with a control movement so that at first the aircraft moves a little in the opposite direction. This is particularly disturbing to the beginner, who may think for a moment that he has made a wrong movement. Alternatively, a small control movement may be assisted by a bump so that an abnormally large change takes place.

Quite naturally, this kind of thing is rather worrying at first, and the aircraft seems a slightly uncontrollable, unwilling beast which threatens to run away out of control at any moment.

In fact, if you do not find it at all worrying to feel a little out of control there is something wrong with your nervous system and you should visit your doctor or give up the idea of learning to fly altogether.

These fears will disappear as you gain experience and learn to respond quickly and to feel in harmony with the controls. Your confidence will then

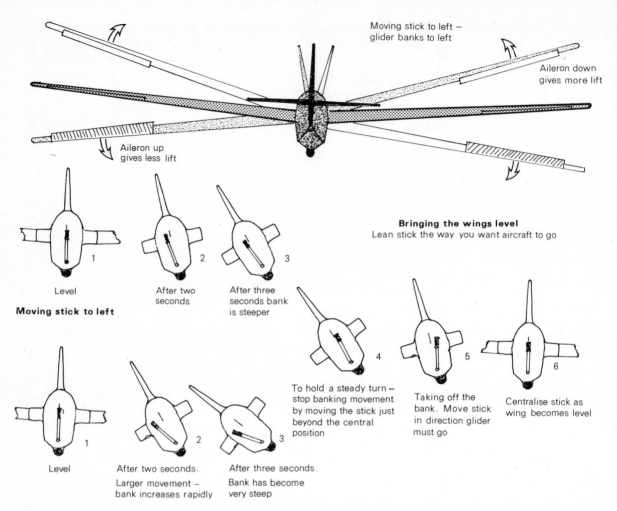

Moving stick to left –
glider banks to left

Aileron down
gives more lift

Aileron up
gives less lift

Moving stick to left

Level · 1

After two
seconds · 2

After three
seconds bank
is steeper · 3

Level · 1

After two seconds.
Larger movement –
bank increases rapidly · 2

After three seconds.
Bank has become
very steep · 3

Bringing the wings level
Lean stick the way you want aircraft to go

To hold a steady turn –
stop banking movement
by moving the stick just
beyond the central
position · 4

Taking off the
bank. Move stick
in direction glider
must go · 5

Centralise stick as
wing becomes level · 6

6 The effect of sideways movements of the stick – banking or rolling. Note that for an accurate turn small rudder and elevator movements are also required. *Lean the stick the way you want the glider to go.*

have the sound foundation of experience and knowledge which is essential for your safety as a pilot.

In these early stages you will also experience some rather disturbing sensations which you had certainly not anticipated in your daydreams about flying. Some of these feelings are a milder version of the various thrill-makers at an amusement park. But whereas you expect that nasty feeling as you zoom over the top of the hump on the Big Dipper there is often little or no warning in a glider and, at first, no apparent reason for the feelings that occur from time to time in flight. Without some explanation these sensations

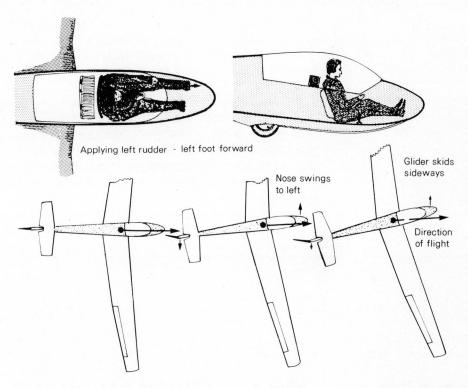

Applying left rudder - left foot forward

Glider skids
sideways

Nose swings
to left

Direction
of flight

7 The effect of the rudder. Moving the left foot forward makes the nose swing to the left. However, after the initial swing, the nose stops swinging even if the rudder is kept on. The glider skids sideways through the air. When the rudder is centralised, the nose swings back almost to the original heading. Unlike the rudder on a boat, the rudder on an aircraft has little real turning effect.

can be very frightening and a few people dislike them so much that even one flight in a glider or small aircraft is one too many! This is a pity because, for the majority of beginners, these sensations are only felt on the very first few flights.

Of course a few people suffer from severe motion sickness and these people are unlikely to want to fly for pleasure. However, just because you have been seasick, or felt ill, in a car or boat it is no reason to expect to be upset in a glider. Whereas a boat has continual movements over which you have no control, there are only occasional bumps in the air on most days and you will learn to counteract them with the controls. If you are rather nervous about your reactions to flying don't be afraid to take a travel sickness pill before your first few flights. Then reduce the dose gradually and soon you will probably find it unnecessary to take anything at all. Most of these preparations seem to have very little adverse effect apart from leaving the mouth rather dry, but, as with all drugs and flying, you should obtain medical advice about which medicines are safe to take since many either tend to put you to sleep or impair your judgement and reactions.

The best safeguard is a better understanding of the sensations which occur so that they do not cause so much worry.

Changes in 'g' or loading

The force of gravity is acting on us all our lives from the moment we are conceived. It is such a normal part of life that it is only if you consciously think about its effects that you notice them. For example: sitting on a chair you can feel the pressure between your bottom and the seat; standing up you can feel the pressure between your feet and the ground. But because these effects of gravity are there all the time, it is only when you think about them that you are aware of them.

This loading of 1g, or gravity, may be temporarily affected by various accelerations. For example, on the Big Dipper at the fair (see Fig. 8) the loading is increased at point A as the car changes direction at the bottom of the slope. You can feel the extra pressure on the seat as the loading or 'g' is

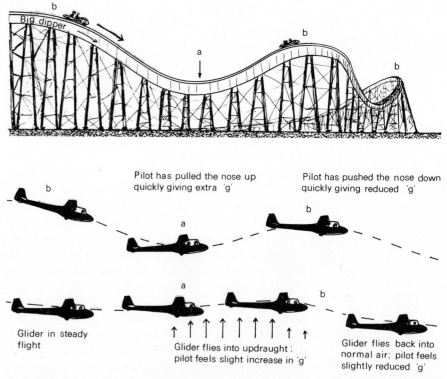

Pilot has pulled the nose up quickly giving extra 'g'

Pilot has pushed the nose down quickly giving reduced 'g'

Glider in steady flight

Glider flies into updraught : pilot feels slight increase in 'g'

Glider flies back into normal air; pilot feels slightly reduced 'g'

8 Variations in 'g' during flight. These may be caused by the pilot moving the stick or by flying through turbulence.

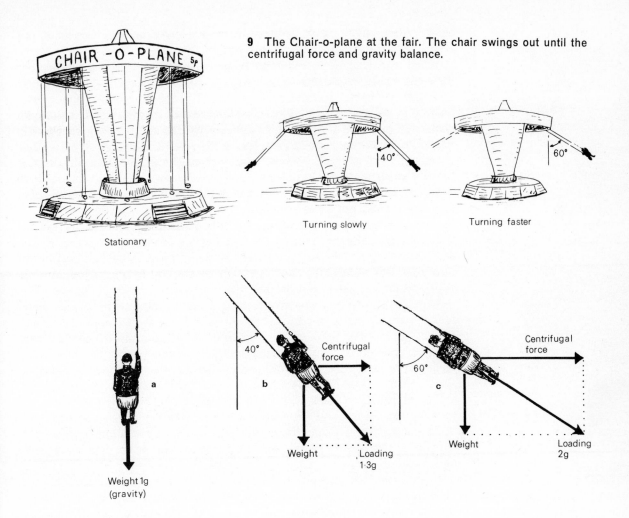

9 The Chair-o-plane at the fair. The chair swings out until the centrifugal force and gravity balance.

Stationary

Turning slowly

Turning faster

40°

60°

a

Weight 1g
(gravity)

b

40°

Centrifugal
force

Weight

Loading
1·3g

c

60°

Centrifugal
force

Weight

Loading
2g

increased at this moment. This is not a particularly unpleasant feeling unless it is rather sudden. If anything, the feeling is one of slightly increased security as you are pressed a little more firmly into the seat. The Chair-o-plane at the fair (see Fig. 9) produces a steady increase in 'g' and helps to explain the lack of sensation during an accurate turn in an aircraft. As the chairs are swung round at speed, centrifugal force throws them out until there is a balance between that force and gravity. The rider feels no tendency to fall inwards in spite of the angle of bank, as the force acting on him is holding him squarely in the seat. The pressure on the seat in Fig. 9b is almost one-and-a-half times the person's normal weight. If the speed of rotation is increased, the chairs swing out to a larger angle until a state of balance is achieved again. In Fig. 9c the loading has increased to 2g and each one of the cables or chains holding a seat has twice the normal, stationary load. For safety, these chains must be able to stand many times the weight of the heaviest person who is likely to take a ride.

When the loading is reduced, however, you experience a completely different sensation and this is not very pleasant. The biggest thrills or most terrifying moments (according to your taste) at the fairground come as the loading is reduced a little. This occurs whenever the movement is a rapid change of direction downwards – either a sudden drop or any change involving a downwards acceleration (point B in Fig. 8). In everyday life, this is what you feel as you drive over a hump-back bridge, or when you are in a lift as it starts to descend.

As the loading on us is reduced, the muscles which normally hold up the stomach against the force of gravity find themselves with less weight to support and we feel our stomachs rise. The pressure on our feet or bottom is also reduced and this creates a definite feeling of insecurity. Some of this feeling may be ameliorated in a glider by wearing the safety harness almost uncomfortably tight. This maintains a more constant feeling of pressure on your bottom and helps to make you feel more secure.

Most people are very sensitive to even a slight reduction in 'g' and small reductions may occur in bumpy conditions or if the stick is moved forward rather quickly. By deliberate movements on the controls the loading can even be reduced to zero for a few seconds. This is rather an unpleasant feeling and, unless you were strapped firmly into your seat, you would float about in the cockpit like an astronaut! The sensation is momentarily like the feeling of falling off the top of a cliff in a nightmare. Very few people seem to enjoy this feeling and fortunately it is one which does not and need not occur during normal flying. However, towards the end of training we should experience this feeling at least once or twice so that we are familiar with it and its causes.

In everyday life, the physical sensations which we feel are used almost unconsciously to help us balance and move about safely on two legs. These sensations are co-related with what we can see so that we can interpret exactly what is going on.

Sensations of tilting or turning in any direction are detected by the vestibular organs or semi-circular canals in our ears. This system is very effective on the ground where the movements are generally restricted to two dimensions and where our eyesight is able to up-date the information and correct any small errors which occur.

Another source of information is muscle sense. If we lean over slightly, the pressure is increased on one foot, or, if we are sitting down, on one side of our bottoms. We recognise the leaning movement by this change in pressure. Experience has taught us that these feelings indicate that we are leaning or beginning to fall over, and without being conscious of them, we react and stop ourselves.

However, in most circumstances our eyesight is the master sense, and without consciously recognising the sensations of leaning, our brain reacts to the combination of feelings and visual clues.

Any slightly misleading or confusing sensations are disregarded by the brain, as it compares what is seen with the other sensations. Without the visual information, however, the brain is forced to rely on the sense of balance and muscle sense, and we suddenly become very aware of them.

For example, in a blacked-out room, our ability to balance is wholly dependent upon our non-visual senses. Immediately, we become acutely aware of these sensations as they take over from our eyesight.

Similarly, if there is only a limited or inadequate amount of information from our eyes, the messages from the other senses are amplified and we become very much more conscious of them.

The sensations of changing 'g' as a lift starts and stops are greatly reduced if there is a door or a small opening so that it is possible to see what is actually happening. The information from our eyes is sufficient for the other sensations to be largely suppressed. If, however, the lift has no windows at all, the sensations will be very much more vivid and upsetting.

During your first one or two flights, the movements of the aircraft are often unpredictable and, because the whole environment is a new one, it is difficult to recognise visually exactly what is going on. In the meantime, since there is no clear visual information, the other senses make themselves felt at several times their normal strength. Furthermore, with the movements occurring in all three dimensions, it is difficult at first to relate the sensations to their cause. This is rather alarming.

After even just one or two flights, the average person learns to recognise what is going on when, for instance, the aircraft is tipped into a bank by turbulent air. The visual sense then becomes dominant again and the other sensations are suppressed to their normal level.

It is best, therefore, to avoid flying in very hazy or cloudy conditions for the first few flights. The sensations can also be minimised by looking ahead over the nose where both up and down and banking movements can be most easily seen against the horizon. Staring out at the wingtips and looking at the instruments both increase the sensations because they make it more difficult for the pilot to recognise what is happening.

An experienced pilot has these kind of problems in poor visibility or in cloud. Without the visual clues, even his sensations are misleading and frightening. In order to fly safely in cloud by means of the instruments alone, he must learn to ignore his sensations and rely entirely on the readings of the instruments.

The feeling of reduced 'g' may occur whenever the aircraft pitches in a nose-down direction or starts to sink rapidly or flies from rising into non-rising air. The same sensation will occur at the top of most car or winch launches and also when the airbrakes are opened. It can also happen during stalls, especially if the pilot overdoes the recovery and pushes the nose down too rapidly. It is important to realise that this feeling is nothing really to do with stalling, otherwise the pilot may continue to push the nose down further and further, trying to get rid of the feeling but making it worse. After a few flights, most of this sensation disappears because your eyes see and identify the change which causes the feeling, and reassure you, for example, that all that has happened is a small downwards movement of the nose.

Sensations of sideslipping

There is one other rather disturbing feeling which occurs during the first few flights. At this stage, one of the biggest problems is to remember to use the stick and rudder together when applying or taking off the bank in turns. Often the beginner will forget the rudder altogether or will use too little too late. The result is that, although the bank is applied, the glider hesitates a few seconds before it starts to turn. At this moment you will experience a very vivid sensation that the angle of bank is continuing to increase and that the glider is going to topple over out of control. This is a very disconcerting feeling and it occurs whenever the glider is slipping, even slightly, towards the lower wing. After a few flights, the rudder movements become much more co-ordinated so that the glider turns correctly and this sensation no longer occurs. Also your eyes learn to recognise immediately that the angle of bank is not abnormal and is not increasing. This visual information helps to suppress the sensation. It is important to look out ahead over the nose of the aircraft as the bank is applied and not in the cockpit or at the wingtip. Looking ahead enables you to see both the angle of bank and any changes in the position of the nose in relation to the horizon.

On the first few turns, beginners are sometimes a little nervous of applying even a moderate angle of bank because of this sensation of sideslipping. Oddly enough, they will often put the glider into quite steep turns without the slightest worry, providing that they happen to get the rudder movement correct so that no slipping occurs. But on the very next turn, perhaps, they will make a gentle bank while forgetting to use the rudder, and be quite alarmed by the feeling.

A similar sensation can occur occasionally in a car. If you drive your car up onto the verge of a country lane in order to park it, even if the verge is only 18 inches high and the car is not tipped up at all steeply, you will experience the same sensation – a vivid feeling that it is going to tip over. Then, a few seconds later, you laugh at yourself for being foolish enough to worry when the bank is so low. When the car tilts, unless you are looking ahead and consciously thinking about the angle, your sensations will suggest to you that you are tilting further, and that perhaps you will roll right over (Fig. 10).

At such a moment, the car is banked over but is not turning, just as the glider, when the same sensation occurred, was banked over but was not turning. In both cases, the feeling of slipping is very real and is caused by the tendency for us to slip across the seat towards the lower side. If the side of the car or cockpit was missing and we were not strapped into our seat, we would tend to fall out! In a correct turn, no slipping occurs since we are held nicely in the seat by the balanced forces, just like the person in the Chair-o-plane in Fig. 9.

10 The sensation of sideslipping which occurs on early flights if the pilot uses no rudder, or too little rudder, as the glider is banked into a turn.

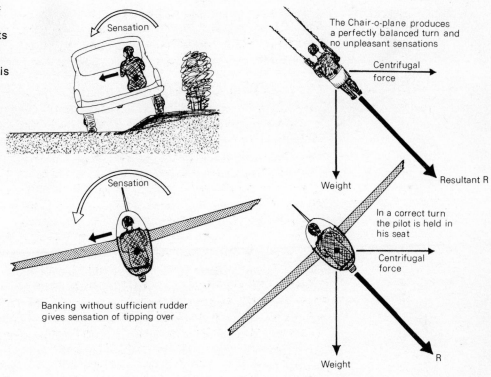

Sensation

The Chair-o-plane produces a perfectly balanced turn and no unpleasant sensations

Centrifugal force

Weight

Resultant R

Sensation

Banking without sufficient rudder gives sensation of tipping over

In a correct turn the pilot is held in his seat

Centrifugal force

Weight

R

Now we have discussed these various sensations and understand when they may occur, it is easier to realise that they will only be really noticeable on our first few flights. As soon as we learn to recognise what the aircraft is doing, most of the vivid sensations disappear, and it does not take long to gain confidence and become less tense and nervous about the whole business of flying.

3 Learning to Glide

Confidence   34   Advice and help at the
The handling stage   35   handling stage   37
Planning and judgement   36   The circuit planning stage   46

Confidence   It is probably true to say that, with flying, the beginner is his own worst enemy. In his comparative ignorance he is usually impatient and also hyper-critical of his inabilities, with the result that he undermines his own confidence. He often analyses his mistakes wrongly, and, by his shyness, fails to get the assistance and help he really needs from his instructors.

Without a clear idea of the pattern of learning it is difficult for him to appreciate the system of instruction and, though learning slowly, he is usually bewildered by the seeming jumble of instructions and happenings.

The instructor who fails to explain the pattern of instruction and the problems which must be solved, deprives his student of the two things which help to reassure him that the task is not impossible. Only the instructor has a knowledge of the difficulties of a number of students and knows how these have been overcome. The beginner himself sees only his own troubles and the magnitude of the undertaking before him. He usually assumes that he lacks aptitude and is making slow progress. He worries that the instructor will tire of pointing out the same mistake again and again.

It is interesting to invite beginners to listen to talks and discussions intended for pilots taking an instructors' course. Whereas the instructors have difficulty in appreciating the beginner's point of view, the explanation of how and why the instructor should adopt a particular method is immediately understood by the beginner. Their comments show conclusively that psychologically they are often left concerned and at a disadvantage because of the failure of their instructors to keep them 'in the picture' about the stages they will go through.

In retrospect, the major deficiency in my previous book of instruction *Gliding* is that, like most other text books, it only deals with the technicalities of learning to fly the glider. It tells you how to move the controls to achieve a manoeuvre but gives no indication or help on how to overcome any of the difficulties which will arise while learning. Most students go through similar stages of learning and need much the same help and encouragement in order to achieve competency. It is most unlikely that you are an exception.

At the risk of dismaying a few of the faint-hearted, consider just what is involved in learning to fly a glider, even without soaring. This list is far from complete but will give you some idea.

Recognition of changes in attitude (nose up and down, banking and yawing).

The effect of controls, co-ordination of the ailerons and rudder, use of the trimmer and airbrakes.

The ability to control the glider safely and reasonably accurately for the take off and launch, turns, and the approach and landing.

The ability to plan and judge the circuit and approach and to vary these to suit different weather conditions.

The ability to recognise the approach of the stall and to recover promptly from stalls and spins.

The ability to deal with cable breaks in all conditions whether the launching is by winch or tow car.

Sufficient experience to recognise and react quickly and calmly to any situation which occurs.

At first sight even this is a long list. If any instructor attempted to teach you all this at once you would be discouraged during the first few flights. His job is to break this down into a logical and digestible sequence so that it is well within your capabilities. Instructors will always differ in exactly how they do this. Also, of course, the type of glider (or motor glider), the length of flight or height of launch and the aptitude of each student may influence how he sets about simplifying the task.

The first step is to divide the list into two stages, the Handling Stage and the Planning and Judgement Stage.

The handling stage　A great simplification is possible if the instructor takes all the responsibility for the positioning and planning of the circuit and the use of the airbrakes for the control of the approach.

The early flights, whether wire launches, aerotows or motor glider, can then be made without any reference being made to the landing field.

After learning to recognise the normal flying attitude and the effect of controls, the student then begins to make turns using all the controls in co-ordination. The instructor, by asking for various turns, ensures that as height is lost the aircraft arrives in a good position for the base leg and approach. After one or two flights, the student is taught how to make the landing and he makes all the early landings without reference to the use of the airbrakes which the instructor operates.

This system has two important advantages. The student can concentrate on the actual landing and the instructor can, if necessary, prevent a heavy landing by reducing the amount of airbrake should the student pilot over-control and 'balloon' upwards instead of flying level. This allows the student to concentrate on the basic control movements, stick and rudder. Apart from the approach and landing, the whole flight may be conducted as though it is many miles away from the field and without referring to the position of the aircraft in relation to the circuit.

With this method, therefore, the student must understand that, for the time being, he is *not* concerned with anything but the basic use of the controls in order to practise handling the aircraft.

The aims at this stage should be: to get accustomed to handling the controls and to become reasonably relaxed in flight; to establish the habit of keeping a good lookout and using the stick and rudder together, and to make accurate steady turns and reasonably consistent landings.

The moment it is clear that the student has obtained a good idea of the landing, i.e. the landings are good, or he corrects slight ballooning so that touchdown is satisfactory, it is time to introduce the use of the airbrakes. However, since these are used to adjust height on the circuit and approach, this involves planning and judgement. He has now reached the second stage.

Planning and judgement

The battle of learning to glide is virtually over when the student has learnt to take all the responsibility for decisions and to act on his own initiative *without* help from the instructor.

The exact moment to start the student using the airbrakes is a matter of opinion. The operation of the lever presents few problems, but because it must be used intelligently, there is little value in just using it when the instructor says so. Every circuit and approach will be different in some respect, and as far as possible the decision to use, or not to use, airbrakes must be made by the student if he is to make progress.

After a thorough briefing and a few circuits with the instructor explaining the routine, the decision should be left to the student, so that he does not unconsciously learn to rely on the instructor to prompt him.

If this method is being used, therefore, the student should not attempt to concern himself, in the first stage, with the positioning of the aircraft in relation to the field, or with the use of the airbrakes until the instructor draws attention to them. He should concentrate on the handling of controls and on learning to land. Unless this is explained to him, he may worry because he cannot keep track of his position with the constant turns one way and the other. Of course, if he has several instructors, it is vital that they all use the same basic method. It would be very demoralising for a beginner who is concentrating on the handling, suddenly to be asked to plan the approach when he isn't really aware of his position in relation to the field. The whole system works rather as though the pilot is being trained in a light aircraft and goes away from the circuit for the early exercises in handling. The method is the same, but in the case of the glider, particularly with launching heights of only 800–1000 feet, a landing is necessary every few minutes. Since each landing is valuable practice, and learning to land may often be a factor which holds up progress, it is quite normal to begin learning to land after only one or two flights. Every landing which is wasted will mean an extra flight on the student's training and this makes it particularly important for the instructor to ensure that the aircraft does arrive back in a good position for an easy approach. (I always suggest to new instructors that they should really offer to pay for every flight on which there is not enough time for the student to settle down and attempt the landing without help.)

Advice and help at the handling stage

During the first few flights, it is particularly important for the instructor to restrict the flying to fairly gentle manoeuvres since the beginner always experiences rather vivid and upsetting sensations at this stage. The first essential is to learn to recognise the attitude of the aircraft by memorising the position of the nose in relation to the horizon and to interpret any changes in attitude quickly. In this mechanical age, the beginner may try to use the airspeed indicator rather than the position of the nose, but this is not the easy way. Whereas a change of attitude can be spotted immediately by looking ahead, it takes time for the aircraft to gather or lose speed so that the airspeed indicator only gives a very delayed indication of a change in attitude. Similarly the changes in sound of the airflow suffer just the same time lag as the A.S.I. as well as being almost unnoticeable to the average person at this early stage.

It is easiest at first to ignore the instruments and concentrate on looking ahead for changes in attitude. This enables both pitching and banking movements to be seen and controlled without the need to watch both the instruments and horizon.

After a few flights, and particularly in poor visibility, it will become necessary to make an occasional check of the airspeed to confirm whether the attitude is exactly right. A glance at the speed is all that is required and if the speed is, for example, a little too fast, the nose should be raised an inch or so and held in the new position. After a few seconds, a further glance at the speed will confirm if the attitude is correct. Do *not* watch the speed while the correction is being made. This will result in too large a correction – due to the delay in a change of speed registering on the instrument – so that the speed will drop right off. Always make the change by looking ahead and adjusting the position of the nose and holding it in the new position. Use the airspeed indicator only as a check and do not look at it for more than a glance at a time.

Keeping the wings level, particularly in bumpy conditions, will seem to be a full time occupation. When you are not looking around to make sure that there are no other machines near by, your attention should be focused on looking ahead. By doing this, changes in both the angle of bank and nose up and down position can be seen at a glance. Small angles of bank may possibly seem difficult to detect at first, but looking out at the wingtips causes even worse problems.

While looking at a wingtip, it is almost inevitable that the nose will move up or down. Looking ahead enables changes to both bank and attitude to be seen and, after very little practice, small angles of bank can be detected very quickly because the aircraft starts to turn soon after a wing goes down.

Almost every student finds the use of the rudder by far the most difficult part of learning to fly a glider. The direction of movement is not at all instinctive and does not relate with any other machine or vehicle in his experience. Furthermore, the rudder on many types of glider has very little feel and does not necessarily recentre itself. In fact, at times when the aircraft is moving sideways through the air (sideslips, skids and spins), the rudder loads may become very light, or even reverse, so that the rudder tends to lock over and requires a push force to recentralise. (This is true of the K7, K13, Bocian and many other gliders.) Any change of feel can be very confusing since the beginner may think that the movement of the controls is caused by the instructor making a correction. It will occur whenever the pilot fails to use the stick and rudder together correctly and if the amount of rudder is too much in a steady turn. The important thing to remember is that whenever the rudder pedals are felt moving themselves, the pilot has always to push back and stop the movement. It is a great help for the instructor to demonstrate this overbalance effect so that the learner knows what to expect.

He should also try not to tense up against the rudder pedals so that pressure is applied to both of them at once. This results in much higher friction and in difficulties in applying the rudder smoothly.

Another problem, if the student is used to driving a motor car, is that he will be in the habit of making rather firm movements with the left foot on the clutch and very delicate movements with the right foot on the accelerator. This seems to be the main reason why at first many beginners find difficulty in making the correct rudder movements for both left and right hand turns.

On a glider, the rudder movement has to coincide with the movements of the ailerons. This means that a habit has to be formed so that the stick and rudder are moved together every time.

Unless the stick and rudder are moved together, the nose will swing in the opposite direction as the glider begins to bank. This yawing movement stops the glider from turning for a few moments, and during this time, the aircraft is slipping sideways through the air (Fig. 11).

Similarly, if the stick alone is used to bring the wings level, the aircraft will again swing slightly and will move sideways for a few seconds. These movements are known as adverse yaw, or the effect of aileron drag, and they are most noticeable with low-speed aircraft, particularly those with a relatively large wing span. Aileron drag is the inevitable result of using ailerons as a means of controlling banking movements. When the ailerons are deflected, to apply bank for example, the downward moving one increases the lift on that wing and therefore increases the drag. (You cannot get something for nothing in this world!) While the banking or rolling movement is being made, one wing is producing more lift than the other one and, as a result, much more drag. This extra drag acting with the leverage of the large wing span tends to pull the nose of the aircraft off to the side. The pilot must apply sufficient rudder to prevent this swing or there will be a very large increase

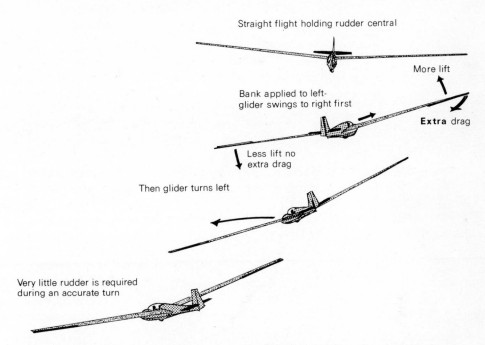

Straight flight holding rudder central

More lift

Bank applied to left-
glider swings to right first

Extra drag

Less lift no
extra drag

Then glider turns left

Very little rudder is required
during an accurate turn

11 The effect of aileron drag when the glider is banked at the start of a turn causes a momentary swing in the opposite direction. For an accurate turn the stick and rudder must be applied together to prevent this swing. (See Fig. 13 for further explanation.)

in the drag of the whole machine as it moves sideways through the air.

Whenever the stick is moved sideways in order to apply or take off bank, the banking movement will be accompanied by some adverse yaw. This is why the stick and rudder must always be used together. The real purpose of the rudder is just to keep the aircraft pointing in the direction in which it is going so that it remains as streamlined as possible (Fig. 12). It is used, as necessary, going into and coming out of turns in order to prevent the aileron drag from swinging the glider sideways. The force which actually turns the aircraft is the lift from the wings once they are banked over. In a steady turn, the lift from both wings is equal (otherwise the angle of bank would be increasing or decreasing) and, therefore, there is no aileron drag or adverse yaw. After the bank has been applied, the amount of rudder must always be reduced. Normally a very small amount of rudder is needed in the direction of the turn in order to keep the fuselage exactly in line with the airflow for low drag.

Faster aircraft do not tend to yaw so much and on most powered aircraft, the adverse yaw caused by aileron drag is usually almost undetectable. At

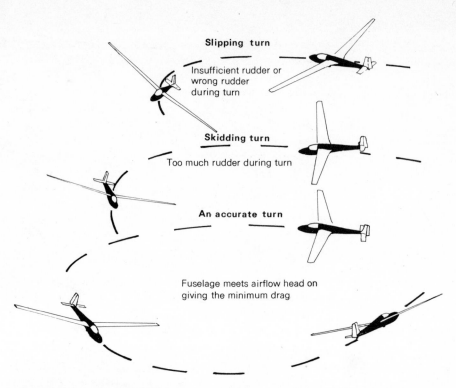

12 Slipping and skidding in the turn. Any inaccuracy causes extra drag and a greater loss of height. In skidding turns there is a marked tendency for the bank to increase.

higher speeds the aircraft is, as it were, gripped in a much more solid mass of air, so that it is more resistant to yawing. Also the shorter wing spans give less leverage to any aileron drag so that it has far less effect than on a glider. On most light aircraft, quite acceptable turns can be made by merely applying bank and then easing back slightly on the stick. It is only at low speeds, on the approach for example, that any rudder is required for turning. In this respect, powered machines are much easier for the beginner since well-co-ordinated rudder movements are not required. Furthermore, most of the time in powered aircraft is spent in straight flight going from *A* to *B* whereas in a glider nearly all the time is spent circling.

The power pilot learns to use the rudder primarily for steering on the ground and to stop the yawing movements caused by the effects of the engine and propeller. That is, he learns to apply a steady pressure as a correction to a more or less constant swinging tendency. Most modern light aircraft have engines which rotate in a clockwise direction as seen from the cockpit and this gives rise to a yawing movement to the left under power. This effect is cancelled out in cruising flight by setting the fin at a small angle (or sometimes by offsetting the engine itself) so that the pilot can relax and ignore the rudder once he is in level flight. However, the same aircraft will need some right rudder applied all the time the aircraft is flying with more than cruising power (climbing) and left rudder all the time when the engine is throttled back (gliding). Since these are not very large effects, they do not require so much skill as the rudder movements required for turning gliders. Also, there is plenty of time to spot the yaw and then to move the rudder, whereas on the glider the movements of the stick and rudder must be exactly co-ordinated for every turn.

Usually on the first few flights a beginner keeps forgetting to use the rudder. A few flights later he develops a random series of faults such as using the wrong foot, being too late, or leaving the rudder on during the turn. Right from the very start, it is important for the instructor to insist on a good look round before starting any turn, and a very common fault is to begin to apply the bank while still looking round. This generally causes trouble for beginners, though it will become normal and desirable a little later on, by which time most of these initial problems will have been overcome.

If the turn is started while looking round, the nose will nearly always get hopelessly out of position. This can be avoided by being a little slower and more deliberate about the whole thing. Sometimes, if the student is having problems with controlling the glider during turns, the instructor is tempted to let the student start the turns without the good look round. Although this may prevent the aircraft getting out of position at the start of the turn, the lookout is far more important at this stage than the accuracy of the turn. Failure to look round may cause a collision, whereas bad turns are seldom, if ever, fatal.

In the early stages, it is easiest to think of the procedure for making a turn as a definite routine. Otherwise the beginner may find himself forgetting vital movements with the result that the turns are spoilt. It is helpful to talk yourself through each turn in order to establish the correct sequence of control movements. The movements will soon become almost automatic (see Fig 13).

A turn is made in the following manner.

First look round and note the position of any other aircraft in the vicinity. Make sure it is clear in the direction you want to turn. Look back to the nose and check that it is still in the normal flying position in relation to the horizon or ground ahead. Re-position it correctly if necessary and then apply the bank using the stick and rudder together, watching ahead as you do so. Just before the angle of bank reaches the amount you want for the particular turn, stop the banking movement with a small counter-movement of the stick and *then* reduce the amount of rudder so that only a very small amount is left on in the direction of the turn. Ease back slightly on the stick or the glider will gradually drop its nose and gain excess speed during the turn. The turn will then continue steadily providing that the angle of bank and the position of the nose are kept constant.

During a prolonged turn, corrections will be needed to overcome the effects

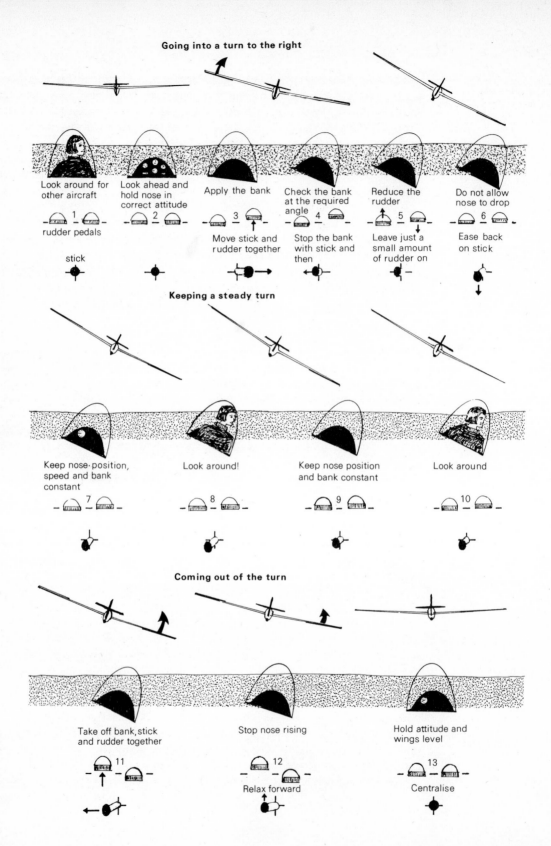

Going into a turn to the right

Look around for other aircraft

Look ahead and hold nose in correct attitude

Apply the bank

Check the bank at the required angle

Reduce the rudder

Do not allow nose to drop

1 rudder pedals

2

3 Move stick and rudder together

4 Stop the bank with stick and then

5 Leave just a small amount of rudder on

6 Ease back on stick

stick

Keeping a steady turn

Keep nose position, speed and bank constant

Look around!

Keep nose position and bank constant

Look around

7

8

9

10

Coming out of the turn

Take off bank, stick and rudder together

Stop nose rising

Hold attitude and wings level

11

12 Relax forward

13 Centralise

13 (opposite) The control movements for a turn. After a few flights the beginner ceases to think about the exact movements on the controls.

of any bumps which may upset either the angle of bank or the attitude. It is also essential to continue to keep a good lookout for other machines and stop the turn and move away if they appear to be getting too close for safety.

Coming out of the turn, the stick and rudder are again used together in order to bring the wings level. The backward pressure on the stick must be relaxed and the controls must be quickly centralised as the wings come level, otherwise the glider will bank over into a turn in the other direction.

Abbreviating this explanation for use in the air:

Look round – look ahead and check that the nose is in the correct position. Apply the bank with stick and rudder together – stop the bank with the stick and *then* reduce the rudder – ease back slightly.

Keep the bank constant – do not let the nose drop – look round.

Take off the bank with the stick and rudder together – relax the backward pressure on the stick – centralise the stick and rudder and hold the wings level.

In gliding, it is particularly important to be able to keep a steady, accurate turn in order to make good use of thermals. Many of the faults in a turn do not show up until the glider has turned at least half a circle, and therefore, it is important to make some prolonged turns rather than just turn through 90°. It is best if the instructor always gets his pupil to maintain a steady turn and to go on turning until told to straighten up. This enables the instructor to see whether the bank is being held constant and whether the rudder has been reduced once the bank has been established. It also helps the instructor with the planning, because he can always ask for the turn to be stopped at an appropriate moment to help the positioning on the circuit. The student will otherwise often take the easy way out by straightening up whenever a bump starts to bring the wings level, instead of making the correction and keeping the turn going. It is very noticeable that beginners who are not given turns of more than 90° or so are seldom capable of really accurate, steady, continuous turns.

Coming out of turns most students have very little trouble in straightening up on a selected point. However, it is much more difficult to learn to make the final turn onto the line of the runway or landing area and this takes practice. After a few flights, the use of the rudder begins to become a little more automatic and is forgotten less often, provided that there is no distraction. Usually when it comes to the approach, the rudder is completely forgotten because of the need to think about the landing. The glider then begins a series of yawing movements from side to side which are difficult to stop without help from the instructor.

This is the stage of training at which the instructor must be particularly vigilant! What appears to be just a minor fault, like leading into the turn with the rudder (moving the rudder before the aileron) or leaving the rudder on without reducing it in the steady turn, will soon be established as a habit which will be very difficult to eradicate. This will often happen if the turns are only short ones, because, although the control movements are not correct, the fault does not show as an inaccuracy in the few seconds of the turn. One fault like this is the failure to ease back sufficiently during the turn. It is only after 180° that the nose begins to drop appreciably and therefore it is only in continuous turns that the fault can be detected easily. Poor turning habits almost invariably show up and become more dangerous during a final turn before the approach, particularly if the glider is getting rather too low or is late in making the turn. Not reducing the rudder in a turn may be almost unnoticeable when the bank is applied gently with only small movements of the stick and rudder. However, when the bank is applied quickly using all the available aileron and rudder, a very violent skidding will occur in the turn if the rudder is left on. This skidding movement, with the fuselage battering its way sideways through the air, creates high drag and, at a time like a low final turn, has much the same effect as opening full airbrake. Similarly, failing to use the correct amount of backward movement in the final turn will result in the nose dropping badly and a large loss of height. If it becomes necessary to turn a little steeper than normal because of leaving the turn too late, much more backward movement will be needed and unless this is applied, the nose will drop rapidly. This will result in a rather undignified dive at the landing area with the speed getting far too fast and with the turn finishing much too close to the ground for comfort or safety.

In the long run, turning habits are the most important part of gliding instruction. They determine how well the pilot can centre in a thermal, how efficiently he flies, and to a great extent how safely he will fly at times of stress when his flying may be semi-instinctive.

Whereas straight and level flight is usually considered to be the basis for good power flying, turning is the basis of all good glider handling. In fact, it is very largely a waste of time to bother with straight flight as a definite exercise in a glider, particularly in smooth conditions and in the early stages of training. This is because the stick and rudder co-ordination has to be very well established before there is any hope of flying straight. It is most important for beginners to realise that the most difficult thing for them to do is to fly straight. Usually, it is only just as the student is reaching the solo stage that he has built up the experience and practice to do this.

The explanation is not hard to see if we consider the glider on an approach in bumpy weather. If the left wing drops a little because of turbulence, unless the pilot brings it level immediately, or prevents it from actually dropping, the glider will start to turn in the direction of the bank. Therefore, in order to achieve a straight approach, the pilot must have almost instinctive reactions to the aircraft tipping and must use both the stick and rudder together (and correctly) to bring the wings level. If the rudder is forgotten or wrongly used, the glider will swing off course as the wings are levelled.

This degree of skill takes time and practice to achieve – much more skill than to make normal turns during which there is almost time to think out the control movement.

In powered flying, straight and level is usually taught as the basic exercise. However, because in smooth air only a few corrections are needed, learning straight and level flight is not so effective as starting with plenty of turning. The use of the controls is grasped much more quickly by a series of turns which gives many more movements and much more practice in trying to use the stick and rudder together. Since any correction to bring the wings level in a glider has to be made with the co-ordinated use of the stick and rudder, straight flight is really a form of negative turning – preventing turns and turning back to level flight after each disturbance.

The early stage of glider training, therefore, consists of turns, turns, and more turns, with the occasional landing whenever the ground comes up. Since it is all a matter of establishing almost automatic stick and rudder movement, there is nothing to be done to help the process except practice!

Do not get too perturbed about your inability to fly straight, it will develop automatically with experience.

During the early flights, while most of your instruction is concentrated on co-ordination and turns, you will also be learning to land. However, it is important to realise that you will still be having problems with keeping straight, particularly on the final approach. Unless the landing area is rather limited in width, or has obstructions which must be avoided, just do the best you can to keep straight. Do not worry if there is some sideways drifting during the landing, provided that there is no danger of hitting anything. This drifting will eventually be corrected by keeping the wings level and using a little rudder to straighten up, or if there is a cross wind, by lowering the 'into wind' wing slightly. Landings are often spoiled by the student seeing the drift and getting so involved in attempting to correct it, that he lets the landing 'happen'. Try to concentrate on the hold off and touchdown. The ability to keep straight at the same time will come after quite an amount of turning practice, and at this stage you may have to be assisted by the instructor making a few deft movements on the stick and rudder. A major problem is that of getting too tense and worried about the landing, with the result that the control movements become jerky. This tendency will gradually disappear as you begin to have success and become more confident. Once the landings are reasonably successful, so that the instructor does not need to change the airbrake setting during the final stages because of ballooning or being too high, it is a simple matter to take over the operation of the airbrakes. Providing that the brakes are opened and set in one position for the final 50 feet or so, the left hand on the brake lever can be mentally cut off, held still, and forgotten, while the right hand using the stick makes the landing as on previous occasions. Only in the event of last minute alterations in the approach or a poor hold off, will there be a need to change the airbrake setting so that both hands have to be used independently. It is easiest to restrict movements of the airbrake near the ground to a reduction of the amount or, in an extreme case, closing them altogether. The lever should then be held firmly in the new position while the other hand makes the landing. Otherwise it is possible to start moving both hands, or the wrong hand, with catastrophic results.

Try to avoid this problem by getting settled on the approach with the airbrakes set, before the start of the round out.

The circuit planning stage

The use of the airbrakes also involves the student with planning and judging the circuit and approach (see Fig. 14). Instead of only being concerned with following instructions on where to fly and which turn to make, the student must now begin to make decisions himself. Now, at a time when he is beginning to feel that he can really manage and that at last he has time to look round and relax a little, all the planning and decisions become his responsibility.

It is quite normal for his flying to deteriorate for a few flights at this point because he has so much to think about. A further confusion may arise because of the variations which occur from circuit to circuit. Each variation requires a slightly different plan of action and it is only after perhaps four or five circuits that the student is able to recognise for himself that there are only two or three basic situations.

At this stage the student will probably begin to feel that he is not making any progress. This happens to everyone. There are many new things to do and, at first, it seems impossible to find time to do them all.

The decision making must be handed over to the student as soon as possible and he must be taught how to think about the planning. This is largely a matter of learning to think at least one jump ahead of the situation. There is little benefit to the student if the instructor just says, 'You are too high. Open the brakes.' Ideally, much earlier in the proceedings, the instructor should have been saying, 'At this stage you should be asking yourself, "Am I going to be too high?" Now, decide what you think. Does it look high to you? Do not use the brakes unless you think you will be unnecessarily high.'

Good circuit planning is largely a matter of learning to look at the situation and then deciding quickly what needs doing. A common fault is to make decisions and judgements, but to be very slow to take action. This is not helped by the instructor prompting the action instead of waiting for the student to take it. It is quite useful if the student gives a running commentary of his thoughts and actions. This prevents the misunderstanding which sometimes occurs when, for instance, the student has chosen one plan of action, and the instructor assumes that he has chosen another. Usually, in this case, any prompting on the part of the instructor then creates a complete mess-up.

Students often become expert at talking as they fly and in this way the instructor knows whether the student is thinking ahead and whether he has seen hazards such as other aircraft. Sometimes it even becomes a slight embarrassment if the instructor can't get a word in edgeways until after the landing!

Probably the most common fault in circuit planning is the tendency to cramp the final stages. This is caused because the glider is apt to bank slightly in the direction in which the pilot is looking, so that it gradually edges in

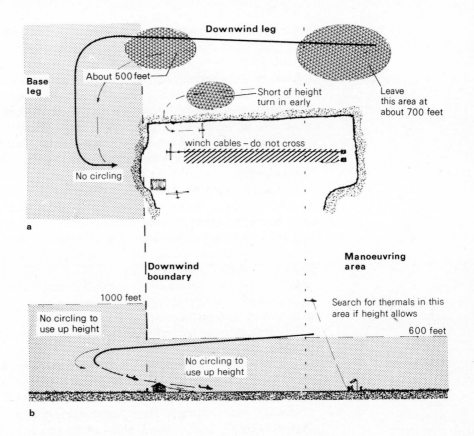

Downwind leg

Base leg

About 500 feet

Short of height
turn in early

Leave
this area at
about 700 feet

winch cables – do not cross

No circling

a

**Downwind
boundary**

**Manoeuvring
area**

1000 feet

No circling to
use up height

Search for thermals in this
area if height allows

600 feet

No circling to
use up height

b

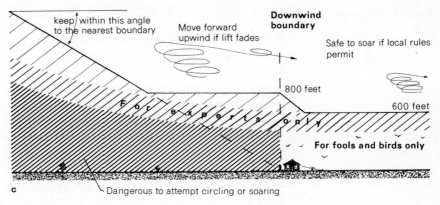

keep within this angle
to the nearest boundary

Move forward
upwind if lift fades

**Downwind
boundary**

Safe to soar if local rules
permit

For experts only

800 feet

600 feet

For fools and birds only

Dangerous to attempt circling or soaring

c

14 Limitations on the circuit and local soaring. **a** Basic circuit planning **b** Height
limits for circling to use up height on the circuit **c** Height limits for attempting to
use lift and soar.

towards the landing area on the downwind leg. This leaves only a very short base leg (that is the part of the circuit just before the final turn, see Fig. 14), so that there is very little time for decisions or adjustments. Usually, the base leg also tends to wander so that the final turn takes place far too close to the landing area. It is absolutely vital that the final turn is not too far back or there may be a risk of undershooting the landing area, particularly if the wind has freshened since the flight began. However, even with powerful airbrakes, the glider is not like a helicopter and cannot descend vertically. The final turn, therefore, must always be completed some distance back from the desired landing point if a spot landing is to be at all possible. Apart from the waste of valuable height, an extra one or two hundred feet is of no embarrassment at the start of the base leg, unless the circuit has been very cramped. With the extra height, a longer base leg is possible, and this allows extra time to assess things and to ensure that the final turn is in the desired position and not too close. There is time to decide whether the final turn looks as though it will be completed unnecessarily high and, if this is the case, to use some airbrake to correct this tendency. There is also time to adjust the base leg by moving back a little to lengthen the approach. Obviously, it is best to have just a little too much height on the base leg and to throw some away with the airbrake. This will put the turn just at the height and position which seems ideal. Then, if the glider happens to pass through strong sink, the airbrakes can be closed immediately, and the extra height will still allow the planned turn and approach. Similarly, if lift is encountered, full airbrake and a slight widening of the approach will cancel out the effect of the lift and also allow the planned approach. This is one of the most important uses of airbrakes. If there is too much height, it is better to use them promptly on the base leg than to wait until after the final turn, when there may be far too much height to get rid of on the actual approach.

Obviously, the airbrakes have to be used with discretion and the situation needs to be constantly re-assessed. If necessary, the airbrakes must be closed again to avoid using up too much height. In order to keep control of the situation at all times, the real requirement is to think ahead. Ask yourself 'Am I going to be back at the start of the base leg at about the right height?' If not, a decisive action is needed. Either the circuit must be extended or widened to try to get rid of the excess height or if it looks as though there is too little height, a short cut must be made to put things right.

By the start of the base leg, it is the position and height of the final turn which should be under review, so that an adjustment may be made to get as near as possible to an ideal situation by then.

During the final turn, a decision should be made on whether the airbrakes will be needed immediately after the turn. If the turn is rather far back, this action may need to be delayed. Thinking ahead like this should enable the student to be ready to open the brakes without delay as the turn is completed, rather than spend a valuable few seconds after the turn making up his mind, during which time the glider floats up the field. Prompt decisions are important because for ten seconds spent dithering, the glider can float two or three hundred yards further up the field!

It is only by this process of thinking well ahead that it is possible to prevent difficult situations arising. In windy and unstable conditions when height may be lost very rapidly and unexpectedly, it is vital to have alternative plans ready to cater for a sudden loss of height. In fact, it is not safe to be in a position where there is no landing area within easy reach should you suddenly lose several hundred feet at any time. This is the reason why circling to use up height on or near the downwind boundary is dangerous. If the glider loses height unexpectedly in the turn and drifts back, it will often be unable to reach the landing area against the wind. Instead of circling, a quick decision to throw away the excess height with full airbrakes and perhaps to make a slightly wider base leg, is always much safer. The loss of height can then be controlled, so that there is no question of getting into a marginal position.

Whenever there appears to be some excess height and there is any tendency for the circuit to be cramped, the first move should always be to improve the positioning by moving out. Then, if there is still too much height, action should be taken to get rid of it. Once the glider is too close, it is difficult to regain a good position without losing sight of the landing area altogether. It is always easier to keep well out, because if it becomes necessary to cut in and make an abbreviated circuit, the landing area can be seen the whole time.

The essence of good circuit planning and of good piloting at any time is the ability to review the situation constantly and make quick decisions. Fig. 15 shows a mythical circuit flight in a glider with notes of the thoughts and decisions which need to be taken. At first, most beginners are only capable of making about one assessment and decision every fifteen to twenty seconds. This is nowhere near fast enough, and leads to a situation where the pilot is left having to take drastic action at the last moment in order to try and bodge up a situation which, with forethought and early action, could have been avoided. Any tendency to over-concentrate on a single aspect of the flying or planning will usually result in something getting neglected. For example, there is not time to allow for more than a quick glance at the instruments from time to time. With practice, the reading of the A.S.I. can be taken in at a glance. This is rather like taking a snapshot and retaining the image in your mind which you interpret while looking elsewhere. This is essential during the base leg, or the correct moment to turn may be missed while looking at the instruments.

At this stage, practice is necessary to prevent the pilot's mind becoming overloaded so badly that his standard of flying is jeopardised, and dangerous situations develop. In order to prevent this chaos, it is essential that he gains the experience and knowledge to understand what is happening and how to deal with it.

At first, of course, this is quite impossible for the average beginner, but, after a few circuits using the airbrakes and doing the planning, the flying

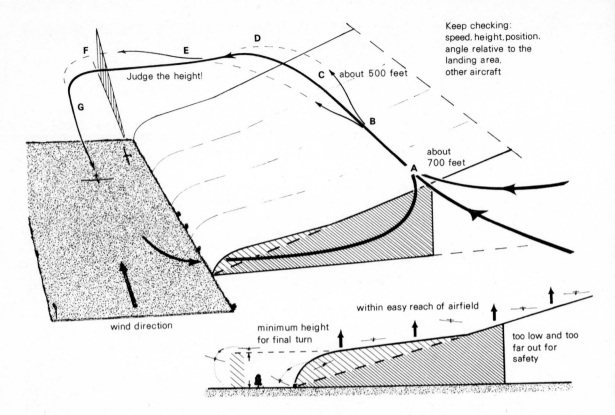

Keep checking:
speed, height, position,
angle relative to the
landing area,
other aircraft

D

F

E

Judge the height!

C about 500 feet

G

B

about
700 feet

A

wind direction

within easy reach of airfield

minimum height
for final turn

too low and too
far out for
safety

15 Circuit planning. **A** Whenever possible, join the circuit at the upwind end of the airfield at about 700 feet. **B** Move in or out to keep within a safe angle to the boundary of the field and aim to use up excess height so that you arrive opposite the landing area at about 500 feet. Lower the main wheel if retracted. **C** Check the landing areas for obstructions, make a preliminary choice, assess the wind strength and check all round for other traffic. **D** Turn onto the base leg, gain speed and retrim, hand onto the airbrake lever and disregard the altimeter in favour of judging the height for the rest of the circuit. Assess if the final turn will be unnecessarily high, and, if so, open some airbrake or move out away from the landing area to correct the tendency. **E** Select the exact line for landing, recheck for other aircraft nearby and move in or out to position the final turn. **F** Make a well-banked final turn onto the approach and during the turn try to assess the amount of airbrake which will be required as the turn is completed. **G** Open the airbrakes as necessary, maintaining the chosen speed and using aiming point technique to judge the approach.

itself becomes less of a conscious effort. Later on, most of the flying will be done without the need for considering the manoeuvres in any detail. The planning then becomes a matter of thinking, 'Now it is time for me to move towards the start of the base leg', rather as a driver might steer his motor car across a field to the gate, the actual process of driving being almost automatic.

A few people do not seem to be able to develop the ability to think quickly about several things which may be happening at the same time. Sometimes, they can learn to fly tolerably well by sheer persistent practice, but the need to think quickly about all the other factors involved in planning is too much, and overloads their system. While over-concentrating on one aspect of the flying, everything else suffers, and chaotic situations are likely to arise. Whereas in a powered aircraft there is usually a possible solution, such as putting on the power and making a further attempt, in a glider there may be no escape from a nasty accident. Experience in dealing with all kinds of possible emergencies may help by making them familiar and routine, but sooner or later in gliding, unpredicted situations always occur and then there is real trouble. Pilots who repeatedly get themselves into difficulties and have incidents are not a good liability and sometimes it is necessary for their own safety to stop them flying gliders. They may, however, become acceptable power pilots, because, providing that the engine does not fail (and this is very rare with modern engines), critical situations do not occur.

Some elderly students have difficulty in believing that the cause of their problems is basically that their hand/eye co-ordination and reactions have deteriorated. They are often active sportsmen who drive fast cars but are still unable to make the quick decisions necessary in the less familiar situations which can occur unexpectedly. Unusually slow progress is almost always an indication that the student is temperamentally unsuited to flying and may never make a really safe pilot.

A few people suffer major hold-ups in their training because of psychological problems – usually nervousness, which makes them very tense. They just have to accept that they will be rather slow learners although this will not necessarily mean that they will not become as competent as the swift learner. However, there is not much truth in the saying that the slow learner often becomes a better pilot. Research with Second World War pilots showed conclusively that, on average, the quicker the student learns to fly, the greater the probability that he will become an above average pilot. The exceptions to this rule will usually be those people with psychological problems which hold up their progress. They are usually the interesting cases as far as the instructor is concerned, because he has to use all his technique and experience to get results. Unfortunately, the student who has natural aptitude is often given very little help. As a result, he may go solo prematurely, and never really achieve the high standard which, with careful supervision, he could attain. Artistic, non-technically minded people and many girls lack confidence unless they have a more complete understanding of how and why things happen. Only when their self-confidence is really established and they have proved to themselves that they can manage any foreseeable emergency, can they safely be sent off solo. There have been numerous cases in the past where students who have not really understood the basic facts about flying have failed to take any action when faced with a new and unexpected situation. Normally, the beginner should be given plenty of practice in dealing with situations where decisive actions are needed. This is far more important than making elegant, copy-book circuits and landings.

Practical problems of gliding instruction are frequently the root cause of the individual student's lack of progress. For example, in some cases he will have flights with many different instructors. This requires him to make a psychological adjustment on the first flight with each new instructor and he will worry that the instructor will expect too much of him. In most clubs, the student has a turn of two or three consecutive flights in order to get back into practice and get more value from the flying. This is really only adequate if the student is flying with a few instructors he knows well, so that a good student/instructor relationship can be built up. This can, however, be taken too far. Women and young people may very easily build up their confidence with a particular instructor. Without knowing it, the instructor may foster this sense of confidence so that very rapid progress is made and then it is easy for him to send them solo prematurely. First solos are often made under this rather hypnotic spell, but it is no real substitute for knowledge and experience, and, if things do go wrong, without the moral support of the instructor a state of panic may ensue. Although encouragement and persuasion may be used in the early stages, by the end of the training the student must have learned to be totally self-reliant.

This is the main disadvantage of youth training schemes where the pilot is trained just to the point where he is sent for his first few solos. Boosted by the encouragement of his instructor, he is assured that he can manage safely and he probably achieves three perfectly safe and well-flown circuits for his A and B certificates. However, unless he is given the opportunity of continuing to fly until he has built up his own confidence, these solos become like a dream. Even after a few days, he begins to realise how little he did know, and how vulnerable he would have been if something unexpected had happened. The more mature student is likely to make the decision not to let himself be put in a situation like that again and gives up flying.

If the student does have any problems on his first solos, it is vital that they are completely explained and corrected by extra instruction before he is sent solo again. Otherwise the incident, however small, may become a source of worry, so that after a few weeks his desire to fly at all may have gone.

This is a very real problem at most gliding clubs. The solo pilot should be given plenty of dual flying and always a daily dual flight before going solo for perhaps twelve or more flights. Each early solo flight and any flight with dubious airmanship or piloting, regardless of the pilot's experience, should be commented upon and any problems should be explained. After a poor landing, it is essential for the inexperienced student to be given extra dual instruction in order to re-establish his confidence and give him the opportunity to reassure himself that it will not happen next time he is solo. Many pilots give up after a few solos because they lose confidence and begin to worry about flying and their ability to cope safely. Here is an example of how this can happen – an actual case some years ago.

During a solo landing, the pilot ballooned slightly, reduced the airbrakes setting, and after floating some distance, flew into the bumpy ground and bounced rather heavily. At the time, the pilot was annoyed with himself and slightly surprised that no one at the launch point seemed to have noticed. The glider was undamaged. The incident happened unexpectedly and the pilot was not really quite sure exactly where he went wrong. During the week, he thought it over and still could not decide. The next weekend, the weather was poor and he could not get a dual check as he had hoped. He was offered the hangar flight in a solo glider. The approach was a little gusty but he managed a reasonable landing in spite of being worried about ballooning after his previous experience. However, he was inclined to think it was luck, not good judgement. By the next weekend, he had realised that he was not at all sure of himself and again, with the weather being unflyable, he spent a rather unhappy day. Another week went by and when he received an invitation to go elsewhere for the weekend, the prospect of another possible non-flying day added to his loss of interest and keenness. After a few weeks he had lost his appetite for flying and was never seen at the club again.

At the early solo stage the pilot must fly regularly to maintain confidence. He still needs the encouragement and advice of an instructor and to feel that the instructor is just as concerned about his flying as he was before he reached solo standard.

Beginners seldom make deliberate errors or try to be clever. Their faults are almost invariably due to misunderstandings, or lack of practice or inadequate training. It is important, therefore, for any faults to be analysed very carefully and criticised constructively. Only the very experienced pilot can be safely criticised for wilful dangerous flying.

Pilots who are not used to having their flying watched and commented upon sometimes tend to take criticism badly and feel that they are being 'got at'. This is a danger sign. Either the training has been poor, so that the pilot has learned to have little respect for his instructors, or else he is getting dangerously over-confident. A mature outlook is essential for safe flying and no one can afford to ignore criticism or advice.

4 Help with Landings

The landing	54	The round out	68
Judging the height	59	The hold off	70
Learning to land	64	The ground run	72

The landing

It may seem surprising that there is still considerable difference of opinion on how a glider should be landed. There are two schools of thought: the 'fly it onto the ground' school and the 'hold it off as long as possible' school.

Many years ago, the majority of gliding instructors believed that trying to teach a tail-down landing would result in many heavy landings when the student misjudged his height and held off too high. At that time it was common practice to level out just above the ground and let the glider land in a rather tail-high attitude without holding it off to lose speed.

Experience showed, however, that the risk of damage was increased by this method, particularly when the landing was on rough ground. The gliders were far more prone to damage if they were flown onto the ground than by being held off too high so that they sank the last few feet a little heavily.

Nowadays, even amongst the Cadet training organisations where minor damage is of little concern to the instructor and where speed of learning is of prime importance, a properly held off landing is taught. It takes very little longer but greatly reduces the risk of damage at a later stage. It also makes it an easy matter for a pilot to convert to normal light aircraft since the landing technique is similar.

If the glider is levelled out and allowed to fly onto the ground straight away it is landing in a tail-high position and has not lost its flying speed. Any bump in the ground, or rebound from the wheel or skid, will throw the glider back into the air. Then, if the pilot is over-anxious to get down or reacts instinctively by moving forward on the stick, he may fly the glider back into the ground onto its nose skid. Since the nose will always rebound on impact, the bounces will tend to continue and get more violent with a real risk of breaking the skid or fuselage structure above it (Fig. 16).

When inexperienced pilots convert onto a new type of glider for the first time, there is an extra risk of damage if they have been in the habit of flying the glider onto the ground. These pilots will nearly always make their first few approaches with a little extra speed in hand and, if the machine is of a higher performance than the one with which they are familiar, it is an easy matter for this 'little extra' to become rather excessive. Naturally they will also tend to be over-cautious about using more than a small amount of air-

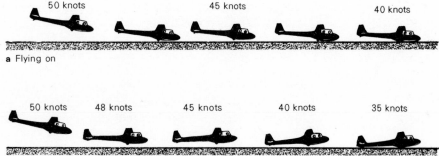

16 Styles of landing. **a** Flying on. After levelling out, the glider is allowed to fly gently onto the ground. This method is still recommended at some American gliding sites but is only satisfactory for landings on smooth ground. The touchdown is fast and the risk of damage higher than with a fully held off landing. **b** Fully held off. After levelling out, the glider is held off the ground for as long as possible until it sinks the last few inches and touches down on the main wheel and tail skid simultaneously.

brake with the result that the glider will float for a long, long way during the hold off. After floating along some distance, the pilot will usually try to make the glider land by pushing it down onto the ground. The strange and unfamiliar view over the nose will generally fool him into believing that he is already in the landing attitude whereas, in fact, the glider is very nose down and about to touch down on the nose skid! Unless the ground is very smooth the glider will cannon off into the air again. Often by this stage, the pilot will be getting a little alarmed and will make a further determined effort to get down by moving the stick forward again. This mistaken action will result in a series of violent nose-down collisions with the ground and very often the skid and nose structure will be badly damaged. This is even more likely to happen if there is any drift or sideways motion at the moment of impact and the front skid at least will be broken or torn from its fittings.

A few gliders of very old design have virtually no shock absorption in the tail wheel or skid and these can be damaged by landing heavily in an extreme tail-down attitude. Most design authorities insist that proper shock absorption is provided for landings in all normal attitudes including a tail down. (It is usually simple to devise and get approval for a modification to strengthen a weak tail skid. However, it must always be weaker than its supporting structure and it must be kept very light. Even a small increase in weight at the tail will necessitate re-weighing the glider and recalculating the minimum cockpit load which will keep the centre of gravity within safe limits.)

In the 'hold it off as long as you can' method, instead of levelling out and allowing the glider to land, it is kept from touching the ground as it loses speed by gently easing back on the stick. Eventually, the glider will sink onto the ground, in spite of the pilot's backward movement on the control. The glider will be in a much more tail-down attitude and the main wheel and tail skid will touch down more or less simultaneously.

In this way, the landing is made at a much lower speed. (Remember that the shocks on touchdown are proportional to the *square* of the speed, so that any reduction significantly reduces the shock and the chance of damage.)

On touchdown, the majority of the load is taken on the main wheel, which is a good shock absorber and will also stand any sideways loads without risk of damage. Furthermore, since the glider has run out of flying speed just as it touches down, there is little or no risk of it bouncing or ballooning up off the ground again.

The great advantage of this method of landing is that it ensures a perfectly safe landing in any glider, or in any type of powered aircraft. However, it is not safe in very high winds with gliders which are not fitted with any form of airbrakes, or those using only flaps to control the approach and landing.

Unless an aircraft touches down very gently, it is likely to rebound from the ground. The type of undercarriage and in particular the position of the main wheel in relation to the centre of gravity (C of G) of the machine largely determines what will happen at this moment (Fig. 17).

Gliders fitted with a main skid at the front under the nose, usually have the wheel just behind the C of G. This acts in a similar way to a tricycle, or nose wheel undercarriage on a light aircraft. As the glider touches down, it tends to pitch nose down a little, reducing the angle of attack of the wing and so reducing the lift. There is, therefore, very little tendency to bounce off the ground since after touchdown there is nowhere near enough lift left to support the weight and keep it flying.

On other machines, the main wheel is well forward of the C of G. Unless a perfect landing is made onto smooth ground, any touchdown made with the tail skid off the ground may result in the rebound pitching the nose up as the front wheel touches first. This will cause bouncing and ballooning. If, however, these machines are held off fully, the touchdown will be on both the front wheel and tail skid simultaneously. Then there will be no tendency to pitch nose up, no bouncing will occur, and, as before, all the excess flying speed of the approach has been used up so that as the machine sinks onto the ground there is not enough speed, and hence not enough lift, for the aircraft to leave the ground again.

With most aircraft, the designer sets the wings onto the fuselage at such an angle that, if the aircraft is held off fully just above the ground for as long as possible, it will touch down correctly for a perfect landing. For example, on most gliders this technique will result in a touchdown on the wheel and tail together. On a tail dragger (a tail wheel aircraft such as a Condor or the Cub) again the landing will be wheels and tail together. On a nose wheel type (Cessna, Cherokee, etc.), the aircraft will settle down on the main wheels with the nose wheel off the ground. In this case the wing incidence is set so

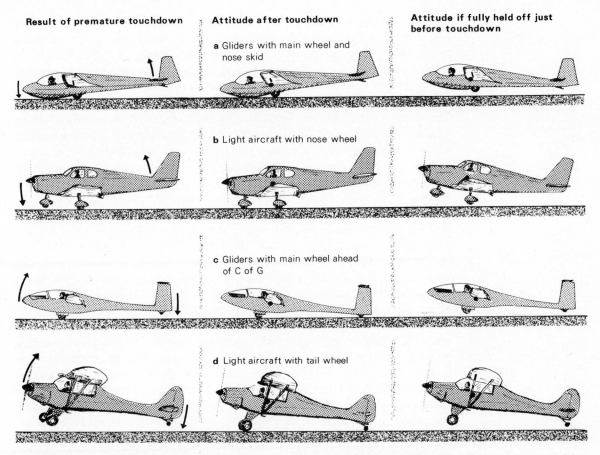

Result of premature touchdown   **Attitude after touchdown**   **Attitude if fully held off just before touchdown**

a Gliders with main wheel and nose skid

b Light aircraft with nose wheel

c Gliders with main wheel ahead of C of G

d Light aircraft with tail wheel

17 Variations in the landing characteristics with different types of undercarriage. **a** Gliders with the main wheel behind the Centre of Gravity and a forward main skid, and **b** light aircraft with a nosewheel, which tend to pitch forward on touchdown so that the angle of attack of the wing is reduced. This prevents the aircraft bouncing. **c** and **d** Aircraft with the main wheel ahead of the Centre of Gravity tend to pitch nose up unless they touch down perfectly with the main and tail wheels together. This increases the wing angle giving more lift and starts bouncing and ballooning.

that it is practically impossible to touch the tail of the aircraft. It lands itself before it can reach such an extreme angle.

The principle of holding the aircraft off the ground as long as possible will result in a good landing in all cases and it is only in very windy or gusty conditions that it needs to be modified. In these conditions there is a possibility of the glider being ballooned up a few feet at the last moment by a gust and this could result in a heavy landing if the gust subsides a few seconds later. It is prudent in very gusty conditions to allow the glider to touch down a little earlier than normal while it has a bit of speed in hand. If the airbrakes are opened fully at the moment of touchdown this will reduce the risk of a gust of wind or a bump in the ground lifting the glider off again.

It is also much safer to arrange for all landings to be made with some air-brake applied. (Usually the instructor will be manipulating the airbrakes in the early stages of learning to land.) Then, if the glider does bounce or balloon and there is a risk of it sinking heavily onto the ground, the airbrakes can be closed (partially or fully as necessary) so that it will float on further for a safe landing. Closing the brakes increases the lift and reduces the drag so that the glider will keep flying a little longer. It is rather like using a burst of engine power in a light aircraft, except that there is only a limited amount available and it can only be used once on any landing! If the air-brakes are opened fully at the moment of touchdown and the stick is held stationary for a few seconds the glider will stay firmly on the ground. This technique for correcting a bounce or balloon cannot be used in gliders or aircraft using flaps instead of airbrakes. Closing the flaps reduces the drag but also reduces the lift as well and if this is done at low speed the aircraft sinks or, in an extreme case, stalls. Special care is needed in gusty conditions for the approach and landing control if you are landing a glider fitted only with flaps. (Some modern gliders feature powerful flaps for this purpose.) On touchdown, therefore, a small forward movement is required to hold the glider down firmly while the flaps are raised to reduce the lift.

When we first adopted the tail-down landing for gliders it was particularly noticeable that the main opponents were instructors who had learned to 'fly on' and who were themselves under-confident about holding off for a proper landing. Now it is almost universal to find that a landing which is not fully held off will be criticised by an instructor. In my own gliding centre, it seems to have greatly reduced the number of bad landings and minor damage and this is well worth the little extra trouble needed during tuition. It is partic-ularly important for cross-country flying, when the surface of the landing area may turn out to be rough and where there is only a limited area available. But quite apart from the risk of damage, there is, I believe, an even more important reason for adopting a proper style of landing.

Many glider pilots convert to powered aircraft at a later date and habits are very difficult to change. Any power instructor who has tried to convert glider pilots onto light aircraft, particularly tail draggers, will tell you that it is often much quicker to teach a student who has done no flying at all. This is because the glider pilots who have never been taught to hold off fully for a landing have become inhibited and frightened of holding off for fear of being too high or stalling the aircraft. Once this fear has become established, it is extremely difficult to overcome. The result is that these glider pilots keep touching down prematurely when they attempt to land any normal aircraft.

Often the pilot has not really learned to judge his height accurately. He merely levels out a few feet above the ground and allows the aircraft to sink and land itself instead of using the controls to check the sinking just as the aircraft reaches the ground. On most occasions this produces a reasonably acceptable landing but it explains the large number of light aircraft and gliders damaged on landing. If the hold off happens to be a little too high or too low, a heavy landing will occur. It is often difficult for the instructor on a nose wheel type of light aircraft to fault the students' landings unless they are really bad. However, with a tail dragger, lack of judgement is obvious since these aircraft will bounce unless they are landed correctly. Similarly, the gliding instructor can tell immediately whether the pilot has really learned to land if he insists on a fully held-off landing.

After proper glider and power training, conversion from one to the other should present no particular problems. The real differences are that the hold-off height must be varied to allow for the length of the undercarriage and that the effectiveness of the elevator declines more rapidly as the speed is lost during the final stages of the hold off in the powered machine.

But for this problem of conversion, glider training might easily have become a normal part of pilot selection many years ago. Unfortunately, tests showed that bad landing and rudder habits learnt in the earlier days on older types of gliders resulted in it taking more flying time to train an ex-glider pilot than an absolute beginner.

With modern machines and good instruction, we know that this is no longer true. Of course, at any time poor instruction leads to bad habits and these are always difficult to eradicate at a later date.

While there still are, and may always be, differences of opinion about the most desirable style of landing, the case for a fully held-off, tail-low touchdown is, in my opinion, overwhelming. In brief it can be summed up as follows:

a It reduces the landing speed and therefore the risk of damage on rough ground.

b The shock is taken on the main wheel which can take very large vertical and side loads and absorbs most of them through the tyre.

c It avoids damage to the front skid (if fitted) caused by flying into the ground, particularly with drift.

d It prevents bouncing and ballooning by ensuring that flying speed is lost by the time that the glider touches down.

e It leads to good landing habits which can easily be adopted to suit any type of machine or conditions.

f It requires judgement and a proper understanding which are essential in the long run, for safe piloting.

Judging the height The key to learning to land is to know where to look and what to look for. Many students suddenly acquire the knack of landing without trying to analyse exactly what they are doing. Others find their progress held up and need all the skill and advice of their instructor to overcome this hurdle.

The explanation which follows is probably inaccurate and in some respects incomplete, but it is simple and it has proved a help to many students both on gliders and on powered aircraft.

At first, most students do find some difficulty in judging when to *start* the initial levelling out movement or round out. This height is really not very critical and even an error of 10 or 20 feet is not serious providing that the move is made too early and *not* too late. Fig. 21 shows the drastic effect of being too late for this movement.

During the initial attempts at the landing, it is usual for the instructor to tell the student when to start the round out. Usually after a few landings the student has learnt to recognise the height and it becomes mainly a matter of the instructor reminding him not to leave things too late.

The main thing at this stage of the landing is to look out at the ground well ahead. Do not look at the horizon, or just over the nose at some particular point on the landing area. Do not allow your eyes to become fixated on the boundary hedge or the spot you think you may land on. If you do, as you get closer or pass over it, you will end up looking much too close over the nose. This is a very common cause of bad landings. The ground will rush up at an alarming speed at the last moment, and you will have to be very quick to level out before the aircraft flies into the ground. It is worth remembering that if the ground does rush up at you suddenly it is a definite sign that you are looking much too close. Below about 200 or 300 feet the position of the nose in relation to the horizon is of little help. On the approach it is a matter of holding a steady attitude. Near the ground and during the hold off, the attitude of the aircraft is no longer of importance and the landing becomes a matter of controlling the height above the ground.

Some instructors and textbooks suggest that, during the final stages of the approach, the detail and movement of the ground suddenly becomes much more apparent. On a grass field, instead of a carpet of green, the individual blades of grass suddenly become visible at a height of about 20 or 30 feet, just about the right height for the initial backward movement on the stick to start the levelling out from the approach.

However, most beginners will find it much easier to judge their height by glancing across and watching the changing appearance of objects on or near to the landing area and of the perspective of the ground ahead.

Some lucky people will instinctively use these clues without being conscious of how they judge their height and without detailed instruction. After only one or two attempts they will be recognising the height at which they should start their round out so that they will very quickly find themselves able to make reasonable landings. Others will need much more experience before they have learned to make this kind of judgement, especially if they are left to their own devices and are given no real help apart from practice.

The major problem is to remain sufficiently relaxed as the aircraft approaches the ground. It is only too easy to stare rigidly ahead instead of glancing very quickly across to near-by objects in order to gather the additional clues which make the judgement of height much easier (Fig. 18).

The actual height at a given moment can best be estimated by glancing across at trees or other objects around the landing area. Once you have seen how easy it is to compare your height with an object and see, at a glance,

100-200 feet	50 feet	15-20 feet. Round out height	5-10 feet. Start holding off

Estimate these heights for yourself. Often a momentary glance across to an object at one side will confirm your height.

18 Aids to judging height for the round out and landing. Two examples of the changing appearance of objects on and near the landing area during the approach and landing. The glider's height can be compared with buildings and other tall objects as it loses height on the approach. During the round out and hold off a glance across to much smaller objects nearby, such as other gliders, cars and people, will give an accurate idea of height. Most of the time, however, the pilot must be watching the changes in perspective ahead to detect any gradual change of height.

when you are just above or below it, there is very little difficulty in judging the moment to start to round out.

Fig. 19 shows how your perspective view of the ground ahead varies with height and how it begins to change much more rapidly during the final 50 feet or so of the approach. When there are no other clues, for example when landing on a very large open area, this change in perspective is almost the only way that the pilot can judge when to start to check his descent and round out for the landing. However, when there are trees or buildings near by, they can be used to judge the descent either by direct comparison or by watching the change of perspective of the top of the objects. In this way the pilot can obtain an earlier and much more accurate indication of his height.

The same methods of direct comparison and changing perspective can often be used during the actual hold off much closer to the ground. Once you can relax sufficiently to glance across the landing area to near-by people

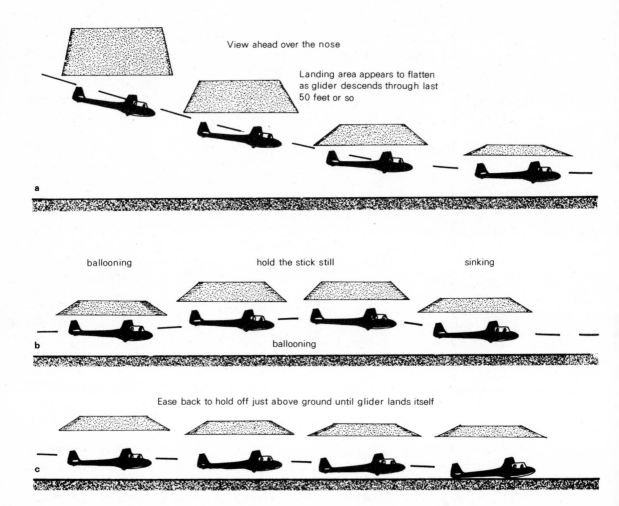

View ahead over the nose

Landing area appears to flatten as glider descends through last 50 feet or so

a

balloning   hold the stick still   sinking

b

ballooning

Ease back to hold off just above ground until glider lands itself

c

19 Detecting changes in height during the hold off by watching the changes in perspective of the ground ahead. Ballooning makes it easier to learn to make the landing. **a** During the final 50 feet or so the perspective changes quickly until, as the glider levels out, the perspective view becomes static. **b** Here the backward movement on the stick has been too large or quick and the glider begins to balloon and gain height. This can easily be detected by the contrasting change in perspective. Do not move the stick forward to try and stop this ballooning. If the stick is held still for a few moments the glider will then sink again and the perspective will begin to change. This is the cue to start the backward movement on the stick to stop the glider sinking and landing heavily. **c** Continue to ease back enough to keep the glider floating just above the ground and the perspective view ahead constant. Finally, the glider will settle the last few inches and land itself.

or objects you can judge your height very accurately. Obviously if you are looking down at the launch point or a group of people you must be rather too high to be holding off, whereas if you are on their level or looking up at them slightly, you must be within inches of the ground.

If you find difficulty in judging the height for the round out and hold off, try to scan more, particularly during the early parts of the approach. This will help to give you an earlier warning that you are almost down to the height where you should be ready to start that minute backward movement to check your descent.

If the glide is gradually flattened out until only a very slight descent is being made, this loss of height can be seen by the gradual change in the perspective of the ground ahead. A similar change may be simulated if you sit a few yards away from a table and lower your head to move your eye level downwards. The descent is seen as a gradual flattening out of the area ahead. Better still, go outside onto an open space and look at the area about 50–100 yards ahead. As you bob down a foot or two by stooping or bending your legs, you will see the changing perspective of the ground. This is the way in which we seem to detect movements up and down during the round out and hold off. However, this does not give us an accurate idea of our exact height above the ground. (Go out and try this now, if possible.)

In order to judge this, it seems that we must make a scanning movement to look for a brief moment at an area much closer and probably a little to one side. It is, of course, easy to see our height by just looking straight down at the ground below (for heights of up to about 20 feet) but this is catastrophic during the landing. Although this enables us to judge our height very accurately at any given moment, it is practically impossible to detect any tendency to go up or down until the movement is quite large. As a result, although we may know at a given instant that the aircraft is, say, 2 feet off the ground, suddenly, without warning, the ground comes up and hits us.

It is very difficult to make a satisfactory landing unless you look well ahead for the majority of the time.

Exactly the same kind of thing happens driving a car in foggy conditions. It is impossible to look ahead very far and it is noticeable that when looking a short distance ahead the exact position in relation to the kerb or white line can be seen, but the car is forever wandering over the road. In other words, looking closely, the exact position can be seen but the trend or change cannot be detected until it is too late. Driving at higher speeds it is essential for the driver to look well ahead. Then he sees the trend and is able to stay on the road, but his judgement of his exact position is not so certain.

Approaching to land in a glider is a similar problem, at similar speeds, and it therefore requires that the pilot looks well ahead to see the changes as they occur. Both student pilots and learner drivers usually start with a tendency to look far too close and therefore you will find instructors repeatedly emphasising 'look ahead' in order to combat this error.

If we now consider the problem of following what is happening during a landing, it soon becomes clear that it will be much easier to spot a ballooning movement than to see the more subtle changes of perspective when the aircraft is flying level and then starts to move up or down. Even the absolute beginner realises that he has overdone the check and started to climb as the perspective change reverses. It is also relatively easy to see the next inevitable change. Once the aircraft is level or starting to go up, it has begun to lose flying speed and within seconds this is bound to cause it to lose height again. Again this contrast from going up to coming down will be easy to see, especially as it is inevitable and, therefore, predictable. The pilot has time as the machine balloons initially to prepare himself for the moment when the descent begins, and to be ready to restart the backward movement to check the descent as the aircraft nears the ground again (see Fig. 19).

Whereas in a perfect hold off and landing the pilot must detect very small changes in height and stop them immediately, if a small amount of ballooning occurs the changes become far more obvious and the pilot knows the sequence of control movements that he is going to require some time before they are actually needed. It is, therefore, important to accept some ballooning as a useful fault in the early stages. If the student becomes worried about ballooning he is likely to go to the other extreme which is to fly the aircraft into the ground while it still has flying speed. This is a serious fault which will temporarily stop all progress towards learning to make a satisfactory landing.

Do not be afraid of ballooning – it is a sign that the aircraft still has too much speed to land. A ballooning movement gives you time to see and understand what is going on and to anticipate the next control movement in plenty of time. By holding the stick *still* for a moment until the aircraft starts to sink again, it is easy then to move it back gently to stop the sinking and so make a good landing.

After some practice in this way, it becomes easier for the eye to follow the changes of height during the hold off. It will then be a simple matter to avoid the ballooning on most occasions and to refine the landing so that at the last moment the aircraft sinks only a few inches onto the ground. The landing will never become a purely automatic subconscious act. It always requires the full attention and skill of the pilot and a really good landing is a real satisfaction and a joy to behold.

Learning to land
By far the greatest hold-up in learning to land a glider is that it is only possible to have one attempt from each launch. In order to make rapid progress, a series of perhaps five or six landings is really needed. This is seldom possible with glider flying since it would take too much time and the flying on most training two-seaters must be shared between a group of students.

Most clubs try to arrange their glider training so that the students get a series of two or three consecutive launches as their turn of flying. By the third landing the student is just beginning to make some real progress and then he must stop to let someone else have a go. Usually by the time he comes to try again it is some days later, so that he has forgotten most of his previous lesson. Progress is rather slow and this is very wasteful and frustrating for both the student and instructor.

Obviously a single landing is of very little value to the beginner who is trying to get his landings right.

The introduction of motor gliders for training has solved this problem. In favourable surroundings, a series of up to ten landings can be made in a half-hour session and any difficulties can be quickly ironed out.

With all glider training, every landing which is not a meaningful demonstration or an attempt by the student, is a landing wasted and one more to be repeated before solo. It is therefore quite normal to start instruction in landing from the very beginning of training – long before the student has perfected the proper co-ordination of the stick and rudder.

(This is not expecting too much from the average beginner. Only a few years ago all glider training was in solo machines. The take off and landing were carried out by the student alone on his very first flight with only a few words of advice from his instructor who stood and watched from the ground. Similarly, all the pioneer flyers like the Wright brothers, taught themselves to fly.)

Because of poor co-ordination of the controls the student will find it very difficult to keep the glider flying straight during the approach. It will probably start to lurch and swing from side to side as he makes corrections, because, at this stage, he completely forgets to use the rudder whenever he has anything else to think about. This usually happens in the early stages even though the stick and rudder movements have been going quite nicely together during the rest of the flight. Every beginner must expect to encounter this difficulty and it often continues to be troublesome throughout almost all the training up to solo standard. Remember that one of the most difficult things of all to do in a glider is to fly straight, particularly in bumpy air.

During the early landings, the instructor can quickly stop any swinging oscillation which occurs by putting his hands and feet on the controls for a few seconds. If he does this at about 100 feet up on the approach, there is usually insufficient time for the glider to start swinging badly again before landing. The landing can then be tackled by the student without the need for further help. (Although this chapter is intended to help the beginner, much of the information and advice is in fact instructing technique, for it is always a help for the beginner to understand more about the way in which his training is being handled.)

Where the landing area is wide enough to allow the glider to turn slightly during the approach and landing, the instructor may choose to allow some wandering rather than interfere with the controls. In this case it is important for the student to understand that he is expected to concentrate on the landing itself and that he should not concern himself too much if the glider starts to drift sideways over the ground or turns slightly during the hold off. Providing that the glider is held off properly so that the drift is taken on the wheel and not on the front skid, no harm will be done. As the student gains experience, his reaction time and co-ordination will improve so that he will be able to hold the glider straighter on the approach.

Obviously, the less there is for the beginner to think about during the approach and landing, the easier the whole thing is and the quicker he can make progress. Most instructors prefer to get the student to concentrate on using the stick and rudder during the landing without involving him with the planning and use of the airbrakes. This simplifies things enormously. Once the landing itself has been mastered it is a simple matter to introduce the use of the airbrakes. Since in most landings they are kept in a constant position during the hold off this should not present any problem.

Good landings are very much a matter of learning to recognise and control what is happening as the aircraft flies along near the ground. After one or two clear demonstrations by the instructor very little more can be learned by following his control movements and the student has to start to make his own attempts.

A satisfactory landing is like a living thing. Each one is slightly different and the pilot is continuously finding out how the aircraft is responding as he moves his controls. Their response varies with the decreasing speed once the glider has begun to level off. Variations in the amount of airbrake being used result in different rates of loss of speed from landing to landing.

It is therefore all a matter of learning to watch and see how the aircraft is responding to the elevator movement and then of varying the rate and size of movement to suit this response. This is a continuous process throughout the landing. Don't be put off by this somewhat complicated description. It is nowhere near as difficult to learn to land as to explain it all. The important thing is to realise that it is hopeless to try and learn just how quickly to pull back on the stick. Each time will be different.

A few apparently slight misunderstandings about the landing can cause endless difficulties and frustrations to both students and their instructors. It is impossible to make a good landing if you are trying to do the wrong thing.

First, consider a landing without worrying about the control movements involved (see Fig. 20).

During the whole of the approach the glider is flown in a rather steeper, nose-down attitude than in normal gliding flight. This gives it additional speed and better control in the rather more turbulent air near the ground. At a height of about 20 or 30 feet above the ground, (we soon learn to guess this height, and it is not critical) the descent is gradually levelled out until the glider is flying level, about 3 or 4 feet above the ground. Since we are no longer gliding downwards, speed is lost and this results in a loss of lift. This makes the glider start to sink and a premature landing would occur but for the action of the pilot who raises the nose very gradually to stop the sinking. Eventually, after floating some distance, the glider sinks onto the ground in spite of the nose being raised. If this is done, it should touch down gently on the main wheel and tail skid together.

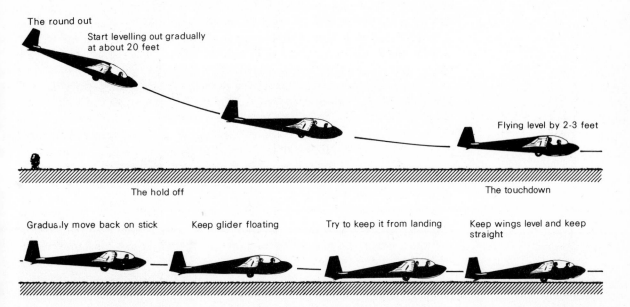

The round out

Start levelling out gradually
at about 20 feet

Flying level by 2-3 feet

The hold off

The touchdown

Gradually move back on stick

Keep glider floating

Try to keep it from landing

Keep wings level and keep
straight

20 How to land. Start levelling out gradually at about 20 feet so that the glider is flying level by the time it is 2 or 3 feet above the ground – not too close. Then try to keep it off the ground by easing the stick gently back as the glider loses speed and tries to sink. Keep the glider floating just off the ground for as long as you can. Eventually it will sink the last few inches in spite of the backward movement on the stick. After touchdown, keep the wings level and keep straight with the rudder. Continue the gradual backward movement to keep the weight of the glider off the nose skid for as long as possible.

Notice that the landing takes place in spite of the pilot trying to keep the glider off the ground. The aim should be to keep it off the ground for as long as possible and *not* to put it down or try to make it land. At this stage of the training, the actual position of the landing is of no concern to the student. This is being controlled by the instructor by means of the airbrakes.

Any attempt to put the glider onto the ground will result in a bad landing with the aircraft flying into the ground in a tail-high position. It is, therefore, essential to disregard thoughts of the long push back to the launching point and aim to make it as long as possible if you are going to make good landings. Later on, the landing point will be controlled by variations of the airbrakes and the positioning of the approach, and the student will learn to land on the spot he has chosen.

For practical purposes the landing can be thought of as being divided into three stages; the round out, or levelling out from the approach; the hold off, or float; and the ground run. Each has its difficulties for the beginner at first, but all of them are easily overcome with practice.

The round out During the final part of the approach, try to remember to glance across to nearby trees and objects in order to tell when you are low enough to start the round out. The rest of the time you should be watching for the change in perspective of the ground by looking well ahead and slightly to one side of the nose.

It is very difficult, if not impossible, to learn to make a satisfactory landing if you are looking just over the nose at the ground only a few yards ahead. At first there is no need to refer to any of the instruments during the final part of the approach or landing. Later, the last quick check on the speed must be made just before the initial round out. In the early practices, the instructor will usually concern himself with the actual speed and can tell the student to lower the nose a little if the speed becomes marginal. This enables the student to concentrate his full attention on the landing itself.

At about 20 or 30 feet (the height has to be judged and at first the instructor will tell you when you get to the right height) a *very* small backward movement is made on the stick. This is *much* smaller than most control movements in normal flight because the glider has much more speed at this moment and this makes the control much more sensitive. In order to give the beginner some idea, this movement is usually about a sixteenth of an inch (two millimetres).

Ideally this movement starts to level the glider out so that it ends up a few feet above the ground, holding a more or less constant height.

The secret of success with the round out is to make it very gradual, and to start in plenty of time. If this is done, during the time that the glider is gradually levelling out it is possible to predict whether it is going to end up flying level at about the right height, or whether an increase in backward movement will be needed to prevent the glider from touching the ground. If it looks as though you will be level too soon and too high up, the backward movement can be stopped for a few seconds to allow the glider to sink a little nearer the ground. It is a great mistake in the early attempts to try to be too precise and level out only a few inches above the ground. Inevitably, the aircraft will sink a few inches or hit a high spot on the ground (unless it is a runway or very smooth grass) and the landing will be made with excess speed and a nose-down attitude.

If the initial movement is left too late, the ground will, by then, be rushing up at you at an alarming rate. You will then be forced to make a very rapid backward movement to prevent the glider from flying hard into the ground. In this situation the chance is very remote that you will make exactly the right amount of movement to end up flying level just above the ground. Having made a sudden movement like this, you will usually overdo it and balloon up badly.

Fig. 21 shows clearly the advantage of starting very gradually and in plenty of time. If the initial movement is late the timing becomes very critical. A split second too late and you have buried the glider! Starting early, it makes very little difference exactly when you start providing that you make the

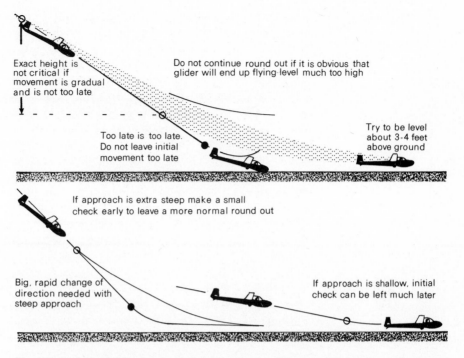

Exact height is not critical if movement is gradual and is not too late

Do not continue round out if it is obvious that glider will end up flying level much too high

Too late is too late. Do not leave initial movement too late

Try to be level about 3-4 feet above ground

If approach is extra steep make a small check early to leave a more normal round out

Big, rapid change of direction needed with steep approach

If approach is shallow, initial check can be left much later

21 The height of the round out is not critical unless it is left too low. The secret is to start the round out early but to make a very gradual movement.

move very gently. It is then possible to follow what is happening and to stop or increase the backward movement of the stick to control the height at which the glider ends up flying level.

If you watch other gliders and aircraft landing, you will notice that just after this initial levelling off they are still in a very nose-down attitude. Frequently, until you have had some practice at landing, you will balloon up away from the ground. This can be caused by a sudden gust of wind but more often by making too large or too rapid a backward movement. Now although the aircraft has gained height it is not, as you might think, in a nose-high attitude. It has climbed bodily on a more or less even keel because it still has plenty of flying speed.

The instinctive reaction of *all* beginners is to move forward on the stick when they realise that they have overdone the backward movement. If you do this, you will find that the ground will rush up at you so quickly that you will seldom have time to stop the glider from hitting the ground hard. Often in a case like this, although the pilot makes a backward movement to stop the machine from striking the ground, there is insufficient time for the controls to be effective and stop the descent.

Do not move forward on the stick unless you have ballooned up 20 or 30 feet. Even then be ready for the glider to descend very quickly or you may fly onto the ground heavily.

If you have ballooned 10 or 15 feet, or have completed the round out at this height instead of a few feet above the ground, just hold the stick still for a moment. Since the glider is gaining height or flying level, it will be losing speed. Within a few moments it will begin to sink. (This is one certainty about all aeroplanes; if you do nothing they always come down!) A backward movement must now be made in order to stop the glider sinking onto the ground heavily. If the ballooning has taken the aircraft well up, the backward move should be delayed until a little of the excess height has been used up. However, when the machine is only a foot or two above the ground, it is necessary to anticipate its sinking and make the movement to stop this just before it actually begins. It always takes time for the aircraft to respond to the control movements and this has to be allowed for, particularly during the landing.

The hold off When the glider has arrived in a position where it is flying more or less level a few feet above the ground, the next stage is to keep it floating to use up its excess speed. A gradual backward movement will be needed to raise the nose a little at a time in order to avoid losing height as the speed decreases. But as the speed falls off, the effectiveness of the controls also becomes less and less, so that slightly bigger movements will be needed at this stage. In fact, a move that at first was far too great and caused the machine to balloon up, may be just about right a few seconds later when some of the speed has been lost.

Do not try to judge the attitude of the machine but keep it flying just above the ground. If it is held off in this position it will eventually sink in spite of the backward movement on the stick, and it will be in the correct landing attitude when it does. If you attempt to judge when the machine is in the landing attitude, you will never hold it off long enough and the landing will be rather nose low. During the hold off, if it is made smoothly, the aircraft is gradually being brought into the landing attitude. It will only reach this position if the hold off is continued for as long as possible.

If the glider tends to balloon or goes on floating, it is still flying too fast for landing. Do *not* attempt to hurry the process of getting down; the machine just has to go on floating until that excess speed has been lost. How long it will float will depend on the speed at the beginning of the hold off and on the amount of airbrake in use at the time. If only a very small amount of airbrake is being used, the drag will be low and it will take a long time to lose speed. In this case you can expect a long, long float with the controls remaining sensitive for longer than usual. Since a long float gives you a long time in which to make a mistake and over-control, there is a far greater chance of your doing this. In fact, landings with very small amounts of airbrake should be avoided if you want to make things easy.

Do not get worried if you balloon up a few feet during the hold off. It is just a sign that you still have too much speed and have overdone the backward movement slightly. Just hold the stick still, watch for the moment when the glider stops going up, and restart the backward movement in time to check the descent just as you are getting close to the ground again. If you overdo the movement a second time or make rather a slow approach, the instructor (or you, if you are already using the airbrakes yourself) will need to reduce the amount of airbrake to prevent the glider from landing heavily. This reduces the drag, so that there is more time available to sort the situation out, and it improves the lift, so that it is possible to carry on flying at the low speed instead of falling out of the air. This could now be a critical situation. If we balloon again, we shall probably end up with insufficient speed and control to check the descent so that we shall land heavily in a semi-stalled condition.

Using a reasonable approach speed, no change of the airbrakes is needed after the first ballooning: it is wise to close them partially on the second; and there just must not be a third time (or you may not be able to avoid a heavy landing!).

Sometimes it is obvious that the speed has become excessive during the latter stages of the approach, or that the approach has become much steeper than is normal. In these cases, it is best to start the round out a little earlier than usual. The steep glide should be reduced to a much more normal one at about 50 feet so that the timing of the proper round out is not so critical. If the speed is obviously rather high, do not try to get too close to the ground. It is much easier to start by getting level at about 5 feet and then gradually lose this height during the hold off until, just before touchdown, you are just off the ground.

Most gliders have very little shock absorbency and rely mainly on the tyre of the main wheel to take the landing shocks. This means that unless you sink very gently onto the ground you will feel quite a bump. Many students make the mistake of getting the aircraft into the landing attitude and then holding the stick in a fixed position during the landing. This does not work very well because as the machine starts to sink, the nose tends to drop. The landing becomes a little heavier than need be and the touchdown is not wheel and tail together and may easily be on the front skid. Only if the stick is being eased back slowly at the moment of touchdown will the glider stay in the tail-low position. The need for this continued movement is best shown at height. If the glider is brought close to the stall with the nose just a little higher than the normal flight position, the stick has to be moved back progressively to keep the nose from dropping. If the stick is held still, although the wing is not stalled, the nose will drop slightly. A further backward move will still raise the nose, proving that the full stall has not yet quite been reached. It is this tendency for the nose to drop that spoils the landing unless the machine is held off *until* the landing occurs. If the stick is held stationary for more than a few seconds during the hold off, a premature landing will occur.

It is easy to see the difficulties which arise if we try to be too accurate and hold off only a few inches off the ground.

During this time, which often involves floating for a hundred yards or so, the glider may start to sink or gain height at any moment. In order to hold the height exactly, a gradually increasing backward movement on the stick is required. When we are so close to the ground, it is necessary to detect and stop even an inch or two of sink. Otherwise a premature touchdown would occur.

A perfect touchdown means therefore, detecting and correcting changes of height of an inch or two in either direction without prior warning, whether the movement will be up or down. Such precision is not required if the hold off is made a foot higher. Then, when the glider starts to sink there is time and height to stop it before it reaches the ground.

The ground run After touchdown, it is important to keep the wings level and to keep the glider running straight. At first many students are so relieved to get down safely that they relax and let one wing touch the ground before they have slowed down.

As a general rule, the backward movement on the stick should be stopped for a few seconds after touchdown. These few seconds will allow a little more speed to be lost and will ensure that the glider does not leave the ground again. In addition, the airbrakes can be opened further to reduce this possibility and to shorten the landing run when necessary.

On gliders which have a nose skid, it should be kept off the ground for as long as possible by moving back on the stick, unless there is a need for a very quick stop. This can be particularly important on rough ground as the shocks will then be taken on the main wheel instead of on the skid, and on a runway, this procedure will save a great deal of unnecessary wear and tear on the skid shoe. In emergency, the stick should be moved right forward after touchdown to use the friction of the skid on the ground to slow down quickly. This is known as rubbing off the speed.

Rubbing off is not recommended as a normal practice on a gliding site but should be used without hesitation if there is any risk of running short of space, or if the ground ahead is uncertain. (Also, if necessary, one wing may be put onto the ground deliberately to make the glider swing and stop, rather than risk running into an obstruction.)

The combination of not holding off properly on the landings with always rubbing off on the front skid, leads to trouble. Sooner or later, the glider will leave the ground just at the moment when the pilot is starting to move fully forward on the stick to rub off. This results in the glider descending very heavily on its nose and was a common cause of damage until a few years ago when fully held off landings began to be encouraged.

Gliders fitted with a main wheel well forward but with no forward skid are liable to bounce, particularly on rough or undulating ground, unless they touch down on their wheel and tail together. The chance of this can be minimised by keeping the tail down firmly on the ground once flying speed has been lost. Keeping the stick back after landing also helps to prevent the tendency for the tail to lift if the wheel brake is applied. Incidentally, while the machine has plenty of speed, there is little or no risk of the glider tipping on its nose, but as it slows down, the elevator becomes less effective and is unable to prevent this happening. This means that the wheel brake must be used with caution as the glider slows down to a stop. An alternative method of preventing the tendency to bounce on these machines is deliberately to lift the tail after touchdown so that the glider is held firmly on the ground. Like rubbing off, this method is not recommended for training or for every-day use, but it can be valuable when landing on bumpy ground in very gusty conditions. It is most effective if the glider is held off normally so that the actual touchdown speed is only slightly above normal.

Once on the ground, all the controls lose their effectiveness very quickly as the speed is lost. The controls are no longer used together as they are for turns in the air. The wings are kept level with sideways movements while the rudder is used quite independently to keep straight or to turn.

In order to stop a slight swing to the left, for example, almost full right rudder will probably be required for a few seconds. It must then be centralised quickly or a swing to the right will tend to develop as the rudder takes effect. All the time the aileron must be used independently to keep the wings level and often almost full movement will be required.

Most motor gliders are fitted with a steering tail wheel coupled through springs to the rudder. This improves the effectiveness of the rudder on the ground at low speeds but may make it rather over-sensitive just after touch-down. Again, any correction must not be held on or a swing the other way may be induced.

It is particularly difficult to detect the start of a swing if the landing area is featureless ground. It helps to look right out ahead to the boundary of the field once the glider is on the ground. Even a slight swing is obvious if you are looking at a tree or similar object in the distance.

In gliders which have the main wheel ahead of the centre of gravity, the inertia of the mass of the aircraft helps to accentuate any swing, as shown in Fig. 22. This effect is greatest in light winds and is worst of all in a light crosswind that is blowing from slightly behind the glider. In these con-ditions the rudder and aileron control are at their worst and the ground speed is high, giving a large inertia effect if a swing starts. Unless the rudder is applied quickly to stop any tendency to swing it may prove difficult, if not impossible, to prevent a ground loop. (This is when the glider swings right round violently, often causing damage to a wingtip or the fuselage.)

This swinging is also resisted by the effect of the tail wheel or tail skid as it slides sideways over the ground. A tail wheel will usually grip the ground whether it is grass or a runway surface so that, if it is kept firmly down by holding the stick back, a swing is unlikely to develop. However, a tail skid is no help whatsoever on a runway or hard ground because it offers so little resistance.

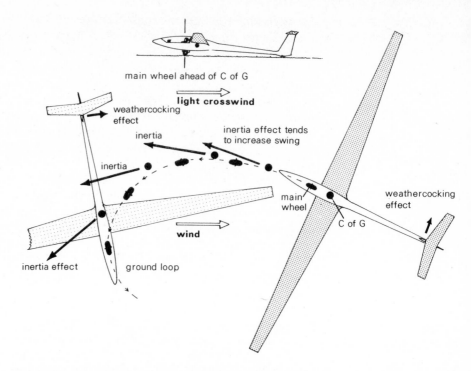

main wheel ahead of C of G

light crosswind

weathercocking effect

inertia effect tends to increase swing

inertia

inertia

inertia

main wheel

weathercocking effect

C of G

wind

inertia effect

ground loop

22 The inertia effect tends to accentuate any swing when the main wheel is ahead of the C of G as in modern gliders. In light winds the inertia effect becomes more powerful than the weathercocking effect.

In strong crosswinds, the tendency to weathercock into wind is often more than the corrective power of full rudder, and the glider will swing into the wind in spite of anything the pilot can do. However, once it is running directly into wind it will not usually swing any further. It is therefore very important to allow for plenty of clearance for a possible uncontrolled swing into wind on every landing which is out of wind.

In light winds the effect of a crosswind is just to induce the start of a swing at a time when the ground speed, and therefore the inertia effect, is large. A swing may also be started by the pilot failing to keep a wingtip off the ground until the glider has slowed down.

It should be noted that once any slight swing has started the use of the wheel brake will only increase the inertia effects and that any fierce braking may lift the weight off the tail skid making the swing even more violent.

These problems are the price paid for the gain in efficiency obtained by eliminating the weight and drag of a forward skid and being able to retract the main wheel neatly into the fuselage.

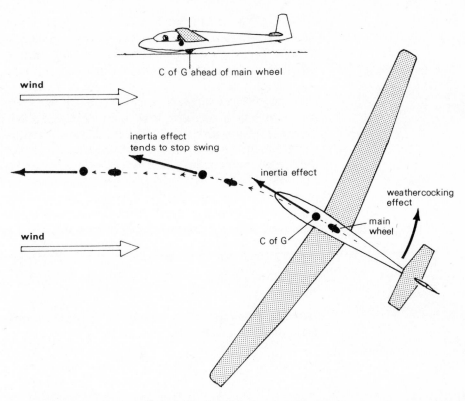

23 With the main wheel behind the C of G the inertia effect tends to reduce the swing on the ground run and the weathercocking tendency is weak.

If the main wheel is mounted on or behind the C of G as in the majority of training machines, the inertia effect helps to *stop* any swing (Fig. 23). Since there is much more side area ahead of the wheel the tendency to weathercock into wind is less marked so that the rudder power is usually sufficient for the pilot to keep the glider straight in any crosswind. On these machines the beginner needs no special skill and can learn to control the machine on the ground without fear of looping. However, it is still prudent to leave extra room for swinging into wind during the landing run.

Steering on the ground is an often neglected exercise in training gliders because they do not often swing badly unless, as shown, they are landing in a strong crosswind. A common fault among students is to attempt to steer in the same way as in the air, by using the stick and rudder together. This only results in the wingtip touching the ground so that a bad swing may develop. It is important to practise steering on the ground as it may enable you to avoid colliding with an unexpected obstruction one day and so save you a costly repair bill.

Towards the end of the landing run, it is difficult to maintain full control on every occasion. It is therefore important to give yourself more than enough room for any eventuality. During your early landings the instructor will almost certainly be selecting the landing area. Later on this will be your responsibility and it is vital to play safe at all times. Choose a completely clear landing area whenever there is one. Do not attempt to land unless you will be at least a complete wing span clear of any obstruction. If necessary make the landing farther up the field, beyond a congested area. Do not land going directly towards an obstruction, even if you think you have plenty of room. You might balloon or bounce badly and then you could be faced with the prospect of either closing the brakes and running into the obstruction, or making a heavy landing in the attempt to get down without closing the brakes. Unlike a motor car, the average aeroplane or glider is not designed for good control on the ground. Both steering and wheel brakes are often rather poor and it is unwise to rely upon them in an emergency. Always remember that if you are tipped by a sudden gust or start to drift at the last moment on an approach, it may be difficult or impossible to keep your glider absolutely straight.

Always allow yourself plenty of room for a possible swing during take off and landing.

5 Spoiling the Gliding Angle

Sideslipping	77	Flaps	83
Spoilers	78	Fuselage airbrakes	86
Wing airbrakes	80	Tail parachutes or drogues	86
Trailing edge airbrakes	82		

Landing in a confined space when the approach involves crossing trees or other obstructions requires a positive and effective means of steepening the glide path without gaining speed.

Height can be lost by putting the nose down and diving to a high speed. However, this does not result in landing appreciably shorter than with a steady glide at a more normal speed. Once near the ground, the extra speed must be used up before landing and the result is just a very long float, defeating the object of diving off the height. The height has been turned into speed, and the speed has been turned into distance.

Theoretically, extra height can also be lost by gliding at a very low speed so that the machine mushes through the air (sinks nose high) at an inefficient angle, creating more drag and spoiling the gliding angle. This is a dangerous solution, since any turbulence or wind gradient effect would result in a stall at a height from which recovery would be impossible.

Sideslipping
(Fig. 24.)

The solution to this problem is to have a means of increasing the drag without a large change in airspeed being necessary. This can be done by sideslipping, when the extra drag is caused by flying sideways through the air to spoil the streamlining. The extra drag reduces the lift/drag ratio so that the gliding angle becomes steeper for the same airspeed. Sideslipping alone is not a very practical method of approach control since it requires a high degree of skill to guarantee a spot landing. Also, it is not safe to sideslip violently at low speed near the ground in gusty conditions to stop the glider floating a long distance before touchdown.

It is impossible to hold most gliders in a steep sideslip because the rudder control is inadequate to overpower the weathercocking tendency when slipping at a large angle. Sideslipping is usually considered as an emergency method of increasing the effectiveness of the airbrakes when the approach has been so hopelessly misjudged that there is a risk of an overshoot.

It is an adequate means of controlling the approach on an old, low performance machine, but if the gliding angle is much above 15:1, some additional form of control is essential, particularly in light winds.

77

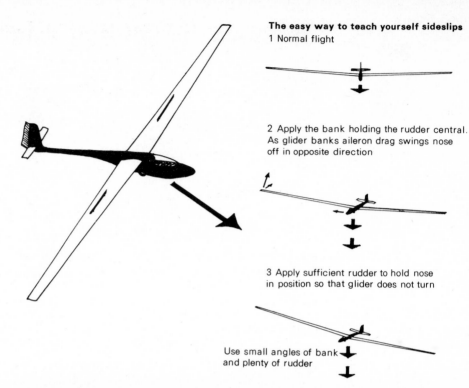

2 Apply the bank holding the rudder central.
As glider banks aileron drag swings nose
off in opposite direction

3 Apply sufficient rudder to hold nose
in position so that glider does not turn

Use small angles of bank
and plenty of rudder

24 Sideslipping. The gliding angle is steepened by sideslipping because of the extra drag created as the fuselage flies sideways through the air. In most gliders a steady, steeply-banked sideslip is not possible.

Spoilers Simple lift spoilers are an inexpensive form of airbrake which spoil the lift of part of the wing, as well as increasing the drag, by creating turbulence. On a rather low performance glider, spoilers will be quite effective in steepening the approach and reducing the float before touchdown. However, the drag at high speeds is nowhere near sufficient to limit the diving speed and therefore they are not effective in these circumstances. When the spoilers are opened, the total lift from the wing is reduced as though a portion of the wing has been cut off. The stalling speed is raised slightly so that some additional speed is needed. Generally, the increase in stalling speed is less than 3 knots, but additional extra speed is also needed because, as soon as the glider starts to level out for the landing, the extra drag of the spoiler results in a more rapid loss of speed than normal and this can cause a heavy landing. As with all forms of airbrake, a few knots of extra speed are a good insurance except when landing in a confined space in a high performance machine when extra speed could result in floating into the far boundary.

The initial effect of opening the spoilers is a rapid sink for a few feet together with a slight nose-down change of trim (nose heaviness) in many

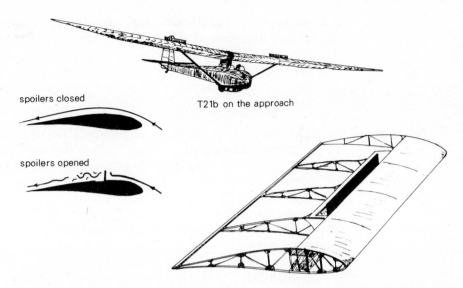

spoilers closed

T21b on the approach

spoilers opened

25 Lift spoilers. Spoilers produce an increase in drag with a marked decrease in the lift over that part of the wing. Opening the spoilers usually results in a nose down change in trim.

cases. This is due to the loss of lift. If the same airspeed is required, the nose of the glider must be lowered a little as the spoiler is opened or the extra drag will slow the glider down. After the first few seconds, the glide settles down to the steeper angle of descent. The angle may be varied by changing the spoiler setting and in this way the glide path can be very accurately controlled in order to land within a few feet of the chosen spot. Care must be used if the spoilers are opened close to the ground and the tendency to sink must be checked with the elevator control, or a heavy landing may occur. Whereas closing the spoilers improves the lift and lowers the stalling speed, opening them at low speed, perhaps after ballooning up a few feet, can be disastrous. The beginner is advised to avoid opening them close to the ground unless he is certain that the speed is more than adequate, or unless there is a risk of floating out of the field.

Although all forms of spoilers and airbrakes create much more drag at higher speeds, diving off excess height with the spoilers open is not recommended since it is very difficult to learn to judge how far the glider will float once it is levelled out. A steady approach at a well-controlled speed is essential for consistent spot landings.

There are many kinds of airbrakes, ranging from the simple spoilers already described, to tail parachutes. Airbrakes are designed to create large amounts of extra drag in order to spoil the gliding angle and often to limit the diving speed. Fig. 27 shows some common types and it will be seen that there are three main categories; wing airbrakes; fuselage drag increasing devices and wing flaps.

Wing airbrakes These are by far the most common and also the most effective means of approach control and they work in a very similar way to spoilers. They are usually effective enough to steepen the gliding angle at a normal approach speed to about 6:1 or 8:1, using full airbrakes, and this makes precision approaches a simple matter. Most types of airbrakes cause some loss of lift in addition to a very large increase in the drag. Considerably more speed is needed when landing with the airbrakes fully opened to allow for the loss of speed during the round out for landing. Airbrakes are usually designed so that there is no trim change when they are opened at speed. If there was a nose-up trim change, there would be a risk of overstressing the machine if the airbrakes were opened at high speed in cloud during the pull out from a dive. The airbrakes fitted to modern machines limit the diving speed to below the maximum permissible, or Never Exceed Speed (known as V_{NE}) in any dive of less than about 60°. Older machines have brakes which limit the speed in a continuous, vertical dive but this is difficult to achieve with a very clean, modern glider. In practice, airbrakes are seldom used as dive brakes, but it is a comfort to know that they can be opened or used at any speed if you get into difficulties in cloud, or want to get down from a great height quickly.

In order to avoid very high control forces which would make it difficult to open them at high speed, airbrakes are either balanced, so that the air load on one set helps to overcome the air load on the others, or they open at right angles to the airflow so the loads are reasonably small at high speed. Fig. 26 shows a very common type of airbrake with the brake paddles opening above and below the wing. When both paddles are fitted into one box the airbrake has a tendency to snatch open as it is unlocked by the pilot. The reduced pressure above the wing helps to suck open the top section while the air at rather higher pressure flows into the brake box and forces the two brake paddles apart. Unless a damper of some kind is fitted in the circuit, the pilot must keep a firm grip on the lever in the cockpit as he opens the brakes at speed, or they will fly to the fully open position. Unless this type of brake is very well sealed and fits perfectly flush to the surface, there will be a serious loss of efficiency. Any slight leakage through from the bottom surface will reduce the lift considerably and cause bad turbulence over the rest of the wing behind the brake. This can be avoided by putting the two brake paddles into completely separate boxes, which also eliminates most of the tendency to snatch.

Another satisfactory solution is to do away with the lower paddle altogether and just fit slightly larger top surface brakes. This is much more effective

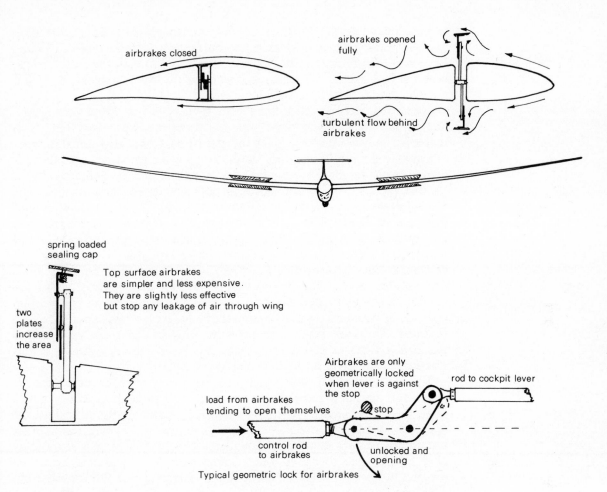

airbrakes closed

airbrakes opened fully

turbulent flow behind airbrakes

spring loaded sealing cap

Top surface airbrakes are simpler and less expensive. They are slightly less effective but stop any leakage of air through wing

two plates increase the area

Airbrakes are only geometrically locked when lever is against the stop

rod to cockpit lever

load from airbrakes tending to open themselves

stop

control rod to airbrakes

unlocked and opening

Typical geometric lock for airbrakes

26 Airbrakes. Unlike spoilers, these airbrakes tend to be sucked open in flight and a mechanical lock is essential to keep them closed. This is usually a geometric, over-centre lock as illustrated.

than using a bottom surface paddle only because the top surface paddle acts as a lift spoiler and so has more effect on the gliding angle than would an increase in drag only.

A geometric lock (see Fig. 26) is usually used to secure the airbrakes against this tendency to be sucked open, and, as an extra safeguard against the pilot leaving them unlocked on take off, it is usual to include a spring in the control circuit to hold them closed at low speeds, even if they are unlocked. (Spoilers do not require such a positive lock because the airflow tends to blow them down flat.)

Many modern designs have a spring-loaded cap to the airbrake. This helps to provide a really good seal, which stops any leakage and allows the wing to bend up and down without risk of the seal being broken. But it does make it much harder to close and lock the geometric lock, with the result that more force is needed to unlock the brakes. When this happens, the snatch of the brakes at high speeds will seem much worse as the lock is suddenly freed and the pilot inadvertently pulls the lever too far.

Converting from a glider fitted with spoilers to one fitted with speed-limiting airbrakes should cause very few problems. The main thing is to remember to lower the nose much more as the airbrakes are opened in order to maintain the approach speed. On the first few flights, always get into such a position for the final approach that you can use at least half airbrake for the final 50 feet or so. Use an adequate approach speed, *not* a marginal one.

The history of wing airbrakes is a chequered one. The Germans introduced them before World War II and by 1950 they were universally accepted. However, the intense competition for higher and higher performance has led to the acceptance of less and less effective brakes, while at the same time most of the machines have become faster and heavier, as well as having a much flatter gliding angle. The introduction of new low-drag aerofoils with more laminar flow necessitated moving the airbrakes back beyond the halfway point along the chord. In this position the boundary layer has already become turbulent. Unfortunately, at this point the wing section is not very deep so that it is difficult to fit a deep airbrake paddle; moreover, airbrakes in this rearward position are far less effective at low speed.

The net result of all these problems is that many of the modern breed of glass fibre machines require above average skill to land accurately into a small field. The ineffectiveness of the brakes makes it vital to control the approach speed very precisely. A few knots too much may result in an uncontrollable float into the far boundary. This kind of error is more likely after training and flying on gliders fitted with really powerful brakes on which a little extra height or speed can be corrected in a few seconds with full airbrake and a dive or sideslip.

This design fashion will probably be short-lived and it can only be hoped that good airbrakes will appear again on even the highest performance machines.

Trailing edge airbrakes

Trailing edge brakes are very attractive since they leave almost all the wing with an unbroken surface for efficiency. It is also easy to provide a really big area so that the brakes are powerful.

The portion of the flap above the wing provides a balancing force to reduce the load on the lever in the cockpit as the flap is lowered. For ease of handling, it is important that lowering the flap does not increase the lift. Otherwise it becomes difficult, if not impracticable, to raise the flap again anywhere near the ground in the event of a need to extend the glide at the last moment to float over a rough patch of ground or perhaps a hitherto unseen electric fence.

This type of airbrake is nice to handle because it does not snatch. Also,

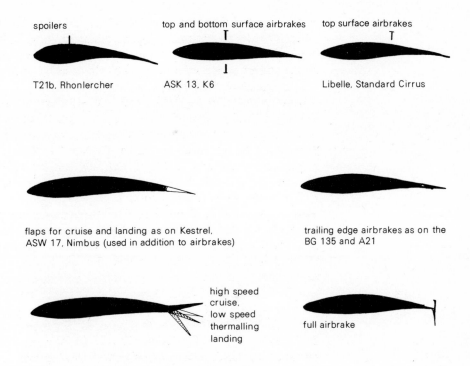

27 Common types of airbrakes and flaps.

spoilers

T21b, Rhonlercher

top and bottom surface airbrakes

ASK 13, K6

top surface airbrakes

Libelle, Standard Cirrus

flaps for cruise and landing as on Kestrel,
ASW 17, Nimbus (used in addition to airbrakes)

trailing edge airbrakes as on the
BG 135 and A21

high speed
cruise,
low speed
thermalling
landing

full airbrake

the operating load becomes progressively greater as the brake is opened further, which gives the control a good feel. At the time of writing only a few machines have this design of brake and it is early days to hazard a guess as to its future.

Flaps Flaps can be another means of approach control for gliders and, despite some of their problems and limitations, it seems likely that most of the competition machines of the next decade will be fitted with them for one reason or another.

Some of the different kinds of flaps which have been tried on gliders are illustrated in Fig. 27. So far, attempts at area increasing flaps, like the Fowler type, have not been very successful. The aim with this type is to increase the wing area and so reduce the wing loading and circling speeds for soaring. It is usually easy to obtain extra lift and reduce the stalling speed, but only at the expense of extra drag so that the gliding angle suffers. Even then, the lowered flying speed may give an advantage for small thermals because it may enable the glider to stay in the better lift and this may offset any small increase in the glider's rate of sink. Unfortunately, there is also likely to be a drag loss at higher speeds when the flap is not in use. Very often the result is that just as useful a performance could have been obtained with less weight and expense by using a clean wing without the complication of the flap. This may well be the case with the well-known Czechoslovakian Blanik

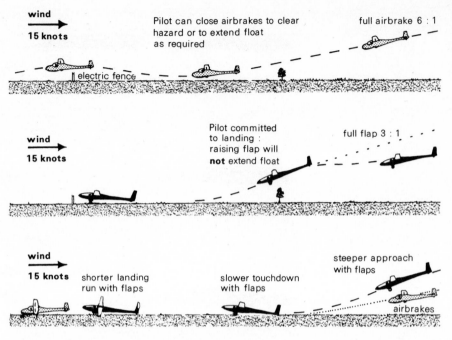

wind
15 knots

Pilot can close airbrakes to clear hazard or to extend float as required

full airbrake 6 : 1

electric fence

wind
15 knots

Pilot committed to landing : raising flap will **not** extend float

full flap 3 : 1

wind
15 knots

shorter landing run with flaps

slower touchdown with flaps

steeper approach with flaps

airbrakes

28 A comparison between the effects of airbrakes and landing flaps. Flaps can produce steeper approaches and lower landing speeds but airbrakes are more flexible and allow more accurate spot landings.

two-seater. The fact is that the drag of the modern glass fibre machine is now so low that only a machine with perfectly fitted flaps is likely to compete with them. However, this kind of problem is always the target for the most enterprising designers so we can expect some progress with area increasing flaps in the near future.

Flaps for approach control are arranged to deflect to a much larger angle in order to create large amounts of drag. Plain flaps are now used on many types of high performance gliders since they have the great advantages of being easy to seal as well as being as cheap, or cheaper to fit, than airbrakes. These flaps are usually made to be moveable through a range of about 5° or 10° up and down to improve the cruising performance, and downwards to 60° or 70° to increase the drag for steep approaches. The ailerons are often arranged to move up and down a few degrees with the flaps so that, in effect, the aerofoil of the whole wing is changed according to the flying speed.

Moving the flap up a few degrees reduces the drag at high speeds when a high lift coefficient is not needed (i.e. when the high speed gives most of the lift and only a very small angle of attack is necessary, the actual wing angle does not have to be reduced to an inefficient degree. Instead, the flap is raised and this reduces the lift so that the forward half of the wing remains within an efficient angle). This results in extending the range of speeds over which the flow remains predominantly laminar, with an impressive effect on the performance.

Lowering the flaps has a significant effect on both the lift and drag. With the flap lowered down to about 10°, there is a considerable increase in the lift with only a small increase in the drag, so that the best gliding angle is scarcely affected. The increase in lift reduces the stalling speed by 2 or 3 knots and also results in a smaller turning radius for thermalling – a useful feature in a fast machine.

As the flap is lowered beyond about 10°, it becomes impracticable to lower the ailerons to match without spoiling their effectiveness. The lift continues to rise steadily but together with an ever-increasing amount of drag, so that the gliding angle becomes much steeper. By about 50°, the lift is almost constant but the drag is rocketing up because of the complete disruption of the airflow behind the flap. On many machines the difficulties of designing a really close-fitting, low-loss flap which can move down beyond about 40° have discouraged the designer and either some form of airbrake or tail parachute has been resorted to, rather than use the flap alone to give steep approach. Without some kind of powered assistance, it is almost impossible for a man to lower the flap quickly against the airflow above about 70 knots, so that the flaps cannot be relied upon in emergency for limiting the diving speed.

However, in many respects the flapped glider has a number of advantages and is impressive in performance when compared with an equivalent machine fitted only with airbrakes (see Fig. 28).

Flaps compared with normal airbrakes

	Landing flaps	Airbrakes
Basic stalling speed	35	35
Stalling speed, full flap or airbrake	32	38
Approach speed, full flap or airbrake	45	50
Best gliding angle	30:1	30:1

Effect of flaps compared with airbrakes on the approach and landing

No wind		
Angle of approach, full flap or airbrake	5:1	8:1
Touchdown speed, full flap or airbrake	35	40 +
15 knot headwind		
Angle of approach, full flap or airbrake	3.3:1	5.6:1
Touchdown speed, full flap or airbrake	20	25

All speeds are shown in knots

The flapped machine may have a stalling speed 6 to 8 knots less than the machine with airbrakes as well as a much steeper glide and reduced float because of the very high drag. The big snag is decreased flexibility near the ground. With skill, airbrakes may be safely applied or closed at any stage of the approach and landing so that the exact touchdown point can be selected or varied during the hold off. However, flaps cannot be raised near the ground unless there is excess speed, and even then only with caution.

If the glider is landing in turbulent conditions and it happens to be hit by a gust so that it balloons upwards a few feet, airbrakes can be closed to allow a safe landing to be made. With flaps this would result in a heavy landing. However, since the shock depends upon the touchdown speed, the risk of actual damage may be lower than might at first appear. Obviously, slightly different techniques must be used with flaps and they must not be lowered fully until the final stage of the approach when the pilot is certain of reaching his landing spot. An added advantage of flaps is that the glider flies in a very much more nose-down attitude, which gives the pilot a better view on the approach.

Where flaps are fitted primarily to improve performance, the technique is to let down some flap to lower the stalling speed before the final approach and then to use the airbrakes or tail parachute for the final adjustments. Where the ailerons are drooped in harmony with the flap, it may be desirable to keep the flap in a position where the ailerons are not affected. The aileron control is usually reduced slightly by drooping them, and at low speeds this, together with the increase in aileron drag, may result in difficulties in keeping the wings level during the approach and landing run. A little experimenting will show whether this is necessary on a particular type of glider.

Fuselage airbrakes   A few attempts have been made to use opening flaps on the fuselage sides, or on the fin and rudder, in order to increase the drag for the approach and landing. Although this is fairly common practice on jet aircraft it usually results in insufficient drag to be effective on a modern glider at low speeds and there tends to be an unacceptable amount of fuselage and tail buffeting with this type of brake.

Tail parachutes or drogues
(See Plate 3.)   In many ways tail parachutes are a very attractive solution to the problem of providing a large increase in drag for the approach. Unfortunately, they are more attractive to the designer than to the pilot. As an emergency means of limiting the diving speed in cloud they are acceptable, but as an approach aid they are too inflexible to be really satisfactory.

The cockpit control normally consists of a knob to deploy the chute and a second release which may be used to jettison it. A few machines are fitted with two independently operated chutes which can be deployed individually or together as required. The parachutes are made from strips of nylon so that the air flows through them, creating a large amount of drag. Without the slots all over the canopy the parachute would oscillate wildly at high speeds and would not create sufficient drag to be really effective.

Compared with airbrakes, the tail parachute has the advantage that it does not affect the stalling speed of the aircraft. Theoretically, no extra speed is required on the approach. However, the drag is very high and some extra speed is essential to avoid losing too much and getting dangerously slow during the round out. When the tail parachute is deployed, it takes a few seconds before it develops and the effect of the extra drag is felt in the cockpit. In order to maintain the speed, the nose of the glider must be lowered immediately. The drag will steepen the gliding angle from 30:1 to less than 5:1 in still air and in most cases a tail parachute has a much greater effect even than full airbrake. Because the drag of a parachute rises rapidly with speed, any tendency to overshoot can be eliminated by diving steeply some distance short of the desired touchdown point.

A tail parachute can only be used safely in certain situations because of its very powerful effects.

Above about 200 to 300 feet, it can be opened at any normal flying speed and there will be ample time to lower the nose steeply to maintain the speed as the drag of the parachute is felt. The approach has to be very steep or the speed will start to decrease. If the airspeed is allowed to fall below a normal approach speed, it will be difficult to regain and a heavy landing will be almost inevitable unless the parachute is jettisoned.

It is essential to realise that the angle of descent needed to maintain speed will be about 1 : 4 even in no wind. This is *much* steeper than with any other normal type of airbrake.

Within 10–15 feet of the ground the parachute may be safely deployed at any speed a little above the normal approach speed. For example, on the Kestrel or Nimbus, a speed of 50–55 knots would be sufficient provided that the glider was not above 15 feet. The landing then takes place before the drag of the parachute has time to reduce the speed too much. With speeds in excess of 60 knots there would be no problem at all in opening the parachute at this late stage.

Above 15 feet and below about 100 feet the situation is much more critical. There is seldom enough time and height to get into the steep attitude required to maintain speed, and although the nose is lowered to what appears to be a steep position, some speed will usually be lost during the approach.

The chute must either be opened with plenty of extra speed to allow for this to happen, or alternatively, the pilot must be prepared to jettison it to avoid getting below the minimum safe round out speed. Fortunately, jettisoning the parachute is almost instantaneous and the systems seem very reliable.

The most common trouble is caused by failure to maintain speed so that a damaging, heavy landing occurs. This can be avoided by remembering the golden rule. If the speed is dropping and has reached the normal approach speed, jettison the parachute immediately. (Of course this can be disastrous unless the glider is fitted with some other additional form of airbrake or flap.)

It can be a great comfort to the pilot to know that in emergency he can use the parachute to get down into a small space. In some cases he can use it to reduce the speed quickly in order to avoid an expensive overshoot. In these situations absolute reliability is essential since any failure is almost certain to result in an accident. Tail parachutes have a rather poor reputation for reliability but in most cases, a failure to deploy can be traced to poor day-to-day servicing and incorrect packing.

Ideally, at the end of each day's flying the tail parachute should be taken out of its stowage and hung up where it can dry. It should *not* be left in the machine day after day because if it does get damp the moisture may freeze the canopy together so that it cannot deploy. Most installations are vulnerable to this kind of trouble. The moisture can run down into the parachute container between flights and this alone may be sufficient to cause a hang up. Many of these chutes will only function reliably if they are packed correctly. Make sure that you do not turn them inside out, as, even though they may look perfectly all right, it can affect the opening. For example, with the research glider Sigma, this was found to be one of the chief reasons for the parachute streaming instead of opening fully. The other main cause of trouble is a tight-fitting fairing. Experience has shown that it is worth getting into the habit of making a sharp rudder movement to and fro at the moment of pulling the knob to deploy the chute. This will help to make sure that the fairing holding the chute in place drops away immediately.

One development is to vary the drag of the parachute by providing a control to deflate the canopy partially. This could make the tail parachute much more acceptable to the average pilot since he could then adjust his approach by varying the amount of drag, as with normal airbrakes.

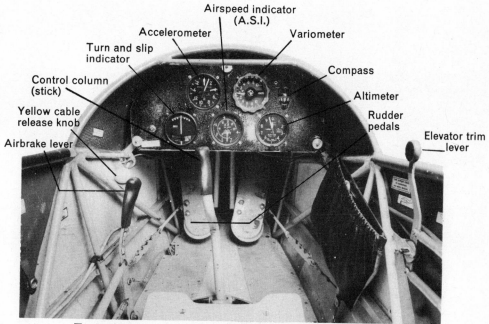

Turn and slip indicator
Accelerometer
Airspeed indicator (A.S.I.)
Variometer
Compass
Control column (stick)
Altimeter
Yellow cable release knob
Rudder pedals
Airbrake lever
Elevator trim lever

Typical cockpit layout of an ASK 13 two-seater training glider
(reproduced by courtesy of Steve Bicknell)

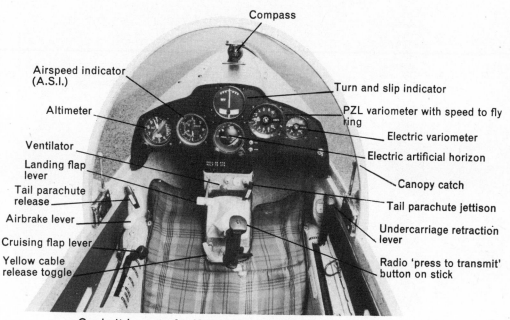

Compass
Airspeed indicator (A.S.I.)
Turn and slip indicator
Altimeter
PZL variometer with speed to fly ring
Ventilator
Electric variometer
Landing flap lever
Electric artificial horizon
Tail parachute release
Canopy catch
Airbrake lever
Tail parachute jettison
Cruising flap lever
Undercarriage retraction lever
Yellow cable release toggle
Radio 'press to transmit' button on stick

Cockpit layout of a Kestrel high-performance sailplane
(reproduced by courtesy of Steve Bicknell)

ASK 13 two-seater training glider
(reproduced by courtesy of Peter M. Warren)

Caproni Calif high-performance two-seater sailplane

19 metre all glass fibre
construction Kestrel
sailplane
(reproduced by courtesy
of *The Times*)

Kestrel using tail parachute and jettisoning water ballast on the approach
(reproduced by courtesy of *The Times*)

A typical two-drum winch
(Copyright BBC)

Preparing for an aerotow at the launch point
(reproduced by courtesy of Steve Bicknell)

6

Using the Airbrakes

The effect of the airbrakes 89
Operating the lever 89
Controlling the speed 91
Approach speeds 91
Use of the airbrakes while
  teaching landings 96

Controlling the float 98
Airbrakes open at the wrong
  times 98
Special advice for beginners
  on using the airbrakes 101

The effect of the airbrakes

The pilot of a glider may think of the effect of the airbrakes in several different ways.

If he is returning from a successful soaring flight and is in a hurry to lose height, or if he is on the base leg of the circuit and is obviously much too high, he will open the brakes in order to throw away the height quickly.

On the final approach he is more likely to think of the airbrakes as the control to steepen his glidepath and to adjust the angle of glide (Fig. 29).

The more powerful types of airbrakes may be used to restrict the diving speed if control is lost in cloud. They can also be used in a limited way to reduce any excess speed on an approach. Even more important, if the approach begins to get too slow, they *must* be closed, or the amount of airbrake reduced, to help maintain or gain speed in order to ensure a safe landing. In a limited sense, therefore, they may be considered as a speed control.

During the actual hold off and float, the distance before touchdown can also be adjusted by a variation in the setting of the brakes, although it requires caution and a little specialised training in order to do this safely.

Spoilers are really only rather ineffective airbrakes which do not limit the diving speed or create very large amounts of drag. Their use and operation is identical to airbrakes but they do not tend to snatch open.

Operating the lever

The operating loads vary with the different kinds of airbrake. With the most common type, illustrated in Fig. 26, there is a definite pull force required to unlock the geometric lock, but once unlocked the airbrakes tend to open themselves. The pilot should keep the left hand very firmly on the airbrake lever to stop the airbrakes from opening further than required. The airbrakes can be unlocked without allowing them to ride open, but this needs care. If this is done on the base leg of the circuit, the airbrakes can then be opened much more smoothly and under much more precise control than if they are opened suddenly from the locked position. The pilot must never take his

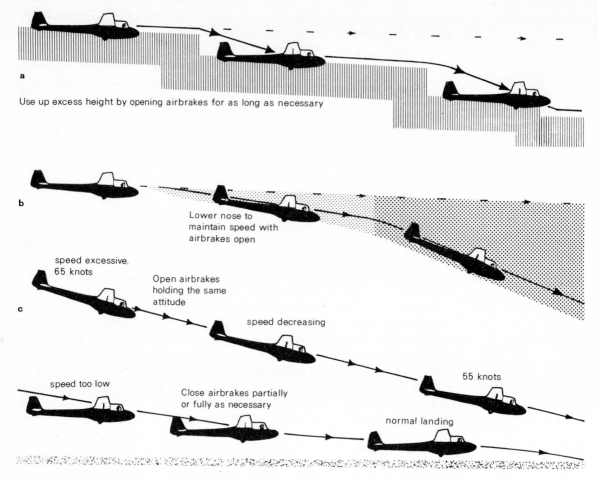

Use up excess height by opening airbrakes for as long as necessary

Lower nose to maintain speed with airbrakes open

speed excessive, 65 knots

Open airbrakes holding the same attitude

speed decreasing

55 knots

speed too low

Close airbrakes partially or fully as necessary

normal landing

29 Ways of thinking about the effect of the airbrakes. **a** Throwing away excess height – the loss of height may be controlled accurately by variations in the amount of airbrake used. **b** Steepening the gliding angle on the approach – remember that the nose must be lowered to maintain speed when the airbrakes are opened **c** Controlling the speed – excess speed can be checked by opening the airbrakes fully without lowering the nose. If the speed becomes too low and there is insufficient height to lower the nose to regain it, close the airbrakes as necessary to allow a normal landing. This is useful in an emergency but has a very limited effect unless the glider has abnormally powerful airbrakes.

hand off the lever once the airbrakes are unlocked, or they may open themselves fully. This could result in the glider undershooting into an obstruction before the pilot has time to find the lever again and close the brakes. Any adjustments to the elevator trimmer must, therefore, be made before using the airbrakes since it is not safe to let go of the stick, and we only have two hands.

The amount of snatching which occurs when the airbrakes are opened depends on the airspeed and also on the strength of the geometric lock. At high speeds the airbrakes will snatch severely and unless you hold the lever and brace your arm firmly, they will fly open with considerable force. Also, if the lock is very strong, you will be applying a considerable backward pressure on the lever as it unlocks so that the brakes will be jerked open suddenly. This problem can be minimised by unlocking the brakes on the base leg, as suggested, and then avoiding locking them again if they are closed for a few seconds at a later stage on the approach. This makes it much easier to obtain a smooth and controlled operation.

Both airbrakes and spoilers have to be held in place all the time they are being used. Unlike flaps they cannot be opened and set in a certain position.

Controlling the speed

Because of the increase in the drag when the airbrakes or spoilers are opened, the nose of the glider must be lowered to maintain the same speed. With powerful airbrakes there needs to be a considerable nose-down change of attitude, particularly if the brakes are opened fully. If the airbrakes are opened even a small amount while the glider is approaching steadily at a constant speed, the speed will start to fall off, and unless something is done about this very quickly a heavy landing will occur because there will not be enough speed to level out properly. If there is time and height to allow it, the nose should be lowered to regain the speed. Otherwise, the airbrakes must be closed, or partially closed, to help reduce the drag and to lower the stalling speed so that, even at the low speed, a landing of sorts can still be made without damage.

There is always a slight tendency to lose some speed on the final approach because of the wind gradient effect (explained in Chapter 9), and when this is severe, extra caution is needed on every approach. An inexperienced pilot is well advised to choose an approach speed which is a few knots faster than is absolutely necessary. The worst result of this extra speed is a few yards of extra float before touchdown. However, this must not be taken to mean approaching at any old speed as long as it is fast. It is important, even for the beginner, to learn to choose a definite speed and try to keep to it. Otherwise the landings will be all over the landing area and will never be really controlled and accurate. The approach speeds need to be consistent in order to learn to allow for the distance which the glider will float before touchdown.

The abnormally slow approach is the real crime since any additional loss of speed at this stage is disastrous and the glider will frequently arrive too slow to be able to round out properly for a normal touchdown.

Approach speeds

On most gliders the ideal approach speed for a light-wind day is the minimum speed which allows the full airbrake to be used for the final approach and the complete round out and landing. At this speed, the glider will only float a few yards before sinking onto the ground. If it floats a long way with full airbrake, this is a sign that the speed was excessive, whereas if the glider arrives on the ground with no float at all, the speed was marginal for safety.

In windier weather the speed will need to be increased to ensure that, in spite of the wind gradient, there is always sufficient speed in hand for a proper landing.

If lower speeds are used, the pilot cannot open the airbrakes fully during the final stages of the approach without the risk of a heavy landing. This can be an embarrassment if you are landing in a small field and find yourself tending to overshoot slightly. Do you open the airbrakes fully and accept a heavy landing and possible damage, or do you leave the airbrakes as they are and risk a rolling into the far boundary? During the hold off and the final stages of an approach, there is very little time to make an actual check on the airspeed. The pilot can only judge by the 'buoyancy' of the machine as he uses the controls to round out and hold off whether it is safe to open the airbrakes further.

Do not attempt to judge the speed higher up on the approach but instead learn to read the A.S.I. at a quick glance so that you can check it just after the final turn and again just after you have set the airbrakes open and lowered the nose to compensate for the extra drag. There is not usually time to check the speed again before starting the round out. The dangers in trying to judge the speed are that neither the sound of the airflow nor the attitude are reliable guides. It is very easy to be deceived by the sound, and, particularly in a modern glider, there is very little noise at all, and only a very slight difference in noise between 50 and 80 knots. The attitude is also not very reliable and there have been a number of accidents in field landings where the pilot has been misled into approaching too nose-high by unconsciously judging the attitude by reference to a false horizon of nearby hills.

It is very noticeable that most students tend to misjudge the attitude and fly too nose-high when the aircraft is below about 300–400 feet. This leads to many stall and spin accidents, particularly when the pilot is unconsciously trying to stretch the flight to get back to the normal landing area after running himself a little short of height in the circuit.

Always check the speed on the approach and lower the nose to maintain it as the airbrakes are opened. If the speed begins to drop off even slightly, either the nose must be lowered, and/or the amount of airbrake being applied must be reduced.

Inexperienced pilots should not attempt to reduce excessive speed on the final approach by raising the nose and flattening the glide. This almost always results in losing too much speed so that the approach becomes too slow. Instead of raising the nose, open full airbrake to increase the drag and limit or reduce the speed. Remember that height and speed are interchangeable. If the approach appears correct to reach the landing area but the speed is excessive, in effect you have extra height and will float too far. The extra speed will result in a much longer float before touchdown and, therefore, you are really in need of more airbrake in order to use up that speed more quickly.

Fundamentally, the attitude of the aircraft, be it glider or jet, is controlled by the elevator and it is the attitude which controls the airspeed. However, adjustments in the attitude have to be made to cater for changes in the drag caused by opening the brakes. For a given attitude, however, the airbrakes will influence the speed and a really experienced pilot can make use of this fact within the limitations set by the power of the brakes on the particular type of machine. Many recent designs are fitted with such ineffective airbrakes that the slowing down effect of opening even full airbrake is too small to save a serious overshoot if the approach is too high or too fast. This makes it vital for the pilot to keep accurate control over the speed as these gliders will float a very long way if the speed is allowed to become excessive.

If the airspeed begins to fall, or the glider seems to be sinking so abnormally fast that it is likely to undershoot, close the airbrake immediately. Do *not* try to check the rapid sinking by raising the nose or you may stall the glider. Closing the brake will reduce the high rate of descent which is almost invariably being caused by a loss of speed. This loss may have been started by failing to lower the nose sufficiently as the brakes were opened, but is most probably being caused, or at least aggravated, by the effect of the wind gradient. If no action is taken immediately, a very heavy landing is likely to occur. The instinctive reaction to a tendency to undershoot or to sink rapidly is to try and check the sinking and to stretch out the glide by raising the nose slightly. This is fatal! If the glider is tending to undershoot the correct action is to close the brakes immediately but to hold the same approach attitude, or even lower the nose to gain more speed. Extra speed is of far more value than extra height and, unless there are tall obstructions ahead, try to turn your height into speed if you are tending to undershoot. The wind speed is always much less close to the ground than at height and by turning your height into speed you gain by reducing the effective headwind. Furthermore, you get an extra bonus because when the glider is flown less than a wing span above the ground (the lower the better in fact) there is a ground cushioning effect which reduces the induced drag. This significantly increases the distance the glider will float, and the glider will go much further this way than if it were flown steadily at the normal approach speed.

Any attempt to stretch the final glide by raising the nose is doomed to failure. At first the glide will flatten out for a few seconds as the glider flies level, losing a little speed. Then the glider will start to sink again, but more rapidly than before, in spite of the appearance of the rather nose-high position. The lowered airspeed will result in less distance being covered against the wind and the higher rate of descent will make the effect of the wind gradient more pronounced. Finally, if the glider arrives near the ground at low speed it will not float very far and there will be little or no bonus from the ground effect or the lighter surface wind (see Fig. 30).

It is common practice to discourage inexperienced pilots from opening the airbrakes at the last moment, when the glider is only a few feet above the ground. This is because most airbrakes cause a sudden loss of height of perhaps 3–10 feet as they are opened and, therefore, a small backward movement is needed at exactly the right moment to avoid hitting the ground at

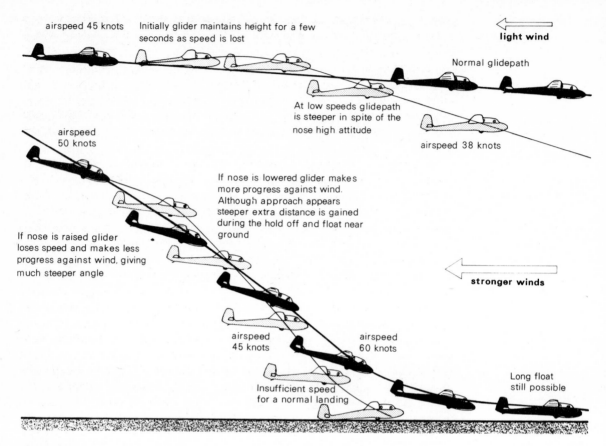

airspeed 45 knots   Initially glider maintains height for a few
seconds as speed is lost

light wind

Normal glidepath

At low speeds glidepath
is steeper in spite of the
nose high attitude

airspeed 38 knots

airspeed
50 knots

If nose is lowered glider makes
more progress against wind.
Although approach appears
steeper extra distance is gained
during the hold off and float near
ground

If nose is raised glider
loses speed and makes less
progress against wind, giving
much steeper angle

stronger winds

airspeed
45 knots

airspeed
60 knots

Long float
still possible

Insufficient speed
for a normal landing

30 The effect of trying to stretch the glide by raising the nose. Never attempt to stretch the glide; lowering the nose to gain more speed will take you further against the wind.

speed and while in a nose-down attitude. However, it is most undesirable to end an approach and landing with no airbrake. This results in a very, very long float before the excess speed from the approach is all used up. It also makes the elevator super-sensitive so that it is difficult to avoid ballooning or bouncing on touchdown. A good landing can be made, but only by being patient and holding off gradually and very gently. Do not try to get the glider down or it will bounce badly. Instead, keep it floating as long as you can and it will eventually sink onto the ground for a perfect touchdown. At that moment, the airbrakes should be opened fully to prevent any sudden gust lifting the glider off again. If there is insufficient space ahead to allow for this long float, the airbrakes *must* be opened and the sooner the better. Keep a firm grip on the lever to stop them flying open and try to open them gradually, easing back on the stick slightly to stop the glider sinking. Even a small amount of airbrake will make all the difference to the distance which the glider will float.

The real answer is not to get caught in a position where you are so short of height that you cannot get the airbrakes partly open by 20–30 feet. Always avoid using up so much height at the start of an approach that you have to close the airbrakes completely to reach the boundary. This will only lead you into the predicament of having to try to get the brakes on at the last moment.

Whereas it is wise to be extremely cautious when opening the brakes at low altitude, they can, of course, be closed at any height. For example, if the approach is a little slow, or the final turn is a mess so that the glider needs re-aligning onto the landing area, or if it is necessary to go further up the field to clear an obstruction, they can be closed at any moment to let the glider float on further and give you more time to get things right.

If the approach has ended up a little slow, or the brakes have had to be partially closed because of holding off too high or ballooning, they should never be re-opened. If there was a real need to reduce the setting because of low speed, this will not result in the speed increasing and opening the brakes again will almost certainly result in a heavy landing.

Over the years there have been many accidents when the airbrakes have been opened fully in the middle of the final turn into the approach. These have occurred because the glider was already desperately slow and in danger of spinning in, and opening the brakes probably raised the stalling speed sufficiently to cause a stall with the result that the glider spun or spiralled into the ground. The real cause of most of these accidents was flying too slowly on the base leg of the circuit so that the speed was quite inadequate for a safe turn in the turbulent air at that height. Most of them might have happened a few seconds later even if the airbrakes had not been opened.

It is quite safe to open the airbrakes during a turn providing that enough speed is ensured by lowering the nose so that the drag of the brakes does not cause a loss of speed. An experienced pilot will have no difficulty in doing this and there are many occasions when he will want and need to do it. The inexperienced student pilot should be a little cautious. The penalty for an error like this can be severe, and the result of delaying the opening of the brakes for the few seconds until he has straightened the glider up is so insignificant that it is probably best for him to stick to some simple restrictions until he has a few hours solo experience. I suggest to my own students that, up to that time, if they already have airbrakes open on the base leg and are settled down at a suitable approach speed, they can turn with the brakes on, providing of course that they still have much too much height and need to lose it quickly. (Caution! Turning with airbrakes on uses up height very quickly and the brakes must be partially or fully closed if it seems possible that enough height has already been used up half way round the turn.) If they are ridiculously high, so that even if they spoil the turn there is no possibility of a problem, then I suggest they open the airbrakes in the middle of the turn. But in all other cases I suggest they should get their final turn over and done with and open the brakes as they are bringing the wings level again.

If the airbrakes are being used a distinct buffeting may be felt on some types of glider. This can be very disconcerting, especially if the pilot is able to look back at the tailplane and see it shuddering. The buffet is usually felt through the elevator and rudder and is caused by the turbulent wake from the brakes hitting the tail.

This occurs on a poorly executed final turn if the airbrakes are open, and is often the result of a skidding or slipping turn. This buffet may in some cases be mistaken for the pre-stall buffet, but it is usually more violent. It will disappear on correcting the slipping or skidding with rudder.

The modern two-seaters gain speed very quickly when the nose is lowered and some students find it particularly difficult to control this speed accurately during the final turn. When there is ample height one solution is to open the airbrakes a small amount before the final turn and keep them on. This tends to stabilise the speed and prevent it becoming excessive. Of course, if necessary, the brakes can be closed immediately if height is lost too quickly and there is any danger of ending up rather low for the final approach.

The actual decision to open the brakes really needs to be made before or during the turn so that they can be opened promptly. At a normal approach speed on a calm day, the glider lands an extra 300 yards further down the field for every ten seconds delay in opening the brakes!

Use of the airbrakes while teaching landings

The actual landing is made by backward movements of the stick and is nothing to do with the airbrakes. The airbrakes are essentially an approach control and determine where the glider will arrive for the round out and how far it will float before touching down. It may be necessary to reduce the brake setting during the landing if the pilot overdoes the round out or hold off so that the glider balloons up. Therefore, while the student is learning and is likely to over-control and make mistakes, it is much easier if the instructor works the airbrake control while the student tries to sort out the landing. Once the student has managed to get fairly consistent landings without ballooning, the airbrakes can be set in position at about 50 feet and held steady for the whole of the landing. Learning to land and also to operate the airbrakes are both made far simpler by breaking down the landing into these stages.

During the initial phase, the instructor talks the student down into an approach with ample speed for full airbrake. He should always attempt to end up with at least half brake to give him some 'stored energy' available to cater for any bad ballooning. If the glider does balloon, the instructor reduces the airbrake just after the crest of the upward movement and as the glider starts to sink again. *Not* before, or the glider will balloon even higher as the lift is improved by closing the brake. The brake setting is again frozen while the student has a further attempt at holding off. If another ballooning occurs, the brakes will probably have to be closed completely to allow one final attempt. This is now a no brake landing with very little, if any, reserve of speed and the instructor should take a hand in ensuring that no more ballooning occurs (Fig. 31).

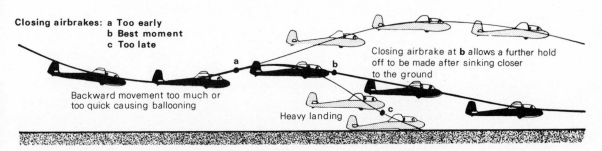

Closing airbrakes: a Too early
b Best moment
c Too late

Closing airbrake at **b** allows a further hold off to be made after sinking closer to the ground

Backward movement too much or too quick causing ballooning

Heavy landing

31 The prevention of a heavy landing by reducing the amount of airbrake at the correct moment. The instructor makes this correction during the initial attempts when teaching the landing.

An initial approach using a lower speed and little or no airbrake will give the instructor no reserve of energy on tap if the student over-controls and balloons. It is, therefore, a very important point for instructors to note, that if they want to teach landings without expensive happenings every now and then they should always arrange for an approach using a fair amount of airbrake.

Sometimes, if the glider is being held off just a few feet high, it is very tempting to open the airbrake in order to make the glider sink those few feet and make a landing. This is all right for a skilled person, provided that they do ease back and continue to hold off for a proper touchdown. Otherwise the glider just sinks onto its nose skid rather firmly. But this is not a good habit to get into because, sooner or later, the glider will be flying a little slower than expected and then when the brakes are opened instead of a relatively gentle sink it will drop suddenly and a really heavy landing will occur.

It takes quite an amount of solo experience in gliders to learn to judge whether it is safe to open more brake during the actual hold off. It is a matter of assessing the elevator response as the stick is moved back gently to hold the glider off the ground. If the movements required are still very small and the aircraft is lively and responsive, then it is safe to open a little more brake. However, as this is done the glider will sink and this has to be stopped by a little more movement on the stick.

A skilled pilot can use the airbrakes, varying the setting throughout the round out and hold off, to land within 5 feet of the chosen spot on every landing. Early solo pilots should be encouraged to concentrate on making their landings perfect before attempting to start touching down within quite such small limits or there will be broken gliders!

Controlling the float

Whereas it is usually safest to discourage the beginner from attempting to open the airbrakes further during the hold off because of the risk of a heavy landing, the pilot who is coming up to cross-country standard must master this technique.

The need frequently occurs when the glider is committed to the final approach into a grass field, and, at the last moment, the pilot sees that his large grass field is divided by an electric cattle fence. For a safe landing he must close the brakes and float on over the fence and then re-open them to make a very accurate landing just beyond in the rather small space remaining. This will demand very smooth and well co-ordinated movements.of the brake and elevator.

When considering the gliding range of a glider on the approach it must not be forgotten that the variation in landing spot is not only governed by the use of the brakes on the approach. The shortest possible landing will occur with full airbrake all the time on the approach and the whole of the landing. Even at the last moment before touchdown, closing the brakes will give a float of several hundred yards. Compared with a steep, full-brake approach, the flattest approach with no brake will take the glider three or four times as far, plus an additional float of many hundred yards in the ground effect. It is much easier to judge a fairly steep approach and to make an accurate touchdown when the glider is decelerating rapidly with a fair amount of drag.

Airbrakes open at the wrong times

Even in this day and age there are still a great many gliders fitted with airbrakes which are difficult to lock and difficult to tell when they are locked, or with systems which allow the brakes to open by themselves if the pilot fails to lock them correctly, or if the locks fail through faulty adjustment.

Many years ago at a British Gliding Association Annual Instructors Conference it was recommended that on future British gliders it should either be impossible for the brakes to open themselves if they were inadvertently left unlocked, or that it should be possible to determine whether the brakes were correctly locked by some kind of visual indication in the cockpit. On many gliders the exact position of the lever is no real indication, and since airbrakes are always arranged so that they close completely before the locking movement occurs, the fact that the airbrakes are flush with the wing surface means nothing.

In most gliders it is a simple matter to introduce a spring or elastic to hold the airbrakes in the closed position in flight. This can be just sufficiently strong to stop them opening and is a great safety device which must have prevented many accidents. However, a pilot going back onto a machine without such a spring is at even greater risk.

Of course, the real solution to this and many other similar problems in flying is for the pilot to have learnt to be systematic and thorough in all matters, and in particular with cockpit checks. However, in spite of instituting a Vital Actions Check which is carried out before every take off, there is always the possibility of an occasional lapse and a serious risk of an accident.

In the old days, before a proper cockpit drill was instituted, the majority of experienced pilots had probably at some time or another taken off with the brakes unlocked so that they had come open on the launch. There were a number of accidents as a result and the fact that the incidents were occurring fairly regularly helped to make all pilots aware of the problem. This probably increased the chance of a pilot realising something was not quite right, and checking the brakes straight away. Later, as the incidents became rare, it was almost unheard of for a pilot to realise what was wrong until he reached for the brake lever to open the airbrakes for the approach, or when he was told after being pulled out of the remains of the machine.

Occasionally a pilot fails to close the brakes before take off. The wingtip holder will usually spot this and point it out but this kind of error shows a lack of the necessary alertness and vigilance for safe flying and, if it happens, I always give the glider to the next pilot and suggest that the culprit takes a rest from flying for a few days!

It more often happens that the pilot has been disturbed during his checks or become slipshod about them, so that although he has closed the brakes, they are not actually locked. In this case, depending on the type of aircraft, they may ride open as the glider bumps over any rough ground, or they may open as the speed reaches 50–60 knots and the suction gets strong enough to pull them open. They usually open quite gently and although they cause a little buffeting and some extra noise, it is almost unknown for pilots to notice anything wrong at this point.

If the pilot gets careless over the Vital Actions Check before take off and just pushes the airbrake lever forward to check that it is closed and locked, without first opening the brakes, there is a risk that he may not have locked them at all. Seeing that the brakes themselves are flush with the surface of the wing is no indication that they are locked. They should *always* be opened first before closing and locking them so that the distinctive feel of the geometric lock taking effect can be felt. Although the strength of the lock may vary considerably, so that on some machines hardly any force is required whereas on others the lock is stiff to operate, the feeling is always distinctive.

The best systems have a spring in the circuit, a geometric lock and a gate for the lever to lock into on the side of the cockpit. The gate enables the pilot to check visually that the lever is in the locked position and it prevents any risk of the airbrakes opening if the geometric lock is faulty or incorrectly adjusted.

I have seen several cases involving Olympias and Capstan two-seaters which show how easily a pilot can be caught out when there is only a geometric lock. The adjustment of these locks is rather critical since they usually rely on the 'give' in the system to provide the load which makes the over centre lock positive. During the season, the locks gradually tend to become lighter and lighter until someone decides that any bump or knock on the lever might be enough to unlock it. By this time every member in the club knows that the locks are very light and that it is difficult to feel them lock as the lever is pushed forward. At last someone decides to readjust the locks and often even with the minimum of half a turn on each rod end the locks become very stiff to operate. They are sometimes so critical in adjustment that the choice has to be between too light or rather too stiff. The glider is now all set up to catch some unwary pilot who is a creature of habit and does not think what he is doing. Eventually one comes along and on his cockpit check he opens the brakes and then closes them as usual by pushing the lever forward – but not hard enough to lock them now that the lock is so stiff. Perhaps he even remembers that this is the aircraft which always had the rather light lock and so he assumes that this was why he did not feel it catch. This time he will be taking off with the airbrakes unlocked and they will open themselves during the take off or early on the launch, as soon as the speed is sufficient for them to suck open.

Easily done, isn't it?

On many machines the flexing of the wings affects the locking of the brakes so that far less force is required to unlock them. This can make a rather light lock very light, so that if the lever is knocked the airbrakes may open themselves. Normally there is a separate lock for each wing and, if they are not locking exactly together, a sudden flexing of the wings may allow one side to unlock, so that the suction is sufficient on that side to unlock the other side also and cause both brakes to fly open.

It is unwise to keep a hand on the airbrake lever during launching because of the risk of opening the airbrakes accidentally instead of releasing the cable at the top of the launch or in the event of a cable break. This could be disastrous near the ground at low speed. However, on some gliders it is easy to keep the left hand close to the release knob and have the brake lever below that hand in such a position that, if the airbrakes did come open during a launch, the lever would hit the pilot on the knuckles and wake him up.

With a car or winch launch, the signaller and the driver are probably the first people to notice the airbrakes open. If they are wise, they keep the launch going and hope that the cable does not break during the first few hundred feet. If that should happen, and even if the pilot is very quick to lower the nose, the speed will be extremely slow and he may unwittingly fly along for a few seconds in what would be a normal attitude, losing speed because of the drag of the brakes. Any turn off or circle is almost certain to mean a stall and spin, and the last thing in the world the pilot is thinking about is the airbrakes. (You can read that how you like!)

If the cable does not break, and the winch driver keeps the launch going, there is more time for the spectators to contemplate. After you have seen a few cases, you begin to believe in modifications to the gliders which have no springs. After the launch the glider usually starts to make a normal circuit and is soon losing height at a desperate rate and heading for a dangerously low final turn. Occasionally the pilot wakes up and tries to find out why the glider is losing height so fast and the brakes go closed and everyone breathes a sigh of relief. Often the final turn ends up on the ground half way round but miraculously without damage. Some pilots lead charmed lives!

The situation if the airbrakes open during an aerotow is even more serious since it can also threaten the life of the tug pilot. (See page 186.)

Special advice for beginners on using the airbrakes

1 Always try to arrange the approach so that at least one third of full airbrake is needed for the last 50 feet and landing.
2 Try to set and hold the position of the airbrake constant for the round out and landing. Choose a speed which is adequate for a full airbrake landing and increase it in adverse conditions.
3 *Do not be afraid* to open the airbrakes, providing there is plenty of approach speed. The round out and landing may be with full airbrake or an intermediate position as required providing that the speed is adequate.
4 *Do be cautious* about opening the brakes if the speed is marginal, or slow.
5 If undershooting or tending to undershoot, close the brakes but hold the nose-down attitude. Never raise the nose to stretch the glide.
6 If the approach speed starts to get slow, lower the nose if height permits, otherwise reduce the brake.
7 If the glider starts to sink rapidly, close the brakes and if high enough, lower the nose; the wind gradient is out to get you!
8 Never re-open the brakes if they have been closed because of a loss of speed or ballooning.
9 Never open more brake to use up the height if the hold off has been started too high; let the glider float down and hold off again normally.
10 Avoid 'no brake' landings whenever you can.
11 Open the brakes fully after touchdown to avoid lifting off in a gust.

If the launch or flight feels abnormal, look out at the airbrakes and check whether they have opened themselves. If the glider is fitted with a tail parachute and there is any risk that it has opened, operate the jettison immediately.

7 Planning the Approach and Landing

Planning and judgement 102
The approach and hold off 103
Aiming point technique 105
The 'play it safe' method of approach 109
Undershoot v. overshoot 110
Judgement and the angle of approach 111
Visiting other gliding sites 112
Hill sites 113
The influence of the launch height 114
The prevailing weather 114
The type of glider 114
Judging the position of the final turn 116
Judging the height for the circuit 116
The height and distance method 117
Positioning by the angle 119
Joining the circuit pattern for a landing 122
Never low and slow 123
Integrated power flying and gliding 127
Preparing to land 130
Suggestions for beginners 131

Planning and judgement

Everyone agrees that the positioning of the glider for an approach and landing is largely a matter of good judgement. However, it is difficult to define how this should be done because of the wide variation of methods used at different sites and from country to country. The best method for a particular site is evolved from practical experience, often as a result of expensive accidents. Sometimes the variations have been introduced for safety reasons, but many of them are the result of the special limitations of the types of glider being flown or the launch height available. It is particularly important that a pilot should understand the factors involved and know why he is encouraged to make his final turn and approach differently at two different sites.

The aim of any circuit planning is to enable the glider to be positioned consistently so that it can complete the final turn at a safe height and in a position from which it can easily be landed at the chosen spot. The shape of the circuit can be very variable and should be considered solely as a means to an end.

The inexperienced pilot will need to follow some kind of plan if the positioning of the glider is going to be consistent. However, in windy and unstable conditions constant reappraisals and adjustments are needed on the circuit because of unpredictable areas of lift and sink. Even the basic plan may have to be modified if correct positioning is to be achieved every time.

Whereas fairly large errors may be quite acceptable for early solo flights on a gliding site or airfield, the pilot must achieve a very high degree of accuracy if an out-landing has to be made in a small field.

One of the biggest problems is that most of us tend to do all our flying from one gliding site with its own special conditions. Without realising it, our methods and procedures become semi-automatic and we do not really use our judgement in order to position the glider for the approach. Instead, quite unconsciously, we use the various landmarks such as farm buildings, clumps of trees, or roads, and relate our circuit to them. Visit another gliding site or land in a strange field without these familiar reference points on the ground, and it is surprisingly easy to misjudge the whole circuit and approach.

This applies whether the home gliding site is a large airfield or a small hill site. The hill site pilot believes that his training and experience will enable him to judge a landing into a small field more accurately, but usually this is not so. He has probably learnt by experience exactly where he must turn in and has no more skill or judgement than the pilot who has been well trained on a vast airfield. However, the first flight of each day is particularly important even at your own site because of the need to assess, and make allowances for, the wind strength. Always make a special effort to land accurately on a chosen spot on your first flight, and be very critical of your judgement if you touch down more than a few yards away from it. On subsequent flights, you will position yourself by comparison with the first one, and instead of making a fresh judgement of the approach, you just place yourself a little further back or a little nearer than before. Although undershooting your spot by a few yards may seem unimportant on a large landing area, if you are already solo, there is absolutely no excuse for not having reduced the amount of airbrake slightly in order to correct this. It is no good kidding yourself that you could have been accurate when in fact you failed. A competent pilot has learnt from experience how careful he must be to make sure of positioning the final turn correctly in strange surroundings.

If we are considering the planning of a circuit and landing, it is often easiest to start at the touchdown and work backwards to the initial positioning. Obviously, an accurately placed landing will be a simple matter if the final turn has been completed in a good position. Also, the final turn will be easier to position if there has been time for adjustment on an adequate base leg and this in turn will be simple to arrange if ample height has been allowed for getting to a good position for the start of the base leg.

The approach and hold off

Assuming an adequate approach speed and a glider fitted with normal airbrakes, the experienced pilot has a surprising amount of control over the position of his landing. The shortest distance to touchdown will be obtained by using full airbrake throughout the whole approach and landing (discounting sideslipping for the moment). The flattest possible approach will be with no airbrake at all. But in addition to the extra distance covered in the glide down, there is the amount that the glider will float after the round out before it touches down.

After the approach and round out using full airbrake, a pilot can change his mind and close the brakes to float on 300 or 400 yards before actually

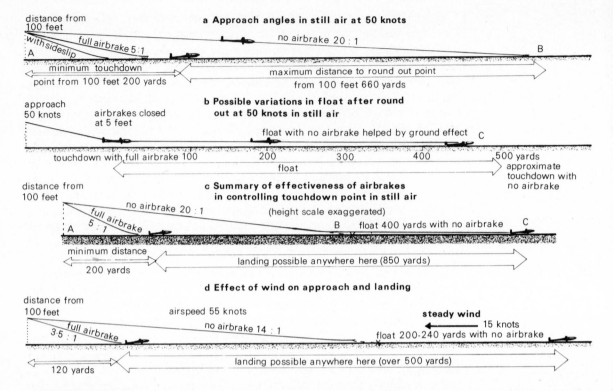

32 Controlling the approach and landing. **a** compares the effect of using the airbrakes on the gliding angles and distances covered by a modern training glider during an approach in no wind. At 50–55 knots, with full airbrake, the gliding angle is about 5:1, whereas with no airbrake the gliding angle is about 20:1. **b** shows that if the airbrakes are closed before or during the round out the float is over 400 yards. Using full airbrake this float is only 20–30 yards. **c** combines **a** and **b**. The horizontal scale is reduced and the height scale is exaggerated for clarity. Against a wind both the gliding angle and the float are reduced. **d** shows that providing that the glider completes the round out at the normal approach speed and *not* below it, the float, though reduced by the wind, is still surprisingly long. However, the theoretical distances are seldom possible because of the loss of height caused by the wind gradient.

landing. (See Fig. 32.) This hidden resource is only there if the approach speed has been maintained until the glider is near the ground. At lower speeds the performance of even a modern glider is seriously affected by any turbulence or headwind and the extra float cannot be relied upon. Most pilots do not in fact rely on this extra float, but keep it in reserve. However, it does mean that with half the available airbrake applied, there is much more scope for extending the distance to the touchdown point than for bringing it closer.

Serious problems occur in field landings when the pilot allows himself extra height, thinking that this is the safest thing to do. The pilot will need full airbrake throughout the approach and this could mean a serious over-shoot if the glider happened to fly through any lift on the way down.

Whenever there are no high obstructions round the field, the aim should be to position the final turn so that, on average, not more than half the available airbrake is needed from then onwards. Unless there is ample space for overshooting the glider should be sideslipped with full airbrake immediately it becomes apparent that the approach is going to need full airbrake for more than a few seconds. In this way the approach can be brought back to within the range of the airbrakes, so that it can be controlled accurately again. Until the pilot has considerable experience at slideslipping, he will have to accept an overshoot if he finds himself a little too high and already using full brake, but as he will be landing on the gliding site, there will be plenty of room to allow this. He will also be advised to try and get the airbrakes set for the final 20 or 30 feet of the approach rather than attempt to make adjustments during the float. Later, when he is more experienced, he will learn to make changes with the airbrakes close to the ground to make his landings even more accurate.

Aiming point technique

It is important to allow for the distance that the machine will float during the round out and hold off. The glider has to be flown down towards a point 100 yards or so short of where you want to touch down, or it will overshoot badly. The position of this point must be selected depending on the wind strength, and, above all, the point must not be too close to the touchdown point if it is important to be really accurate or there may be a risk of overshooting.

In many cases the pilot is not so much concerned with making an accurate spot landing as with landing as soon as possible after clearing a hedge or trees on the boundary of the field. In this situation he will probably use the boundary itself as the aiming point for the approach, and will open the airbrakes fully just as the obstructions are being crossed.

Unfortunately, the glider does not fly in exactly the same direction in which it is pointing. In still air at the normal gliding speed the glidepath is very close to the line of the fuselage, but this is the *only* time when this is so. Against a strong wind, for example, the attitude of the glider remains the same, but the glidepath will be much steeper. The direction in which the nose is pointing can also be very misleading when the attitude is changed quickly during the approach. For instance, if the nose is raised a little, the glidepath is checked briefly. However, after a few seconds the glidepath becomes even steeper than it was in the original attitude and the glider mushes down at low speed. Similarly, when the nose is lowered more the glider descends much more steeply for a few seconds as it gains speed. The final glidepath is somewhere between the two angles as in Fig. 33.

These factors make it impossible to predict exactly where the glider will arrive by looking over the nose and seeing where it is pointing. There is only one method which can always be used to judge exactly where the machine will arrive during the final approach and this is known as Aiming Point Technique. Fig. 34 explains the system and shows how the pilot can see if he

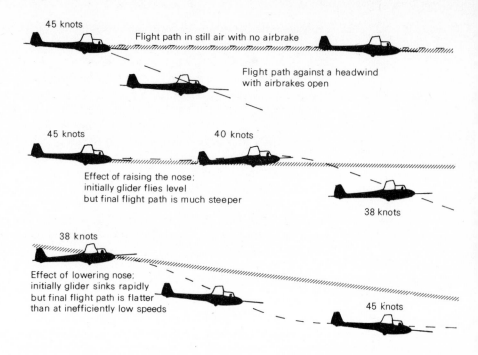

45 knots

Flight path in still air with no airbrake

Flight path against a headwind
with airbrakes open

45 knots   40 knots

Effect of raising the nose:
initially glider flies level
but final flight path is much steeper

38 knots

38 knots

Effect of lowering nose:
initially glider sinks rapidly
but final flight path is flatter
than at inefficiently low speeds

45 knots

33 The initial changes caused by raising and lowering the nose are deceptive. The glider seldom flies along in the direction of the longitudinal axis of the fuselage.

is under- or overshooting his aiming point.

If the glider is held in a steady attitude, the point towards which it is gliding is the only point on the landing area ahead which appears stationary in relation to the nose. Objects beyond this point will appear to move upwards in relation to the nose, and those which are nearer move downwards, eventually disappearing under the aircraft as it flies over them. During an approach, the pilot watches his aiming point, which ideally is an obvious feature or mark on the ground that be seen clearly. If it appears to move downwards, indicating that he is overshooting, he should open more airbrake to compensate. Since the nose must be lowered a little to maintain the speed with the extra drag of the brakes, the position of the aiming point in relation to the nose will have changed completely when this was done. A new assessment must be begun in order to decide whether any further corrections are needed.

After each change of attitude the position of the aiming point, as seen by the pilot, will have changed, and this makes it important to minimise the changes and to hold a steady position while assessing which way the aiming point is moving. Unless the approach is very long, the beginner may find that

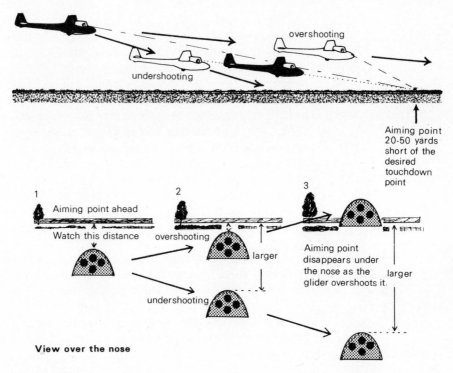

34 Detecting undershooting and overshooting on the approach by aiming point technique.

he hardly has time to make these judgements with all the other things he has to think about on an approach. However, it is important to grasp the method, because it is the only one which can determine where the glider is going. He will find that he can use it to reassure himself that he can safely open the airbrakes after the final turn when he is using the 'play it safe' method described later. The rapid downward movement of the boundary hedge will be very obvious, and no finesse is needed to spot this indication that the glider is overshooting by a large amount.

Of course this whole process can be made much easier with a longer approach, since there is then more time to see what is going on. However, even with a proportionate increase in height, it is not wise to make very long approaches. If the pilot is unaware that the wind has increased since take off for instance, perhaps some hours before, extra height and length of approach just increase the time during which the glider may meet the sink or turbulence which are more likely in a stronger wind. In other words, doubling the height and the length of the approach tends to double the chances of meeting trouble.

The pilot also obtains some further information about his glidepath by relating his angle of descent to nearby objects such as trees. If a very long approach is made (perhaps on the hangar flight at the end of flying) it is noticeable how difficult it is to make any true assessment of the situation until the glider gets down to about 100 feet or so. Then, suddenly, the pilot is able to interpret the situation more clearly, and he knows how much airbrake he needs to get down exactly where he has chosen. This suggests that there is little or no advantage in making very long approaches.

Fig. 35 shows another useful way of aiding your judgement both on the approach and during the round out and hold off. When approaching over obstructions, a change between the relative positions of the top of the obstruction and your aiming point or another mark on the ground will indicate whether the glider is over- or undershooting. It is also much easier to judge your height by comparing it with tall trees, or, lower down, by watching the changes in perspective of objects near the landing area, as in Fig. 18.

Once the beginner has flown solo long enough to become relaxed and confident about getting himself up and down safely, he should make an effort to start to use this aiming point technique on every flight. It will be only a matter of practice to get used to spotting what is going on, and making the necessary changes quickly. This is the method he will have to master before he can land safely away in a strange landing ground of limited area.

35 Using obstructions on the approach to help detect under- and overshooting.

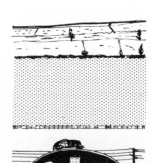

View ahead during initial approach. Note relative position of top of trees and wires in relation to fence and watch for any change

Gap between treetop and fence is increasing indicating that glider will clear fence easily. Use more airbrake to prevent overshoot

Treetop has moved above fence indicating that glider is undershooting. Close airbrakes immediately!

The 'play it safe' method of approach

When a very accurate landing is not essential and strong winds and bad downdrafts are known to exist in the approach area, the 'play it safe' method can be used (Fig. 36).

In these special conditions, even a high performance machine might undershoot what would normally be a perfectly safe approach. The policy to adopt on these occasions is to keep very close to the edge of the field, so that an undershoot is impossible however much height is lost in sink. After the final turn, the height is 'thrown away' with full airbrake to land as short as is still possible from such a close position.

The only judgement involved then is in positioning the turn so that it is completed immediately above the boundary at a sensible height for the prevailing conditions. In very windy weather, this may be 500 or 600 feet, but the glider will still land only a few hundred yards into the field.

At most hilltop sites there is a very bad area of strong sink behind the crest of the ridge when a ridge wind is blowing and the conditions are good for hill soaring. For example, at the Derby and Lancashire club site at Great Hucklow in the Peak District of England, it is dangerous to fly behind the back wall on the downwind boundary of the landing ground. The curl over, or 'clutching hand' effect is so strong that the glider can lose hundreds of feet in a few seconds, so that it may end up in the very rough ground behind the wall, or on the stone wall itself. The only safe procedure, regardless of how much height you have, is not to allow the glider to drift back at all. The curl over produces an area of sinking air and very steep wind gradients which can give rates of descent of several thousand feet per minute. Almost every year pilots trained at flat sites come to grief unless they are carefully briefed by the local instructors and *do as they are told*.

Keeping very close to the downwind boundary and then using up the excess height on the final approach is also the only really safe method to use

36 The throwing away height ('play it safe') method of approach for use in high winds and at hilltop sites. The glider is kept within easy reach of the downwind boundary so that there is no risk of an undershoot in adverse conditions.

with very low performance machines like the Grunau, Tutor and T21b, except in light wind conditions. These were slow flying machines with a good soaring performance at low speed, but with a poor gliding angle and a high rate of descent as soon as the speed was increased. This made them much more vulnerable to the effects of the wind and any turbulence or sinking air on the approach. Flying at a higher speed only resulted in a much steeper approach, so that an error, such as flying a little too far downwind for the base leg, could not be redeemed by flying faster and penetrating the wind. The policy, on anything but a calm day, had to be to keep close to the landing area at all cost.

The experienced pilot will use both basic methods of making an approach, choosing the second method in high winds or hill site situations, but using a much longer approach and 'aiming point technique' at other times when precision landings are essential and there are no severe downdraughts about.

Undershoot v. overshoot

Except in very difficult conditions it is most unlikely that any pilot in a modern glider, other than an absolute beginner, would misjudge the approach so badly that he would undershoot his chosen field. Long before this situation was reached he would realise that he was getting very low, and, by closing the airbrakes, he could call upon that extra 300 or 400 yards of float. This assumes that the approach speed was maintained and no attempt was made to stretch the glide during the approach (Fig. 37).

The real problem occurs if the approach is started a little too close or too high. It is much more difficult to judge whether the glide with full

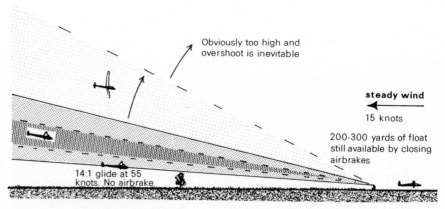

Overshooting unless full
sideslip and full
airbrake applied

Too high
Full airbrake 55 knots
4:1 glide

Ideal but looks rather low

Looks very low

Obviously too low

Obviously too high and
overshoot is inevitable

steady wind

15 knots

200-300 yards of float
still available by closing
airbrakes

14:1 glide at 55
knots. No airbrake

37 Approach angles, even against a 15 knot wind, are remarkably shallow. Always get rid of excess height so that the approach can be made with an average of about half airbrake. (Scale drawing showing achieved gliding angles for K8/ASK 13 class of glider.) In light winds it is easier to detect a tendency to undershoot and, therefore, excess height should be avoided when landing in a confined space.

airbrake will be steep enough to avoid overshooting the landing spot. By the time that the pilot has realised that the glider is overshooting slightly there is often too little approach left to correct this error by sideslipping. This is a serious problem for the student who has learned to fly on a low performance machine, or on a hill site where he has always had to keep very close to the landing area. As he progresses to better machines his technique and all his instincts will have to be modified, or he is bound to have trouble with field landings in open country. This lack of adjustment is the cause of many field landing accidents every year. Usually, the pilot will get himself too high, and too close, for a normal approach. Finding himself in that position, he would almost certainly attempt a violent sideslip or S turn in an attempt to get down in time, and it is during manoeuvres like this that the glider may end up, still turning or slipping at low altitude, close to the boundary hedge. Any mishandling or misjudgement can easily result in the wingtip hitting something, with disastrous results. In a case like this, the glider may often still be flying at an excessive speed so that, if it had not hit the obstruction, it would almost certainly have hit the far boundary.

Because it is absolutely impossible to regain lost height to order in a glider, it is essential not to run short of this valuable commodity. However, it is only too easy to 'play safe' with some extra height and then find, at the last moment, that you are overshooting and cannot get rid of height quickly enough to redeem the situation.

The aim in the circuit planning should be to position the final turn somewhere in between the extremes of glidepaths possible with full or no airbrake applied. On a calm day it will be desirable to have a rather flatter approach, with more airbrake available to foreshorten the float and landing. In windy weather the aim should be to arrange for the approach to be steeper, but still with less than full airbrake, so that there is more height in hand to cater for the effects of turbulence or sink.

Judgement and the angle of approach

During the student pilot's early attempts at planning the approach it becomes apparent that it is very much easier to assess the accuracy of a steep approach than of a very shallow one. This is because, in a steep glide, small changes in the angle of approach can be more easily detected by watching the aiming point. Fig. 38 shows that in a shallow glide even a very slight change in angle changes the touchdown position by a large distance. This means that it is noticeably easier to judge an approach which is against a strong wind, as this has the effect of steepening the approach path. The landing run and the float are also drastically reduced in a strong wind and this makes things less difficult to judge also. Powerful airbrakes make a glider very much easier to land accurately because of the much steeper angles of approach and reduced distance of float achieved with them fully opened. High performance machines with ineffective brakes are much more difficult to land with precision as the airspeed must be carefully controlled during the final stages of the approach. Even a few knots of excess speed will result in a long and rather unpredictable

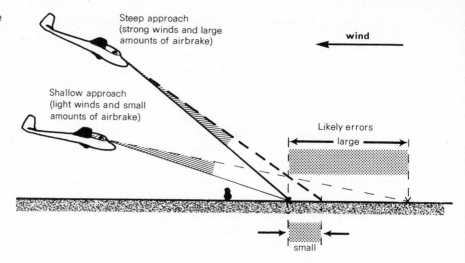

38 Judgement and the angle of approach. A shallow approach is more difficult to judge accurately than a steep one.

Steep approach
(strong winds and large
amounts of airbrake)

wind

Shallow approach
(light winds and small
amounts of airbrake)

Likely errors
large

small

float before landing, and this can cause real trouble when attempting to come down in a small field. The inexperienced pilot is recommended to restrict his cross-country flying to machines which have powerful airbrakes. This will allow him to gain experience of field landings in a machine on which he can make the occasional error and get away with it. Powerful airbrakes can often prevent an expensive overshoot and they certainly take most of the worry out of field landings. However, as the pilot gains experience he should train himself to limit his use of full airbrake and learn to control the approach speed really accurately. He should also practice sideslipping regularly, ready for the occasion when he flies a really modern, high performance machine and may need to supplement the rather ineffective airbrakes by this method.

Visiting other gliding sites

The pilot who travels around and visits other countries and other gliding sites will notice the variations in the methods used in getting the glider into the correct position for the final approach. At some sites the final turn will be at 400 or 500 feet and hundreds of yards behind the boundary of the site. At others, the final turn will seem dangerously low and only just above the boundary fence. Unless you do not mind being kept on the two-seater for the rest of your visit, you are advised to do as the locals do. The style of approach which has been adopted by each club has been influenced by a number of factors over the years. Lessons learned from accidents and near misses usually dictate the local flying rules, and no club wants a visitor who thinks he knows better than their own instructors. So your motto when visiting another club should be to ask for a comprehensive briefing, and then 'when in Rome, do as the Romans do'.

Given a few facts about the site and equipment, it is a simple matter to anticipate the style of approach which will be encouraged.

Hill sites It has already been explained why on a hilltop site the final turn has to be very close, if not over the edge, of the landing area. Except in very windy conditions this will encourage rather low final turns in order to avoid a serious overshoot. The pilots will tend to 'throw away' the height on the approach instead of using 'aiming point technique'. This, combined with the rather high approach speeds generally necessary, tends to encourage pilots at these sites to dive off excess height using full airbrake. It is very common to find that pilots who have been allowed to do this regularly have lost the ability to control their approach speeds accurately. In extreme conditions when approaching through a curl over it is almost impossible to be too fast. In calm conditions, approaching by diving off height is quite unacceptable and makes it impossible to achieve a spot landing. It is the worst possible training for landing a modern machine in small fields.

Equally important, of course, is the need for the flat site pilot to adapt his circuit to the special conditions at the hill site. At first he is likely to think the locals are exaggerating about the turbulence and the 'clutching hand' effects (Fig. 39). However, it is vital that, regardless of what he thinks of this advice, he obeys it to the letter while he is flying their aircraft. It is a matter of courtesy and respect for the experience of the person who is briefing you and who is, after all, only trying to prevent you from having an accident that you do as he suggests, even if you have your own private machine.

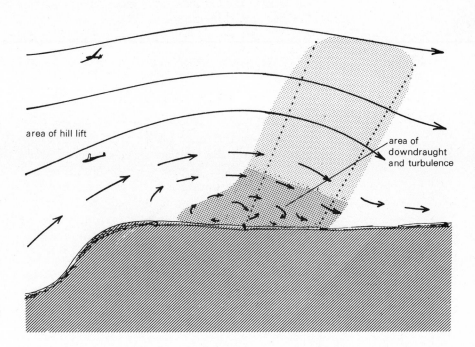

area of hill lift

area of downdraught and turbulence

39 The 'clutching hand' effect in the lee of a hill top is an area of severe downdraughts and turbulence behind the hill top.

The influence of the launch height

A further encouragement towards a style of circuit flying with a low final turn is poor launching heights. On a small gliding site in light winds it is inevitable that the average winch launch will not be very high. For example, before the site was enlarged a few years ago even at the London Gliding Club site at Dunstable, one of the largest and oldest clubs in England, a launch to over 600 feet in a T21b seater would be considered a good launch on a calm day. Inevitably, such low launches must encourage very low final turns, or the glider would never be able to get back to the launch point for a landing. The local rules about minimum heights for thermalling or attempting to use lift will also be influenced by the average launching height. It is particularly noticeable that where all the launching is by aerotow, thermalling is usually considered to be dangerous below about 800 feet, compared with 500 feet at small sites where the launch height is very limited.

It is very easy to see that a pilot's style of circuit planning changes even for the one flight when he takes an aerotow instead of a winch or car launch. Instead of making the best possible use of every foot of height to search for lift before joining his circuit, he will almost always arrive back with excessive height in hand and throw away hundreds of feet of valuable height with the airbrakes. The final turn will usually be completed by at least 300–400 feet and the whole circuit after an aerotow tends to give the impression that the pilot has had a change of heart and is trying to get down as quickly as he can, instead of trying to stay up!

Remember when you visit an all-aerotow site, you can expect to be severely criticised for a low final turn, while a similar turn at a hill site or small flat field with limited launching facilities, might have raised no comment from the most critical instructor.

The prevailing weather

The prevailing weather has a similar effect on the accepted style of approach. Fortunately, strong winds give much higher wire launches and better conditions for hill soaring. This allows more height for the circuit and approach at a time when turbulence is far worse and more height is essential for safety.

In more tropical climates the cloud base is higher and the thermals are often stronger and much further apart than in England. The areas of sinking air between the thermals are then both larger and more severe. These conditions often make winching or car launching uneconomic and, in places where the average wind is light, the ever-changing wind direction near the thermals makes aerotowing the only really practical method of launching gliders. The rather unpredictable conditions together with the strong turbulence make a much higher final turn necessary.

The type of glider

The performance and speed of the glider also influence the choice of circuit and approach. The faster the cruising speed the less the circuit will be upset by the effects of rising and sinking air. This is because less time is spent in flying across the area concerned and reaching the more normal air beyond it.

The very low cruising speeds and the rapid deterioration of the glide angle with any increase in the speed made the low performance machines, like the Grunau Baby, Tutor and T21b, very vulnerable to the effects of turbulence or sink. After a few expensive undershoot accidents, it became obvious that the only safe procedure with these types of machine was not to go more than a very short distance behind the downwind boundary in any weather. This naturally encouraged a rather low final turn in order to avoid landing in the middle of the gliding field every time. In light winds this does not create problems because the slow speed still allows the pilot plenty of time to make his corrections and to adjust the airbrakes during the rather short final approach. Furthermore, with the rather slow and steep final approach of these early machines, the judgement itself was easier.

As the approach speeds and performance of gliders have increased, the approaches have had to be lengthened to allow the inexperienced pilot time to assess the glide angle, and to adjust it with the airbrakes. Therefore, although it is no more dangerous to finish the final turn at 60 or 70 feet in a modern machine than in a T21b, it is more practical to have two or three times that height in order to have enough time to adjust the approach and land really accurately. The extra speed and better performance also make it safe to go much further back.

Please do not think that I am advocating low final turns. I am just explaining why there is such a wide variation of ideas on what is safe and acceptable. At my own site I have seen the changes over the past twenty years and the way in which my own opinions have been influenced by all these factors. Even the most skilled pilot flying in calm conditions must leave some allowance of height for the possibility of misjudgement, and, therefore, it is quite unacceptable to arrange the approach regularly so that the final turn is completed below about 50 feet, or the height of the very tall trees, which is far too low to give a pilot sufficient time to guarantee an exact spot landing. Twice this height seems to be about the minimum for a well-controlled approach with a modern machine. In windy or turbulent conditions, this height would be the absolute minimum for *safety* and the desirable approach height would be much more. With the normal errors in the indicated height on the altimeter, plus the need to learn to judge the height for at least the last 500 feet or so, it is unwise even to think of the height for the final turn in terms of 'so many feet'. Preferably, you should blank off the last 300–400 feet on the instrument so that you cannot refer to it. All that really matters is that you finish that turn by a safe height for the conditions in which you are flying. The altimeter will normally stick slightly and over-read by a hundred feet or more. This makes it very misleading below 400–500 feet. You must be within easy reach of the landing area and finish the final turn above the minimum safe height, i.e. twice the height of the hangar, or twice the height of tall trees, for a light wind day.

Judging the position of the final turn

The position and height of the final turn must be within certain limits if the pilot is to be able to adjust the final approach and make his spot landing. Fundamentally, this is a matter of learning to judge your angle in relation to the landing area and how it must be varied according to the wind strength. Most instructors will be unable to give you much real advice on how to do this apart from telling you that it will all come to you with more experience. This is not much help and, frankly, most instructors are still uncertain of the easiest way for a beginner to start trying to learn to recognise whether the angle is about right. The average angle of the approach could be learnt by repeatedly drawing it, or referring to a wedge of the same angle. Alternatively it may be easier to learn a simple distance/height method to get the glider to the average angle. In this case, the glider is positioned at a consistent height for the final turn and at a certain distance back from the edge of the landing area. This will give the required angle.

The majority of pilots unconsciously refer to their actual position over the ground, and position their final turn in relation to ground features making variations to allow for the wind strength. However, they may believe that they are judging their angle to the landing area because they are looking across at it. In this case they will only discover the truth when they are trying to spot land at a strange site or in an unknown field. When they attempt to assess the angle without the aid of their familiar features they will usually tend to overshoot so badly that they are lucky to get down safely with full airbrake. To be successful when using a height and distance method, both the height and the position of the final turn have to be judged correctly within certain limits to 'insert' the glider into the approach. A good feature of this method when it is used in a strange place is that it prevents the pilot from putting himself far too close to the field for a reasonable approach, which can easily happen when concentrating only on the angle itself.

Since the pilot can never be absolutely sure that his next landing will not be in a strange field, it is important to try and regard every circuit and landing as if it were a field landing and to position the final turn accordingly.

Judging the height for the circuit

As the pilot becomes more experienced he should make a habit of estimating his height, both over the gliding site and also away from it on local soaring flights. This is not difficult to do on the circuit because we become so familiar with the look of the airfield and the various buildings and hangars. It is easy to assume that you can judge heights accurately but this is usually far from the truth, as you will quickly find out if you fly at another site or have to make an away landing in strange surroundings.

Reliable judgement of heights can only come from experience in many different and unfamiliar places and may take years to develop.

Above 600 or 700 feet variations in the visibility and light cause serious inaccuracies and it is common to find that in poor light or hazy conditions there is a tendency to overestimate the height by a considerable amount.

Below 400 or 500 feet, the problems become far less. It is possible to look across at nearby trees or buildings and to start to make a direct comparison between their height and the glider. It is not necessary or desirable to think in terms of actual heights once the glider is below about 500 feet. The normal errors with any altimeter can so easily lead the pilot into believing that he still has height to spare, when in fact he is desperately short. On a long flight the atmospheric pressure will have changed during the day, and this, together with a tendency for the instrument to stick slightly and therefore to over-read, can make the altimeter over-read by several hundred feet. Of course, once the glider leaves the home site and is landing away in a field, the altimeter is no longer much help in telling the pilot how high he is above the ground. The new landing ground may be hundreds, or even thousands, of feet above or below the point of take off!

Provided that the final turn is not dangerously low the exact height is never critical and will need to be varied in conjunction with the wind strength and the position of the turn. Whenever possible it is best to judge the height for the final turn in terms of some convenient unit of height which can be seen or visualised on most circuits. For example, the minimum height for *completing* the turn might be defined as twice the height of *those* tall trees or *that* large hangar in light winds, and more in windy weather. I always make a point of refusing to give an actual height for a final turn and have the first 350 feet or so of the altimeter permanently blanked off so that there is no point in the student trying to use it as a guide. After a very short time they cease to want to use it and rely on looking and seeing instead.

The beauty of this method of comparing your height against a familiar object is that it is impossible for the pilot to descend below it and fail to recognise the fact that he is already desperately low. It takes very little practice to spot that you are just above the height of the obstruction as you look across to it. The same method is easy to use away from the home site because we are all familiar with the heights of common objects which are found in the country. However, there are many wide open spaces which have no convenient object to help us judge height. Fortunately, in such places the fields are usually larger and have good approaches, which make landings less critical.

Using this method of comparison it is obvious that our judgement of height becomes more and more accurate as the glider gets lower. In other words, if we play safe and allow ourselves extra height, we are far more likely to have a larger error of judgement. Together with the natural tendency to position the final turn too close rather than too far back, the extra unwanted height becomes a serious embarrassment and could easily result in a complete overshoot.

The height and distance method
(Fig. 40.)

Using a height and distance method, the surest technique is to choose a position or feature back from the landing area behind which to place the final turn. For example, if the fields are about 400 yards long, as in many parts of England, this position could be just beyond the downwind boundary

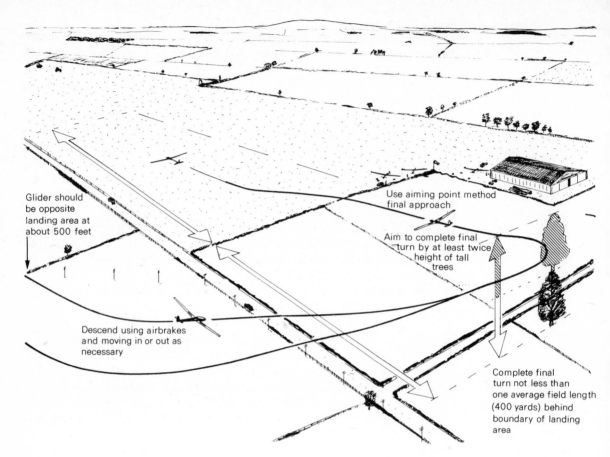

Glider should
be opposite
landing area at
about 500 feet

Use aiming point method
final approach

Aim to complete final
turn by at least twice
height of tall
trees

Descend using airbrakes
and moving in or out as
necessary

Complete final
turn not less than
one average field length
(400 yards) behind
boundary of landing
area

40 Using the height and distance method of positioning for the final approach.

of the next field, which leaves a complete field length for the final approach. You will notice if you analyse where you normally turn in for a landing on the gliding site that this is about 300–400 yards behind the touchdown point. This distance should be consciously related to the length of the landing area in the same way as, later on, it will be related to an average field length for an away landing.

On the base leg of the circuit the procedure is then deliberately to throw away height by using the airbrakes, to make certain that by the time that the glider has reached the turn in point, it has no excess height at all. In light winds the final turn should be no higher than on the airfield or home site, and it is better to err on the low side if anything. In practice it is much easier to detect any tendency to be too low, and, therefore, the pilot can place the turn at a consistent height with very small errors if he does it in this way. It takes very little practice to learn to select the position for the final turn with reasonable accuracy, and it is usually excessive height which causes the problems, if any. Of course, during the final stages of the circuit, if it is apparent that there will be a shortage of height, the position of the final turn can easily be brought nearer to the field.

In windy weather, the final turn must be brought a little nearer to the landing area and the approach speed must be increased. The extra approach speed is most important, since without it the distance that the glider will float is drastically cut and the effects of the wind gradient may cause an undershoot. When the wind is above about 20 knots, unless the field is very small, the 'throw away height' method is probably safest.

Whatever method of positioning the final turn is adopted, it is important to practice using it for normal flying on the gliding site in a way which will relate to landing elsewhere at a later stage. The pilot should try to select the turn in point by relating to the distance back from the edge of the landing area, as though the landing area itself was a field and did not extend more than a few hundred yards beyond the touchdown position. It is easy to get out of the habit of doing this during the period of local soaring after soloing. The pilot will then make accurate spot landings and good approaches on his home site, without realising that he is positioning the approach by habit, and not by judgement and reasoning. Away from the familiar surroundings, he may place the final turn much too close and so run into serious trouble. The best prevention is plenty of practice at picking and making approaches into fields in a motor glider, or if that is impossible, some practice landings in an odd corner of the gliding site where the pilot is unfamiliar with the approach and landing areas.

Positioning by the angle

The alternative to positioning the glider at the correct angle by a height and distance method, is to learn to recognise the angle itself. Most instructors encourage their students to try and do this, but it is common to find that on the whole the beginners just put their final turn in a position from which they know they cannot possibly undershoot, without consciously trying to judge the actual angle itself. It may then take a very large number of flights to learn to make this judgement with any degree of accuracy and, in the meantime, the likelihood is that the pilot may have become so familiar with the field from which he is flying, that he will unconsciously position his approach in relation to familiar landmarks, rather than by the angle.

In some countries a few instructors appear to have adopted a system of teaching definite angles, right from the start of the student's instruction in circuit planning. It may be that more or less standardising on an average approach angle and teaching the student to recognise this angle, is easier and quicker than just letting him muddle along in the hope that eventually he will develop good judgement.

The student is required to learn to recognise two angles; the final approach angle of about 8°, and an angle for positioning the final stages of the circuit and the start of the base leg of about 16°. Once the decision has been made to land, the glider is positioned by moving closer or further away from the selected aiming point on the landing area, until the angle is approximately 16°. By keeping this angle the glider will be brought round the landing area to a key point for the start of the base leg. This point may be at almost any height at an inclination of 16° along a line 45° to the landing direction starting from the aiming point, as in Fig. 41. During the base leg this angle is reduced by using the airbrakes to use up height or by moving the glider further back until the angle of 8° is obtained for the final turn. On the final approach, the normal aiming point technique is used and it will be found that the approach has been made with an average of about half airbrake for most types of glider in use today.

No allowance is recommended for the effects of winds up to about 10–15 knots, apart from increasing the approach speed in the normal manner. With stronger winds the angles are not changed but instead the reference point

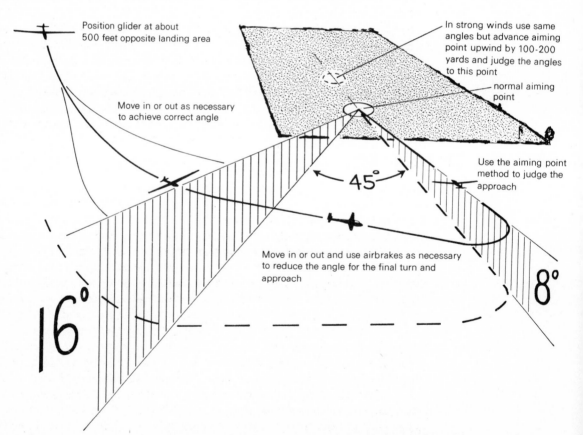

41 Using the angle method of judging the positioning for the final approach.

to which the angles are measured (the 'aiming point' in light winds) is moved several hundred yards upwind along the landing area. This brings the final turn closer to the field, and so steepens the final approach angle.

This means that the student only has to learn the two basic angles which can be both defined and shown very easily.

Many readers may doubt whether these angles will work for all gliders. Obviously there will be exceptions, either because the particular type of glider has a much worse gliding angle than 8° against a wind of 10–15 knots, or because it has such poor airbrakes that 8° is rather too steep for an average approach path. However, these angles are suitable for all the modern training machines as well as single-seaters such as the K6, K8, Pilatus B4, and many other well-known types.

After learning to use this method any slight variation needed for a particular type of glider should cause no problem. The pilot is more likely to go on looking analytically at the angle, instead of being misled into relying on other ways of judging his approach.

It would be an easy matter to make up aids to learning these angles, or to have a simple indicator to refer to on early flights. For instance, a wire frame could be mounted ahead of the pilot in the cockpit as a reminder of the two angles. This would be very easy to use when the wings were level during the base leg, as a direct comparison could be made. In fact there is no real reason why such an aid should not be permanently installed, as any worthwhile aid to judgement would be welcome unless there was a tendency for the pilot to over-concentrate on it at the expense of his lookout (Fig. 42).

Using this method, the pilot does not refer to features on the ground at all and he does not have to make any accurate judgement of his height. It is therefore reasonable to assume that he would find less difficulty in landing in strange surroundings than the pilot who has been allowed to develop his own technique. It is also an advance for the pupil to be given a clear idea of how he is to judge the angle to the landing area, and what it should be.

As with all other methods of circuit planning, the glider must start with enough height to be able to reach the vicinity of the landing area with some height to spare. Ideally, this approach procedure needs to be started at about 500–600 feet, upwind, and well to one side of the landing area. A problem does arise if the glider has lost too much height before entering this pattern. If the student is hell bent on using the angle only, he may end up with a dangerously low and slow final turn without realising what is happening. With any method using angles it is important to distinguish between having excessive height and having the landing area at too steep an angle to be able to avoid an overshoot. If the height is not sufficient to allow the glider to be positioned for a normal base leg well back behind the edge of the landing area, the angle to the landing area may be very steep, indicating that an overshoot is inevitable. In a situation like this the pilot will be sorely tempted to open the airbrakes to stop the overshoot, without stopping to consider how much height he has to complete the turn. Many dangerously low final turns

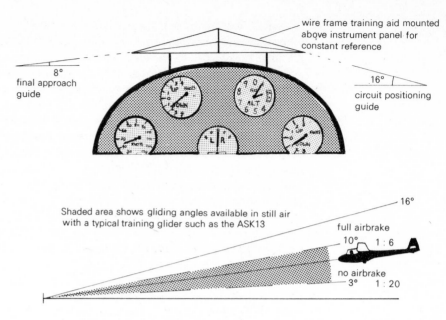

wire frame training aid mounted above instrument panel for constant reference

8°
final approach guide

16°
circuit positioning guide

Shaded area shows gliding angles available in still air with a typical training glider such as the ASK13

16°

full airbrake
10°   1 : 6

no airbrake
3°   1 : 20

42 The suggested wire frame training aid and a comparison between the frame angles and actual approach angles in still air.

occur because the pilot has mistaken being too close for being too high. If the airbrakes are being used before the final turn in order to throw away height there must be some height to spare in the first place. If necessary, the turn must be completed at a safe height *before* using the airbrakes, even if it means a landing further up the field. If you are short of height on the circuit do not use the airbrakes unless you can see that you will still be able to complete your final turn by at least the minimum height required for safety. If by using the brakes the turn would end up too low, do not use them until the turn has been completed.

Joining the circuit pattern for a landing

The rules and recommendations for the upper part of the circuit will vary according to the site and the conditions. If the launches are high enough, each flight will consist of the launch, a period of searching for thermals or other forms of lift or of practising training exercises, and the stage during which the pilot is getting the glider back to the position opposite the landing area with sufficient height for the approach to be planned.

Once again, this may be done either by a height and position method, or by judging the angle to the landing area. The essential thing is to arrive somewhere opposite the landing area at 500–600 feet. This will allow height for a good length of base leg, with plenty of time for the pilot to make adjustments to his position and use up excess height with the airbrakes if necessary. On most average-sized sites or airfields in light winds it will take about 200 feet of height to fly downwind from a position opposite the upwind end of the site. This will mean starting to fly downwind at about 700 feet to be sure of getting back. A little more height may be needed on a dead calm day, because not only is there no help from a following wind, but the glider must be flown back to a position a little further beyond the landing area for a longer than normal approach. In windy weather it might be thought that less height would be needed, but in practice arriving back with extra height is a good insurance against the effects of turbulence and sink. There is seldom any difficulty in using up the extra height against a strong wind as the approach can be so much steeper than normal.

If the glider does seem to be running rather short of height on its way downwind, do not just try to judge the angle to the landing area and decide if it is within gliding reach. The glider must reach a position above the normal turn in point and complete the turn by a safe height. If you imagine a radio tower over your turn in point and look at the angle to the top of the imaginary tower, you will get a much better idea of your chances of reaching it (Fig. 43). If there is any doubt, a new landing area must be selected immediately. On a gliding site there may be plenty more room upwind of the normal landing area, in which case, once the speed has been adjusted ready for the approach, the turn can be made when there is just comfortable height for an ordinary approach and landing. Since the turn is through 180° instead of the normal final turn of 90°, it must be started even higher than usual.

Never low and slow This sounds easy and sensible enough, but it is an unfortunate fact that the average beginner will almost always indulge in wishful thinking instead of taking the necessary action to turn in for a landing while he has plenty of height. In an effort to get back to the normal landing area he will, quite unconsciously, fly the glider a little slowly and this may be his downfall. It may appear that he still has plenty of height, but in order to make a safe final turn, he *must* have extra speed. This may cost most of his remaining height and leave him dangerously low for the turn (Fig. 44).

While the glider is still cruising at its normal gliding speed or less, it may be getting dangerously low, even though it is several hundred feet above the ground. At least half this height will be used up reaching a safe speed for the turn.

The likelihood of running right out of height is further increased by the Yates effect if the glider happens to meet sinking air. (See Appendix A and page 162.) Then the further loss of speed will bring the airspeed to well below the optimum so that the glider loses height even more rapidly. Even from 300 or 400 feet the glider can lose so much height within a few seconds that there will be insufficient left to gain a safe speed for the turn. In this case

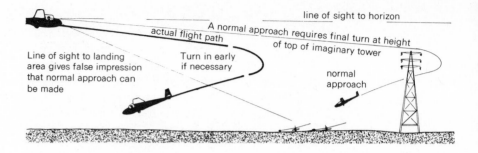

43a   If height could be marginal to get back for a normal approach, imagine a tower just beyond the landing area and estimate whether the glider would reach the top of this tower. If it could, the height is sufficient for a safe final turn. Do not look at the landing area alone as it is not enough to reach it unless there is sufficient height in hand for a safe turn. Always turn in before the height becomes marginal and land further into the field if necessary.

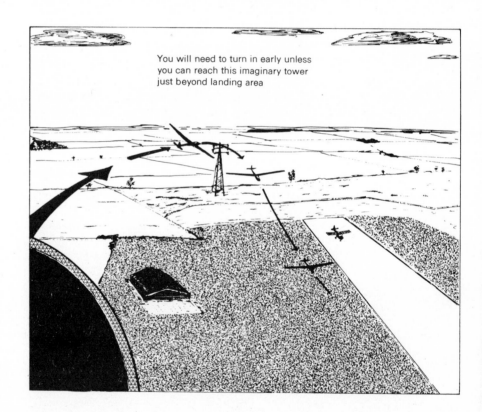

43b   Running short of height on the circuit.

there is bound to be an accident since any attempt to get round at low speed will result in stalling and spinning off the turn.

Clearly this is a situation which must *never* be allowed to arise. The essential precaution is to gain the extra speed by at least 400 or 500 feet. This will mean overcoming the normal instinct to fly slowly in order to stretch the glide a little further.

Once having gained the extra speed the situation is much safer. The height remaining is *real* height and the pilot can safely fly on if there is still more height than required for the final turn and approach. The effects of any sink are greatly reduced because the glider is well above its minimum cruising speed and also because it spends less time in the sinking air (see Fig 45). Above all, even if the pilot does misjudge his height or happens to lose an unexpected amount, the glider will still have sufficient speed for the turn.

In a nutshell, the glider must *never* be allowed to get into a position where it is **low *and* slow**.

Since it may fly into sink and lose an unexpected amount of height at any time, the only real guarantee of avoiding trouble is to gain extra speed *while* there is ample height. Flying slowly below 300–400 feet, any sudden loss of height would leave the glider in a critical, if not disastrous, position and therefore the glider must *never* be flown below that height at a low speed.

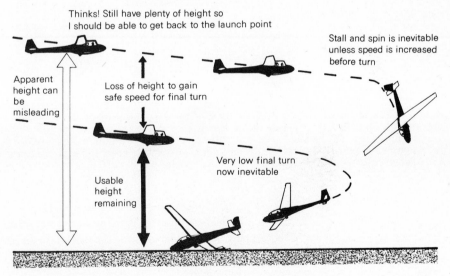

44 For safety, extra speed is essential below 300–400 feet. This is the only way to guarantee that you will never run out of height *and* speed. It is only too easy to forget that while the glider is still flying slowly you have far less *real* height and may already be desperately short of height for a safe final turn.

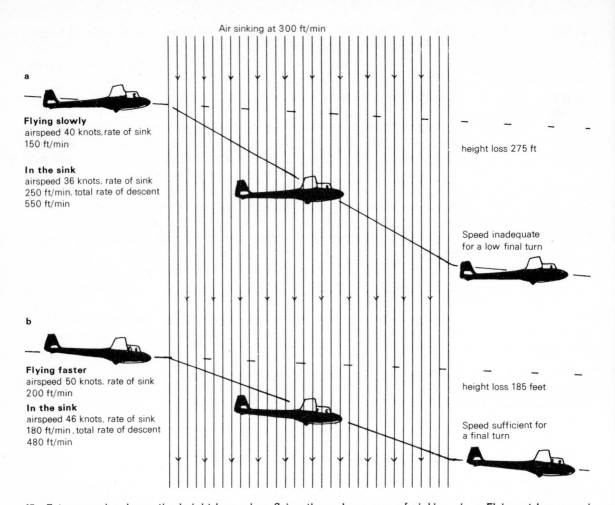

Air sinking at 300 ft/min

a

Flying slowly
airspeed 40 knots, rate of sink
150 ft/min

In the sink
airspeed 36 knots, rate of sink
250 ft/min, total rate of descent
550 ft/min

height loss 275 ft

Speed inadequate
for a low final turn

b

Flying faster
airspeed 50 knots, rate of sink
200 ft/min

In the sink
airspeed 46 knots, rate of sink
180 ft/min, total rate of descent
480 ft/min

height loss 185 feet

Speed sufficient for
a final turn

45 Extra speed reduces the height loss when flying through an area of sinking air. **a** Flying at low speed, for example at 40 knots, when the glider flies into sink it loses speed and has an increased rate of sink. This is in addition to the effect of the sinking air. At low speed it takes extra time to cross the area and loses more height. **b** Flying faster at 50 knots, the loss of speed to 46 knots has far less effect on the rate of sink and the time taken to cross the area is less than before. Less height is lost and the glider has sufficient speed for an immediate turn if necessary. *Moral – always have extra speed when flying below 400 or 500 feet. You never know when you may meet sinking air.*

It is vital that every beginner understands this problem and gets some experience in dealing with it. Briefing is not sufficient because of the serious consequences of not recognising the situation in time. Any indecisiveness is fatal and the real test is to put the student into a position where there will be just too little height to get back to the normal landing area and for the instructor to sit back and see what he does. Until the instructor is confident that the student will spot the situation and take the necessary action without prompting, there should be no question of the student flying solo.

Integrated power flying and gliding

The circuit procedure will frequently be dictated by the need to fit in with the operations of other aircraft. For example, if the club site is also a field used by a flying club, or a commercial airport, very strict traffic patterns will need to be adhered to for the safety of everyone (Fig. 46).

The usual system is to put all gliders and glider towing aircraft on one side of the runway in use, and to restrict them to making circuits and to soaring on that side of the airfield, while making the flying club aircraft operate on the other side, with their circuits in the opposite direction. Soaring is usually restricted to certain areas upwind and on the glider side, with very definite lower limits in the vicinity of the airfield.

Operations like this are made much safer if it is made mandatory for visiting aircraft to have radio, or at least to have to telephone for prior permission and instructions for landing. Most non-gliding pilots are completely thrown by the sight of both gliders and powered machines making approaches at the same time from opposite circuits!

Generally speaking, winch or tow car launching is not safe on a site with much power flying going on. Sooner or later an early solo pilot or a visitor

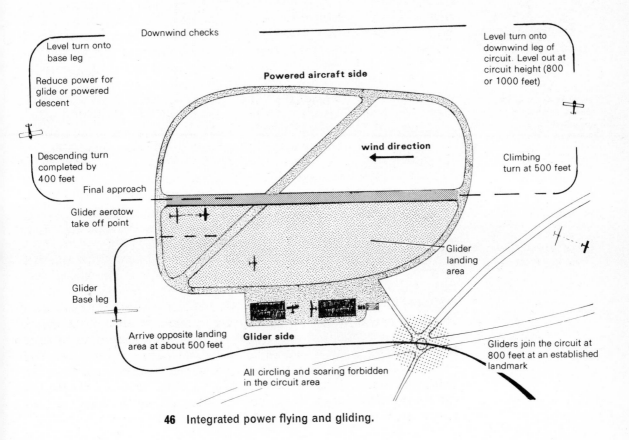

46 Integrated power flying and gliding.

who does not understand the gliding operations will swing, or fly across the launching line while a glider is being launched. If it happens to hit the launching cable, there will be an expensive, if not fatal, accident to the powered aircraft. However, on a gliding site where visiting powered aircraft are discouraged it is practical to have mixed launching and motor gliders all operating together.

For example, at the Lasham Gliding Centre we operate three or four tow planes, three two-seater motor gliders and a two tow car, wire launching system at the same time. On a busy day, this gives a launch rate of about twenty aerotows and between fifteen and twenty car launches per hour during peak periods. Visiting pilots who are not glider pilots are not really welcome, and they often go away without landing when they see thirty to forty gliders soaring close to the airfield, or four or five gliders plus tug aircraft all on the approach to land at the same time!

At a shared site where all the gliders are launched by aerotow the circuit is usually joined at a point just upwind and to the side of the field at about 800 feet. In this case, a long downwind leg is made parallel with the runway in use, and once this has been started no further attempts at soaring are permitted and a rectangular (known as a square) circuit is made, like a light aircraft. Often the local rules make it mandatory for the pilot to gain an extra 5–10 knots (known in the U.S.A. as the 'pattern' speed) at the start of the circuit. This extra speed greatly reduces the effects of sink because less time is spent in traversing an area of sinking air, with the result that less height is lost than at a low speed. The glider should always be retrimmed for this extra speed so that it will not tend to slow itself down again if the pilot is distracted for a few moments on the circuit. The aim with this kind of circuit is to fly a regular pattern so that the other gliders and powered machines know what the glider is going to do. No attempt is made to keep the glider up and, if the glider is arriving back too high, the airbrakes would be opened rather than make any diversion from the normal circuit. It would be quite usual, and a good practice, to have several hundred feet to lose on the base leg before making the final turn. Of course in the unlikely event of losing all this excess height because of flying into strong sink, the circuit would be cut short to avoid the risk of an undershoot.

This is a very safe kind of procedure, and if we all flew gliders launched by aerotow in conditions where it was usual to be able to find lift on every flight, there would be little point in trying to soar at 600 or 700 feet, and we would probably all adopt a circuit procedure of this kind. The very early increase in flying speed on joining the circuit reduces the effects of turbulence and sinking air and avoids any risk of the pilot forgetting to gain speed so that he ends up 'low and slow'.

(A few modern high performance gliders, on which the airbrakes are rather ineffective, have to be brought in to land at a speed which is not much above their normal minimum cruising speed. For example, on the Standard Class

Libelle, Cirrus and ASW 15 an approach speed of 50 knots is ample, and any more will result in a very long float before touchdown. This could be embarrassing in a small field. However, it is still sound practice when cruising at low speed to increase the flying speed at about 500 feet. The final turn will need to be a little further back on these machines as the pilot will need to slow down to the correct 'threshold' speed during the approach.)

In places where the soaring is rather limited by the climate, it is a serious restriction to prohibit all soaring below 800 or 900 feet. Experience shows that this is seldom justified, even where gliding and powered aircraft are flying intensively from the same site. In most cases, provided that the gliders keep to their side of the field, no restriction need be put on their operations.

For example, at the Wycombe Air Park at Booker (less than fifteen miles from London Airport) the gliders have complete freedom on their side of the runway and may even soar on the power side of the runway in use as long as they are more than 500 feet above the power circuit. Although both the gliding and the flying club traffic is very intensive (over 100,000 movements in 1972) good airmanship, good flying discipline, and common sense result in a happy co-operation and safe movements in spite of the small size of the airfield.

In the interests of safety every gliding club has to decide on its Local Flying Rules, and define at what minimum height pilots will be expected to cease attempting to soar. Below 500 feet any thermalling becomes dangerous for inexperienced solo pilots and, in any case, it is seldom worthwhile because the thermals are usually too small to be used. There is always the risk of losing several hundred feet unexpectedly by falling out of the edge of the thermal, and, therefore, any attempts must be restricted to an area close to the field and away from the downwind boundary.

In Denmark only fully licensed glider pilots (cross-country standard and about thirty to forty gliding hours) are permitted to attempt to soar in the downwind half of the gliding sites, regardless of height. Beginners and inexperienced solo pilots have to treat the halfway line as a barrier which cannot be penetrated except to make an approach and landing. If they are soaring and drift back to this line, regardless of height, they must leave the lift and move upwind again to look for another thermal. This eliminates any risk of the student pilot drifting away into a critical position downwind of the field – a constant worry to every instructor. By the time that the pilot is fully qualified it is expected that he will appreciate the dangers of trying to soar at low altitude and of drifting away downwind.

In England we tend to favour a less rigid rule, but this means spending much more time teaching student pilots to use their judgement about where they soar. As my Danish friends point out, our instructors almost certainly have more stomach ulcers worrying about the students who get carried away with the joys of soaring and drift out of reach of the airfield.

Preparing to land   Perhaps the most important thing of all is to make sure that the glider is not being flown too slowly for the last part of the circuit. There is always a great temptation to fly too slowly when the glider is a little short of height and the pilot is trying to get back to land in the normal landing area near the launch point. Unless the speed is increased at about 500 feet, regardless of where the glider happens to be at the time, there is a grave risk that any turbulence or strong sink will leave it short of height *and* speed, and still facing the wrong way for the landing.

The pilot will tend to forget that until he has gained an extra 5–10 knots above his minimum cruising speed he will appear to have plenty of height for his final turn. This extra speed is essential for any turn at low altitude because of the effects of turbulence or of any inaccuracy during the turn which might cause a loss of speed. The pilot must remember that until he has gained more speed he must allow himself an extra 100 feet or so for this purpose. If he does forget, he is liable to find himself dangerously low at the last moment, when he tries to gain speed and turn in for the landing.

For safety, extra speed is needed *all* the time the glider is flying below about 500 feet, so that any unexpected sudden loss of height cannot possibly leave the glider 'low and slow'.

This increase in flying speed is the most important preparation that the pilot must make before landing but there are several others. They can be done as a definite drill or check, or as a matter of routine, good airmanship.

If a formal downwind vital actions drill is carried out (such as the B.G.A. recommended USTAL check) this should be completed by about 500 feet, or at the start of the base leg, whichever happens first.

The essential preparations for landing are:
1 Lower the main wheel and lock it down (unless the field is rough enough or soft enough to warrant a wheel-up landing to reduce the risk of breaking the undercarriage).
2 Lower the nose a little to gain an extra 5–10 knots above the minimum safe cruising speed. Maintain this speed until the final turn has been completed.
3 Retrim the glider to fly hands off, or retrim approximately, by moving the trim lever forward an appropriate amount.
4 Hold the airbrake lever, unlock the airbrakes and momentarily open them enough to make sure they are free. Then hold them in the closed position ready for instant use as required. *Never* take that hand off the lever again until the landing has been completed.
5 Ignore the altimeter readings and judge your height.

Long before this the pilot should, of course, have made a preliminary assessment of the landing areas to see if they are clear, and have looked for other traffic which might be landing on them before him. He should have already decided roughly how strong the wind is and this will determine to a large extent how far behind the landing area he makes his base leg. Once he is down to 500 or 600 feet he must be careful not to over-concentrate on any one thing. He needs to keep glancing across to the landing area to judge his angle to it in order to make sure that he will reach it safely, yet he must also position himself for a good approach.

Suggestions for beginners

Always try to stay at the upwind end of the site until you need to move back for the approach. The wind will keep drifting you back before you have used up your height unless you make a point of finishing any turns facing into wind each time. As soon as you drift back to the downwind end of the field with excess height, the planning of an approach becomes more difficult. If you are trying to thermal soar, search for your lift upwind of the launch point and do not allow yourself to be drifted away out of easy reach of the landing area. Fly back upwind as soon as possible to find the next piece of lift. It is just as easy to soar upwind of the gliding site so that you are always within easy reach of it, as to drift away downwind, where you may have difficulty in getting back to safety against the wind.

Remember that the wind is fickle and may change very quickly through a large angle. Check the windsock, or any smoke, and try to notice which way you are actually drifting as you circle. The wind will seldom blow directly along the runway or take off and landing direction. If it is at an angle be careful not to drift away out of reach to the side of the landing area.

Never fly for more than a few seconds when you are on the circuit without referring by a glance to the position and angle of the nearest landing area. If necessary, turn the machine so that you can see it and keep within easy reach all the time. A sudden loss of height can be detected more easily by looking across and seeing the rapid change in angle, rather than by trying to spot an actual change in the height.

A common mistake is to keep far too close to the field so that there is no room or time to adjust things on the base leg. It is far easier to start your positioning from somewhere well to one side of the field, so that, as you move downwind, you can see the landing areas clearly. If you are coming back too close it is difficult to move out and improve your position without losing sight of the landing area completely as you turn away. If you are both too high and too close to the field, always move out away from it *first* and then, if it is still necessary, use up some height. Always improve your position first, as being cramped on top of the landing area is much more embarrassing than just being a little too high.

Never circle to use up height, or attempt to use lift to soar once you are on or near the downwind boundary of the landing area below about 600 feet. Make a definite decision to land, and once you have made the decision, ignore all lift and carry out the circuit and landing.

Circling is a drastic way of using up height because the loss of height per turn is so variable and the glider always drifts back with the wind. Do not circle unless you can afford to lose about 200 feet and drift back with the wind. Be wary of the tempting little bits of lift which you meet just before you start the base leg. When you circle to try and use them you often go up at first, as you start to circle, and then fall out of the lift into the adjoining strong sink a few seconds later. This can cost you several hundred feet of height and you will have drifted much further downwind by the time you have completed the circle. You will be left in a very dodgy situation if you were already close to the downwind boundary when you started to turn. In an extreme case you might find yourself out of reach of the landing area because of the strength of the wind against you. (See Fig. 47.)

Never circle on, or near, the downwind boundary at low altitudes. It is easiest and safest to use up excess height in this position by widening the circuit, or just by opening the airbrakes fully for a few moments.

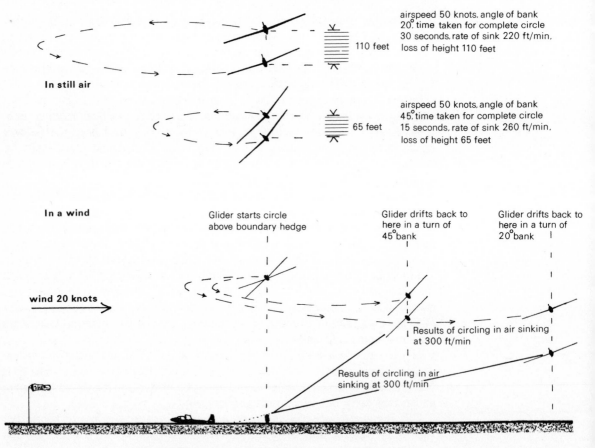

47 Loss of height and distance drifted downwind are reduced by using well-banked turns.

Think at least one jump ahead during the circuit and try to make adjustments to avoid problems, rather than let things develop badly and then try to extricate yourself.

Choose your landing area carefully in plenty of time and avoid landing anywhere near another glider or an obstruction. Never land towards an object and do not approach low over something, unless it is absolutely unavoidable. Do not take chances, give yourself room for errors.

Do not worry about your present height flying downwind to position the glider for the start of the base leg. Try to think how things will be by the time that you have arrived there. Ask yourself, 'Will I be higher or lower than I would like to be?' Almost invariably you should need to make an adjustment to try and correct things by widening or tightening the circuit a little. By the time you arrive opposite the landing point it is too late to worry about this any more, and you need to be thinking about the positioning of the base leg.

On the base leg, it is the position and height of the final turn that you should be thinking about. Does it look as though it will be finished much higher than you really need to be for a safe approach; will you have room for the turn and a proper approach; or will you be too close? (Remember that the final turn brings you towards the landing area by the radius of the turn on a calm day.)

Always try to make corrections by using the airbrakes and moving back a little if the turn is going to finish a bit too high or too close, so that the error is corrected before the final turn.

During the final turn, the pilot should be making a decision about the need for airbrake on the final approach. Then, as he completes the turn, he can open them immediately if he is obviously too high, instead of having to think about it after the turn and waste valuable seconds. Every second of delay means up to 30 yards of overshoot!

If the landing area is obviously way below you at a very steep angle you will need most of the airbrake unless there is a strong wind, so start by opening them fully immediately after the turn. Look at the edge of the landing area, or your aiming point short of where you want to touch down, and check whether you are under- or overshooting it. Is it moving downwards under the nose? If so, open the airbrake, keeping the same attitude. Then readjust the airbrakes to bring the glider down accurately towards the aiming point. Glance at the airspeed indicator and, if the speed starts to drop below your chosen approach speed, lower the nose, or if you are already getting close to the height for rounding out, reduce the airbrake setting to help the glider regain speed. Do not stare at the aiming point as you get down below about 20–30 feet, or the ground will rush up at you and you will fly into it and make a bad landing. Remember, look well ahead as you get near the ground.

Try to avoid approaches which end up with little or no airbrake as it is difficult to judge how far the glider will float in these cases. If the glider has powerful airbrakes a little extra speed and plenty of airbrake will make the landings easier. A few types of machine have very powerful brakes and are a little critical with them fully opened. For example, both the K7 and the Skylark 2 require extra speed for a proper round out using full airbrake, and caution is necessary.

Unless he has been specifically trained to do so, the beginner is advised not to open the airbrakes further during the hold off. Instead, he should try to get them set for the last 30–40 feet and hold them still. Last moment adjustments are something that every pilot must learn to do but which can lead to trouble if he fails to stop the glider sinking as the brakes are opened. If the glider has already lost most of its speed, opening the brakes will result in a heavy landing.

Above all, if you are short of height, pick up extra speed in plenty of time at about 500 feet and prepare for the approach then. Do not try to stretch the glide back to the landing area. Leave yourself plenty of height to complete that final turn by at least twice the height of tall trees!

Never run out of height and speed.

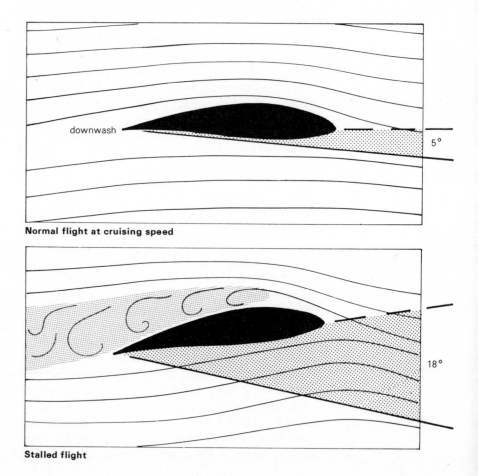

Normal flight at cruising speed

48 The airflow over an aerofoil in normal and stalled flight.

Stalled flight

Stalling and Spinning

8

Stalling 135
Stalling in a turn 138
Incipient spins 138
Spiral dives 140

Full spins and recoveries 140
Spinning off steep turns 142
Practice spins 144

Stalling The normal lift is dependent on maintaining smooth airflow over the wing. However, if the airflow meets the wing at too large an angle, it breaks up and becomes very turbulent above the wing causing a serious loss of lift and extra drag. The wing is then said to be stalled (Fig. 48).

In flight, this means that if the wing is pulled beyond the stalling angle the aircraft will have insufficient lift to fly properly and support its weight. It will lose height rapidly until the wing is allowed to return to a smaller angle so that it can unstall and make lift normally (Fig. 49).

Fortunately, with most aircraft there is a distinctive nose-down pitching movement as the wing stalls. When the airflow breaks up over the top surface of the wing some lift is still being produced and this remaining lift acts further back along the wing so that the nose-down pitching movement occurs as the aircraft sinks. This nose-down movement reduces the angle of attack of the wing, helping it to unstall itself. In fact, almost all gliders will unstall themselves if they are allowed to do so – that is as long as the pilot does not attempt to stop the nose from dropping by moving the stick even further back.

Whereas in normal flight the pilot has learned to move back on the stick to prevent the nose from dropping, this would not only delay the recovery if the glider is stalled but also aggravate the situation. It is therefore essential for every pilot to learn to recognise the symptoms of the approach to the stall and how to recover with a minimum loss of height.

A stall can occur at any time when the wing is meeting the airflow at too large an angle, whether the aircraft is in level flight, turning, or pulling out from a dive. Normally the wing is brought to a large angle by moving the stick back, and a harsh or large backward stick movement is the most likely cause of stalling.

In straight flight the stall occurs at a low speed and the pilot of a glider is given ample warning by the quietness and the poor control response. There

135

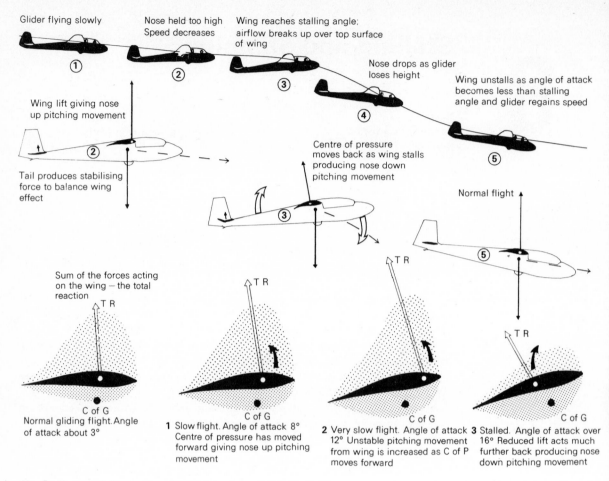

Glider flying slowly

① Nose held too high
Speed decreases

② Wing reaches stalling angle;
airflow breaks up over top surface
of wing

③ Nose drops as glider
loses height

④ Wing unstalls as angle of attack
becomes less than stalling
angle and glider regains speed

⑤

Wing lift giving nose
up pitching movement

②

Tail produces stabilising
force to balance wing
effect

Centre of pressure
moves back as wing stalls
producing nose down
pitching movement

③

Normal flight

⑤

Sum of the forces acting
on the wing — the total
reaction

T R

C of G
Normal gliding flight. Angle
of attack about 3°

T R

C of G
1 Slow flight. Angle of attack 8°
Centre of pressure has moved
forward giving nose up pitching
movement

T R

C of G
2 Very slow flight. Angle of attack
12° Unstable pitching movement
from wing is increased as C of P
moves forward

T R

C of G
3 Stalled. Angle of attack over
16° Reduced lift acts much
further back producing nose
down pitching movement

49 Stalling and the centre of pressure movements in flight.

is usually an obvious vibration or buffet as the airflow breaks away and becomes turbulent near the wing root at a speed a few knots above the stall. Finally, the nose of the glider drops about 15° to 20° in spite of any further backward movement on the stick. For a few seconds the glider loses height rapidly but, providing that the backward pressure on the stick is relaxed, it will unstall itself and regain speed. Reducing the backward movement on the stick allows the nose to drop and helps to reduce the angle at which the wing is meeting the air. Most gliders have a very gentle and docile stall and lose about 50 feet during the period of a stall and recovery.

Since the lift from the wing depends entirely on the airspeed and the angle of attack (that is the angle between the wing chord and the airflow which is meeting it) there is a direct relationship between speed and this angle in steady flight. Virtually the same amount of lift is required to support the weight of the glider over a wide range of speeds and, therefore, at high speed

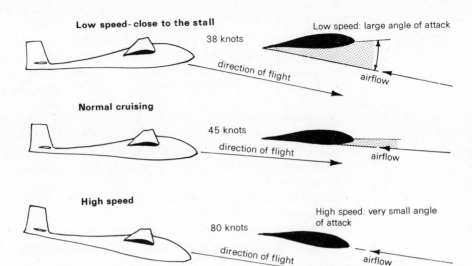

Low speed - close to the stall

38 knots

direction of flight

Low speed: large angle of attack

airflow

Normal cruising

45 knots

direction of flight

airflow

50 The relation between speed and angle of attack in steady, straight flight.

High speed

80 knots

direction of flight

High speed: very small angle of attack

airflow

the angle of attack is small whereas at low speed it is always large. This means that the wing is close to the stalling angle whenever the glider is flown below its normal cruising speed (Fig. 50).

Flying too slowly is the result of flying with the nose too high or even with it in a more normal attitude, if there is excessive drag. The most likely reasons for extra drag are skidding sideways through the air or flying with the airbrakes open.

51 The variation in stalling speed with the angle of bank in accurate turns.

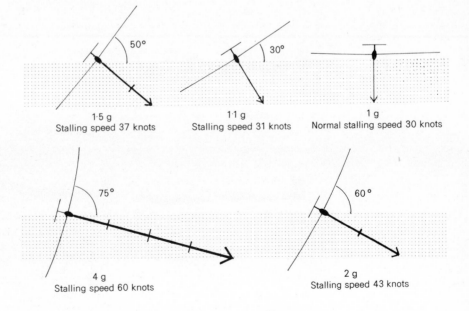

50°

1·5 g
Stalling speed 37 knots

30°

1·1 g
Stalling speed 31 knots

1 g
Normal stalling speed 30 knots

75°

4 g
Stalling speed 60 knots

60°

2 g
Stalling speed 43 knots

Stalling in a turn During a turn or sudden change in direction the wing must develop much more lift to do the extra work of pulling the glider round the turn in addition to supporting the weight (Fig. 51). The stalling speed is raised temporarily during these manoeuvres so that some of the symptoms of the normal straight stall do not occur. For example, the quietness is not so obvious and the controls remain effective until the moment of stalling because of the higher airspeed. Again, at the moment of stall the nose cannot be raised by a further backward movement on the stick and there is usually a tendency for the inner wing to stall and drop first if the glider is turning. This is known as an incipient spin.

If the backward movement on the stick is relaxed immediately the stall occurs there will be little or no loss of height, since there is ample flying speed and therefore good control once the wing has been allowed to unstall itself. However, if the pilot keeps the stick back the incipient spin will tend to develop.

Incipient spins In normal flight the glider tends to resist any tendency for turbulence to tip it over into a banked position. However, once the wing is stalled the glider becomes unstable, and, if a wing starts to drop, it will tend to continue. This uncontrolled rolling movement is known as autorotation and is the cause of a spin.

It is important to realise that a spin can only occur as a direct result of stalling and that the moment the wings become unstalled the glider will become stable again and will stop rotating.

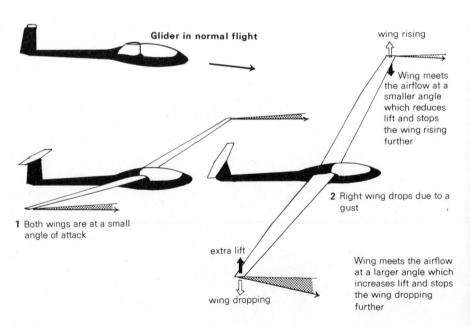

52 Lateral damping in normal flight.

Glider in normal flight

wing rising

Wing meets the airflow at a smaller angle which reduces lift and stops the wing rising further

2 Right wing drops due to a gust

1 Both wings are at a small angle of attack

extra lift

wing dropping

Wing meets the airflow at a larger angle which increases lift and stops the wing dropping further

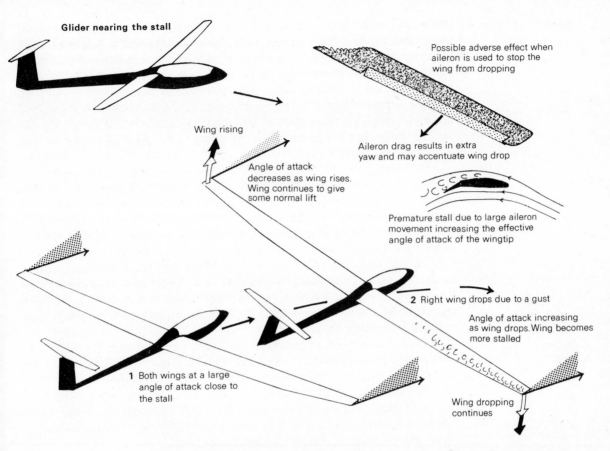

Glider nearing the stall

Possible adverse effect when aileron is used to stop the wing from dropping

Aileron drag results in extra yaw and may accentuate wing drop

Wing rising

Angle of attack decreases as wing rises. Wing continues to give some normal lift

Premature stall due to large aileron movement increasing the effective angle of attack of the wingtip

2 Right wing drops due to a gust

Angle of attack increasing as wing drops. Wing becomes more stalled

1 Both wings at a large angle of attack close to the stall

Wing dropping continues

53 Lateral instability during stalled flight. Compare this with **Fig. 52** which shows lateral damping in normal flight.

While most beginners soon become accustomed to any sensations which occur during the stall and recovery, the sudden dropping of the wing during an incipient spin takes more time to get used to. At first the glider seems destined to roll right over but once you have learned to make the correct control movements to recover promptly you will soon gain confidence. It is best to look ahead over the nose during all stalling and spinning manoeuvres since you can then see exactly what is happening at a glance. Any sudden up-and-down or sideways movements of your head, particularly during the full spin, can cause giddiness and nausea which otherwise would not occur. However, you must expect to find the full spin a somewhat disturbing feeling at first. Try to imagine that you are a part of the cockpit and do not try to resist as the glider starts to tip over. If anything, try to lean across towards the dropping wing as this reduces the strength of the sensations.

To start with, it is best to learn the recovery actions as a sequence of movements, so that they can be made almost automatically. Since the cause of all the trouble is the initial stalling of the wing, it should be clear that the one thing we must never do is to keep the stick back. This would tend to keep the wing stalled and delay the recovery or even result in a full spin developing.

The rudder is a very strong anti-spin control and if the glider is stalled and begins to drop one wing the rudder should be applied to try and stop the aircraft from yawing towards the dropping wing. Usually a fairly large movement is needed.

The order in which the controls are moved is unimportant unless the aircraft is in a fully developed spin – that is after at least one complete rotation. The most rapid recovery from the incipient stage is to apply the opposite rudder and ease forward on the stick at the same time. Above all, the stick must be moved sufficiently to allow the wing to unstall. This is usually a matter of easing forward a little, or of relaxing the backward pressure on the stick. Failure to unstall the wings may result in a violent flick in the direction of the rudder movement. This sometimes occurs if the pilot becomes confused and makes the recovery action required for a full spin, accentuating the pause between applying the rudder and the progressive forward movement on the stick.

It is only natural in an unintentional stall to try and stop the wing from dropping with the ailerons, as in normal flight. This usually only delays the recovery by causing further yawing but sometimes it results in a more violent wing drop, instead of lifting the wing and assisting with the recovery. Try to avoid using any aileron until the wings are unstalled. Once this is done the glider is in normal flight again and the wings should be brought level without delay by means of the ailerons.

Spiral dives
If no recovery action is taken at the incipient stage, most gliders will spin for a turn or so before unstalling themselves and gaining speed in a steep, diving turn. This is known as a spiral dive. The recovery is simply a matter of centralising any rudder, bringing the wings level, and easing the aircraft out of the dive. A spiral dive can be recognised by the obviously increasing speed and the increase in 'g' loading and it is important to stop it before the speeds and loadings become dangerously high. Both spins and spiral dives are very steep, diving spirals in which height is lost very rapidly. A spin can be recognised by the rapid rotation and low, fluctuating airspeed. However, the low airspeed may not be obvious because in many cases the airspeed indicator misreads during the spin, so that although the actual speed is very low, the needle may have moved back through the zero position to indicate a fictitiously high figure. During the spin, however, the 'g' loading is only slightly above normal and remains more or less constant.

Full spins and recoveries
A continuous full spin will normally only occur if the stick is kept right back, and even then only when the centre of gravity of the glider is near its aft

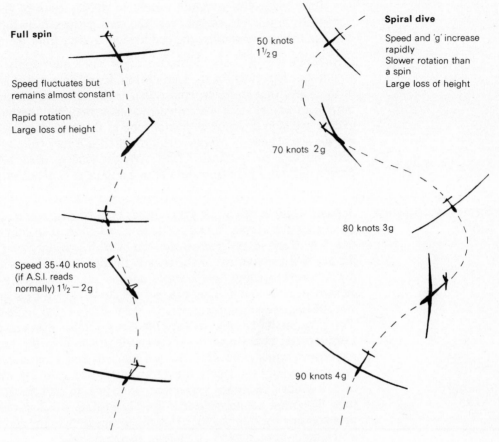

Full spin

Speed fluctuates but remains almost constant

Rapid rotation
Large loss of height

Speed 35-40 knots (if A.S.I. reads normally) $1\frac{1}{2} - 2$ g

50 knots
$1\frac{1}{2}$ g

Spiral dive

Speed and 'g' increase rapidly
Slower rotation than a spin
Large loss of height

70 knots 2g

80 knots 3g

90 knots 4g

54 The differences between a spin and a spiral dive.

limit. Heavy pilots usually find that a continuous full spin is impossible because their weight makes the glider so nose-heavy that the wings cannot stay stalled. However, an unintentional incipient spin can use up several hundred feet and may be just as disastrous as a full spin if it occurs during the final turn onto the approach. Obviously prevention is far better than cure.

The standard method of recovery from a fully developed spin is important because it is effective with all types of powered aircraft and gliders. It is the method used during airworthiness tests and the aircraft would not be cleared as safe for spinning unless it recovers promptly when this action is taken. On a few types of aircraft the order of movement is particularly important and therefore it is standardised for all machines. The standard method of recovery is as follows.

First apply **full** opposite rudder to the direction of the spin – then, with the ailerons central, ease the stick progressively forward until the spin stops – centralise the rudder and recover from the dive.

Although it is desirable to have a slight pause after applying the rudder, do not wait hopefully for the spin to stop. Remember that it is the unstalling of the wings that stops the spin and therefore it is the progressive forward movement of the stick which will normally have the desired result. Most gliders will stop spinning almost as soon as the stick starts to move forward but the actual amount of movement required will vary from type to type and with different cockpit loads. This makes it vital to think of it as being a progressive movement forward and to continue it *until* the spin stops.

Spinning off steep turns

A point which is often not appreciated, even by instructors, is that it is far easier to stall and spin from a gentle turn in a glider than from a well-banked one. There are several reasons for this. On the majority of gliders most of the backward movement of the stick is already in use in a well-banked turn (25° or more) leaving only a small amount left to pull the wing to a large enough angle to stall it. The stick can usually be moved back gradually to the stop without anything more serious than the pre-stall buffeting occurring. This is certainly the case with steeper turns of more than about 40° of bank. Furthermore, because of the higher stalling speed in the turn the control response remains good until the last moment and a recovery can be made instantaneously by relaxing the backward pressure on the stick. Usually it takes a sudden backward movement, or snatch, to stall the glider in a steep turn. The most common fault in steeper turns is to allow the nose to drop by not easing back on the stick *enough* but this is 'fail safe' and merely results in the nose dropping and an increase in speed.

In straight flight or a shallow, banked turn there is always a large amount of backward movement on the stick in reserve which can bring the aircraft to the stall if the wing is pulled to a much greater angle of attack. This is much more likely to result in a sudden wing drop if one wing happens to stall first. Furthermore, it is in gently banked turns that the inexperienced pilot is most likely to be tempted into using too much rudder in an effort to increase the rate of turn. This will result in much more drag as the glider skids sideways through the air. The extra drag, just like opening the airbrakes, will cause an excessive loss of height, and a serious loss of speed unless the nose is lowered. If the glider does stall in this situation the extra rudder in the direction of the turn will make the aircraft begin to spin immediately.

In contrast, the pilot making a well-banked turn is never tempted to over-rudder because the rate of turn is already adequate. In any case, it would probably only result in the nose dropping and a gain in airspeed.

An inexperienced pilot with his head in the clouds has an uncanny knack of producing the exact conditions and control movements most likely to result in a spin. This is most liable to happen if the glider is a little short of

55 The full spin and recovery.

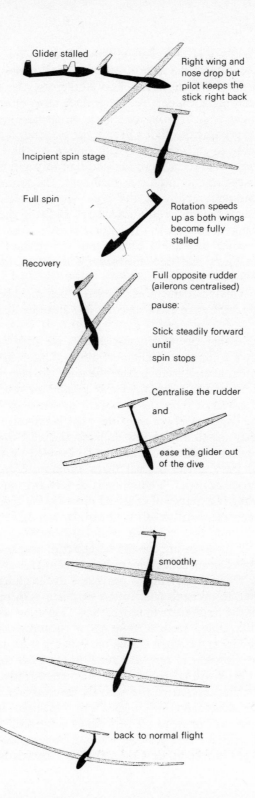

Glider stalled

Right wing and nose drop but pilot keeps the stick right back

Incipient spin stage

Full spin

Rotation speeds up as both wings become fully stalled

Recovery

Full opposite rudder (ailerons centralised)

pause:

Stick steadily forward until spin stops

Centralise the rudder

and

ease the glider out of the dive

smoothly

back to normal flight

height and the pilot is flying it rather too slowly in an effort to keep up. Because of the lack of height he will almost certainly start a gently-banked turn and then, in an effort to increase the rate of turn, he will apply more and more rudder. As the rudder takes effect it will look as if the turn has tightened, but this is only a momentary result. Without realising what is happening the pilot will stop the tendency for the bank to increase and for the nose to start to drop (both caused by the excess rudder and both warning signs that the aircraft is skidding badly and is near the stall). Within seconds, especially if the air is turbulent, the aircraft will stall and the bank will increase rapidly as the nose drops. Unless the pilot recognises the stall immediately, he is bound to try and stop the nose dropping by pulling right back on the stick – the worst possible reaction he could make. In order to recover and avoid diving into the ground he must overcome his natural instincts and ease forward on the stick first to unstall the wings before levelling out of the dive.

Obviously this is a situation which must be avoided, and the best way is to fly with some extra speed at low altitudes and to use plenty of bank in turns.

Practice spins The majority of training gliders are very docile and it is often difficult to give a convincing demonstration of incipient and full spins. The glider will often unstall itself before the pilot has had time to take the normal recovery action and the beginner may get the impression that there is no need to ease forward or relax the backward pressure on the stick. This impression could be dangerous because if the pilot continues to hold the stick back the glider may restall after a few seconds and flick over into an incipient spin in the opposite direction. This can be avoided by always moving the stick forward at least to the normal flight position, even if the glider appears to have unstalled itself. The amount of forward movement necessary to unstall the wing is a matter of trial and error on the type of glider concerned. Too little movement will result in the glider rolling further over into a steeply banked position, or recovering while still buffeting. Too much forward movement will result in unpleasant negative 'g' and an unnecessary steep dive at high speed so that much more height is lost.

When attempting to provoke a docile glider into dropping one wing at the stall in order to practice an incipient spin recovery, there are several tricks of the trade used by instructors. The most violent wing drop usually occurs from almost straight flight and is encouraged by a very small amount of extra rudder and a slight snatch back on the stick just as the stall occurs. It is quite unnecessary to raise the nose an excessive amount and more than about 5° of bank will probably upset the demonstration and prevent the characteristic flicking motion of the start of autorotation. Slightly inaccurate flight with the wings more or less level and that slight, last-moment snatch back on the stick will often result in a rapid wing drop which is difficult to anticipate. This is the best possible training because the student expects a straight stall while in fact either wing may drop. Alternatively, excessive rudder used in a

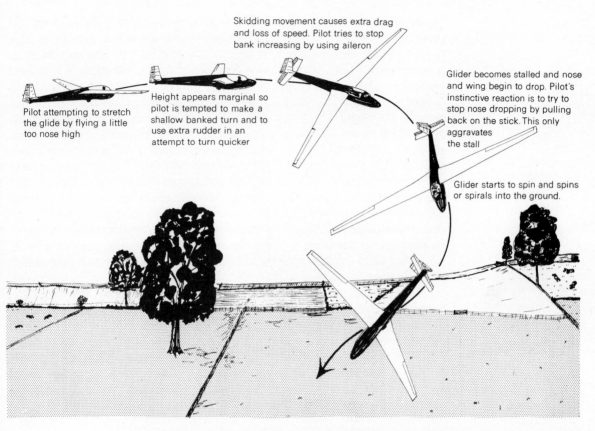

Skidding movement causes extra drag and loss of speed. Pilot tries to stop bank increasing by using aileron

Pilot attempting to stretch the glide by flying a little too nose high

Height appears marginal so pilot is tempted to make a shallow banked turn and to use extra rudder in an attempt to turn quicker

Glider becomes stalled and nose and wing begin to drop. Pilot's instinctive reaction is to try to stop nose dropping by pulling back on the stick. This only aggravates the stall

Glider starts to spin and spins or spirals into the ground.

56 The results of flying too slowly and over-ruddering in a turn at low altitude are serious. Always make well-banked turns with adequate speed.

gentle turn at low speed will result in a predictable wing drop and a realistic lesson on the results of over-ruddering in a slow turn.

When attempting to practise a full spin the problem is again one of getting the spin established. With most gliders full spins are only possible when the centre of gravity is near the aft limit. During the spin there is a tendency for the airflow to move the ailerons. The stick will usually move inwards towards the direction of the spin. With many modern machines the position of the ailerons is critical and often they will not spin for more than a turn or so unless the ailerons are held central. Again it is essential to get the glider fully stalled but it is not necessary to pull the nose much higher than the horizon. The rudder should be applied fully about 5 knots before the stall in order to start the glider yawing before so much speed is lost that the rudder becomes ineffective. Above all, the stick must be moved *right* back and kept there or the spin will not develop.

It is often difficult to obtain sufficient practice with full spin to become fully competent and confident about them. The essential thing is to be competent at recovering from stalls and incipient spins and to build up experience with full spins whenever the opportunity arises. A student who is really upset or scared of spinning is not safe for solo flying. The only solution to this kind of problem is first to understand all about it and then gradually to become accustomed to the sensations involved by repetition. It is general practice to leave incipient and full spinning until the student has become thoroughly acclimatised to the normal sensations involved with flying. This means that he may have little or no experience of the sensations of low or negative 'g' until he starts to practice stalling and recoveries. There is a risk that this feeling may then become associated with stalling so that the student thinks that the feeling means that the aircraft is stalled. In fact it is nothing to do with stalling but would occur at any time and at any speed if the pilot moved forward on the stick quickly. The sensation occurs because of the nose-down pitching movement which tends to throw the pilot (and his stomach) upwards out of the cockpit. The same sensation can occur when the glider sinks suddenly for a few seconds even without any nose-down pitching movement.

It is important to realise that there is no *sensation* of stalling, there are only symptoms. Usually the sensation of negative 'g' only happens when the pilot has made an excessive forward movement on the stick during a stall recovery and this results in an unnecessary gain of speed and loss of height. Remember that all these sensations will be minimised by looking ahead at the horizon so that the movements of the aircraft can be clearly seen. They will seem amplified if the visibility is poor or if you look at the instruments instead of watching what the aircraft is doing.

9 The Effects of the Wind

Flying in a steady wind 148
Ground speed and airspeed 149
Circling flight in a strong
  wind 150
Flying across the wind 152
The effects of variation in
  the wind 152
Wind gradients near the
  ground 154

Surface obstructions 161
Stability of the air 161
The effects of changes in
  airspeed 161
The effects of thermal activity 163
Dynamic soaring 168
The behaviour of model
  aircraft in a wind 170

It is simple enough to understand how an aeroplane or glider flies but when trying to explain the effects the wind has on them it is easy to become confused. So far most of our explanations about flying have assumed a lack of wind in order to avoid complications.

Anyone who has had anything to do with flying model aircraft is almost certain to have watched the influence of the wind on the models and come to erroneous conclusions about its effects. Similarly, without a clear and logical explanation about wind effects, the average glider pilot would be lucky to reason out for himself the truth of the matter.

Because 'seeing is believing' and because some things which appear to happen do not seem to agree with theory, there are a large number of experienced pilots who have very vague, and often completely erroneous, ideas about the effect of the wind on an aircraft.

If you want to hear some really muddled thinking and hair-brained theories, try introducing the subject in the bar at your flying club.

One common misconception is that, since the aircraft has a very high speed over the ground as it flies downwind, all that energy has to go somewhere when it makes a turn into wind. Pilots will often claim to have experienced this increase in speed as they turn into the wind, particularly when hill soaring.

Other pilots, and even some instructors on powered aircraft may comment on the dangers of losing speed because of turning downwind at low altitude and on the loss of climbing rate going downwind.

In all these instances there often appears to be evidence to support the contention that an aircraft is affected by even a steady wind. The real causes of change in airspeed under these circumstances are often difficult to identify and even more difficult to prove.

Flying in a steady wind

The first important **fact** is that if the wind speed is constant the only effect on any kind of flying machine, be it balloon, airship, glider or jet, is to drift it away in the direction of the wind. However strong the wind, there will be no changes in *airspeed* as the machine turns into wind or downwind. In fact, above a layer of fog the pilot of a glider or other aircraft would have no idea in which direction the wind was blowing.

In effect, it is as if the aircraft circles or flies all the time inside a huge block of air. On a still day the block is stationary, whereas on a windy day the block is drifting across the countryside (Fig. 57). Another way of visualising this is to think of the aircraft circling in its block of air while the earth below moves off steadily with the speed of the wind.

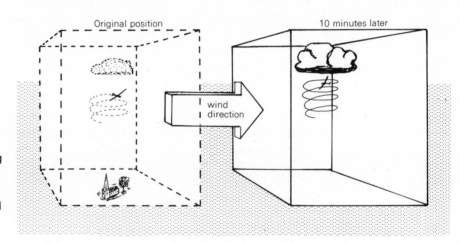

57 Circling in a strong wind. Glider circles under the cloud while the block of air is moved over the ground at the speed of the wind.

A few examples of similar situations in other areas of life may help the reader to grasp this concept and make it more credible.

Think of the situation as you walk to the dining car of an express train. Providing that the train is travelling smoothly, we have a situation similar to flying in our block of air in a steady wind. It is as easy to walk up or down the train as to move across the carriage. We are inside the train just as we are inside the block of air when we are flying. However, if the train is accelerating or braking, or taking a sharp bend, the situation is very different. In the same way, the aircraft is affected by gustiness or sudden changes in the wind.

As another example, imagine yourself about to swim across a wide river on a day with patchy fog. Standing with your feet on the bottom you can feel the current trying to sweep you downstream. As soon as you start swimming you cannot feel the current and can only see that to reach the landing stage on the far side you will have to aim upstream of it to allow for the effect of the current. If you stop swimming and float you will be drifting along with the river within a few seconds. You will feel no movement at all and there will be no 'slip' between you and the water. You would travel at the exact speed of the river and if the fog came down you would have no idea which way to go for a bank. It would not be any easier to swim downstream than upstream and *never is* except when you can see the bank and are concerned with reaching a particular point on it. If the current is strong and we are not making much progress it will become harder work if we swim faster to go upstream against the river. However, if we swim steadily it is just as easy to swim heading in one direction as another – regardless of the strength of the current.

A flight in a balloon is a wonderful experience which has some unexpected pleasures. In level flight there is absolute silence because the balloon is floating stationary in the air, although the air is moving all the time at the speed of the wind. It is as though the basket is suspended stationary while the earth is moved along below! The only wind that can be felt in a balloon is caused by any up or down movements as it gains or loses height. Very occasionally the effects of severe gusts may be felt but most of the time you sit virtually stationary while the earth moves silently along below.

Ground speed and airspeed

The lift from the wings depends solely on the angle of attack of the wing and the airspeed. It is nothing whatever to do with ground speed, or what is happening down below on the ground.

The airspeed is a measure of the speed of the air as it meets the aircraft and in still air this is the same speed as the speed over the ground.

If the aircraft is flown steadily at the same airspeed but against a strong wind, the speed over the ground will be reduced.

Flying downwind, although the speed of the airflow over the wings is the same, the speed over the ground is much higher. For a given loss of height, therefore, the glider will always fly much further downwind. The glider pilot cannot afford to ignore the effect of the wind or he will soon end up too far downwind of the landing field to be able to get back against the wind. This is probably the most common cause of landing *au vache* ('with the cows', as the French would say).

Taking a rather extreme example, if the wind is 40 knots and the glider is flown at an airspeed of 40 knots against the wind, the glider will have no forward movement over the ground. However, by increasing the airspeed to 60, or even 80 knots against this very strong wind, the glider will begin to penetrate and make progress. This is a very important principle to remember if you allow your machine to be drifted back too far behind the airfield. Of course, flying at the higher speed uses up the height more rapidly, but if it gets us back to the field safely and spares us the wrath of the C.F.I., who cares?

The rate of descent of the glider is unaffected by flying into wind or downwind and only varies if rising or sinking air is encountered or if the airspeed is varied.

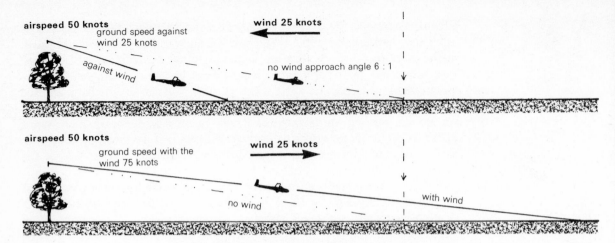

airspeed 50 knots
ground speed against wind 25 knots
against wind
wind 25 knots
no wind approach angle 6 : 1

airspeed 50 knots
ground speed with the wind 75 knots
no wind
wind 25 knots
with wind

58 The effect of the wind on the approach angle and ground speed. Into wind the approach angle is much steeper and the touchdown speed much lower. Whenever possible, landings are always made into the wind.

Flying downwind with a 40 knot wind, the speed over the ground would be 80 knots. Whatever happens, the pilot must not be influenced into attempting to slow down because of the high ground speed. The normal airspeed must be maintained or the aircraft would be in danger of becoming stalled.

Fig. 58 shows how the flight path of a glider is changed by the wind. It is not uncommon on a very windy day to be able to slow down so much that the glider is drifted backwards across the countryside. It is also possible to 'kite' on the winch cable to a phenomenal height in strong winds. This is done by launching normally and then slowing the glider down to its minimum flying speed so that it drifts backwards while the winch cable is paid out again. A further launch can then be made to a much greater height and this process repeated several times, in the same way that the string is let out on a kite. (The maximum legal height in most countries is 2000 feet but heights of almost 5000 feet have been recorded.) Unfortunately, there is not much point in trying for great heights in strong winds because, having released, one circle will take the glider out of reach of the field! Also, if the cable breaks or the winch driver cannot wind the cable in quickly, it will fall across every power and telephone line downwind of the field, besides being a serious hazard to motorists on any near-by roads!

Circling flight in a strong wind
(Fig. 59.)

A steady circling flight results in a gradual drift downwind, so that each circle appears elongated in relation to the ground. While it is difficult to see any effect of wind as the glider circles at height, at low altitudes the aircraft appears to slip sideways as it turns across the wind. It is very tempting to try and stop the apparent slipping with the rudder, but this will only result in a bad turn with very much higher drag. This can cause serious trouble,

150

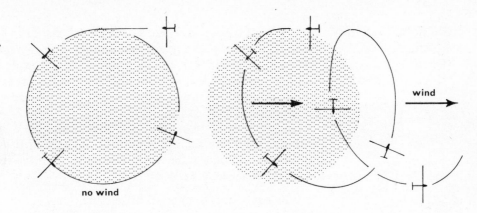

59 Track over the ground while circling.

no wind

wind

particularly in a rather low final turn, and when hill soaring at low altitudes. Always try to ignore this apparent slip and skid if you are turning in a high wind and concentrate on using the controls quite normally so that an accurate turn is made.

However, the actual drift must never be ignored, particularly at low altitudes. A common cause of serious accidents with light aircraft is to forget to allow sufficiently for drift. All the time an aircraft is turning it is being drifted by the wind and, once the turn has been started a little too late, even tightening the turn cannot save it from being drifted into trees or other obstructions. Whereas the radius of turn may be very small as the machine turns into the wind, it will be much, much larger turning from downwind to crosswind. This must always be allowed for, particularly when turning onto the base leg of the circuit in windy conditions (see Fig. 60).

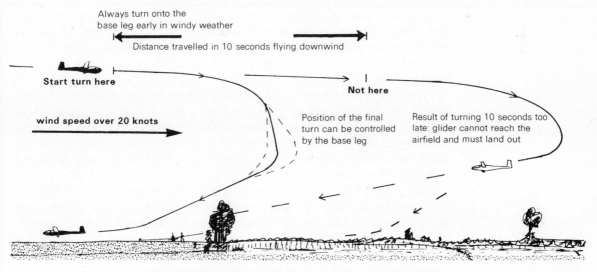

Always turn onto the base leg early in windy weather

Distance travelled in 10 seconds flying downwind

Start turn here

Not here

wind speed over 20 knots

Position of the final turn can be controlled by the base leg

Result of turning 10 seconds too late: glider cannot reach the airfield and must land out

60 In strong winds, turn onto the base leg before reaching the downwind boundary and stay within easy reach of the field.

Again, all that is necessary is to fly the aircraft normally and to take no notice of the apparent slipping across the ground. In order to arrive at a certain point over the ground, therefore, a normal turn is made to point the aircraft in the direction needed, so that, allowing for the drift, it will arrive there. Any corrections are made using normal co-ordinated turns and never by means of the rudder alone.

Even experienced pilots find that they must check the accuracy of their flying when hill soaring at low altitudes because of the tendency to correct this sideways motion quite unconsciously with a little rudder. Summarising the effects of a steady wind:

1 The airspeed is unaffected by circling.
2 The ground speed *is* affected and this affects the gliding range, reducing it drastically when flying into a strong wind.
3 The drift must be allowed for by turning and heading the aircraft upwind a little when flying across wind.
4 At all times the aircraft must be flown normally and accurately at a safe airspeed.

**The effects of
variation in the
wind**

Even as glider pilots we have surprisingly little detailed knowledge of the fluctuations and eddies in the atmosphere. There are so many variations caused by thermal activity and disturbances from hills and other obstructions that it is practically impossible to predict or account for changes in wind, particularly near the ground.

Because these variations break up the steady movement of the air they *do* have an effect on aircraft. Gliders are particularly affected because of their low flying speed and relatively poor control response.

In some conditions there may be quite significant changes in the wind speed and direction where two distinctive masses of air are moving at different velocities. This will sometimes occur if there is a very strong temperature inversion or a stable layer of air which is preventing the usual mixing of the air.

This effect can sometimes be detected in a glider during a winch or car launch. At low levels the air is cold and often hazy with a light wind. Then, at a certain height, a change of wind strength makes itself felt by a jump in the airspeed as the glider climbs up. At precisely the same height near the top of each launch, there will be a jump of 5–10 knots in the airspeed as the glider hits the stronger wind.

During the glide into wind, there will be a noticeable drop in airspeed and a sudden sinking feeling as the glider flies down into the lighter wind again. After a few seconds the rate of sink and airspeed will return to normal. These effects will only happen if the change in wind speed takes place in a very shallow layer of air. Had the same change been spread over a depth of several hundred feet it would have been virtually undetectable. The glider would have regained any lost speed almost immediately and the only change

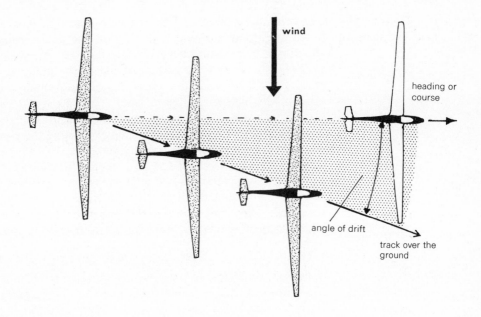

wind

heading or course

angle of drift

track over the ground

that the average pilot would have noticed would have been a slight increase in the rate of sink for a few seconds.

When a large change of wind speed occurs in a layer of air only 50 or 100 feet deep, the glider moves from the top to the bottom of this layer in a very short time. Due to its inertia the aircraft tends to resist any change in its speed or flight path, and, therefore, the drop in wind speed *does* affect the airspeed. One moment the aircraft is flying steadily into a strong wind and a few seconds later this wind has dropped. Had the change been gradual the aircraft would have just lost height a little more quickly for a few moments as it regained its former speed and settled down to a steady glide again.

This recovery will be automatic, providing that the drop in speed is not sufficient to leave the aircraft stalled. As the speed is reduced by a change in the wind such as this the glider sinks more rapidly, both because of the immediate reduction in the lift and because the normal stability comes into play at the same time and lowers the nose a little. Then, as the speed increases, the stability results in a return to the original attitude and a steady glide again.

If the pilot reacts instinctively and tries to stop the sinking by raising the nose a little, there is a very grave risk of stalling. The rapid sinking increases the angle of attack as the air comes up to meet the wing and any raising of the nose may pull the wing beyond the stalling angle. This is a particular hazard if the glider is near the ground.

Wind gradients near the ground

The wind at 2000–3000 feet is almost entirely governed by the variations in the atmospheric pressure which are associated with the changing weather situations. Below this height, the airflow is slowed down by the friction between the air and the surface of the earth, and is also deflected by high ground and other local influences. Since the friction is greatest close to the ground, the biggest change in wind speed occurs in the first few hundred feet. Fig. 62 shows the changes in wind speed with height on a typical strong wind day. Notice the very rapid change close to the ground and the almost insignificant rate of change above 500 feet.

There is also a change in the wind direction and, in the Northern hemisphere, the wind veers as it becomes stronger with heights up to about 2000 feet. Veering and backing are explained in Fig. 63 and the easy way to remember what they mean is to remember that backing means anti-clockwise. This change in wind direction with height may be as much as 20° on a windy day.

Unless the wind is very strong there will be a bigger difference first thing in the morning between both the strength and the direction of the wind near the ground and the wind at about 2000 feet. Then, as the heating of the sun begins to start convection and the thermals begin to mix up the lighter lower winds with the stronger upper winds, the surface wind becomes a little stronger and the direction changes a little. This is a useful fact for the Duty instructor to remember as he wonders which way the wind will be blowing later in the day as he sites the winch before breakfast. The wind will normally veer and strengthen a little during the morning as the thermal activity starts.

The severity of the wind gradient depends upon several factors. Obviously if there is only a very light wind at 1000 feet, any change in wind speed will be insignificant. A steep wind gradient can only occur in a fairly strong wind.

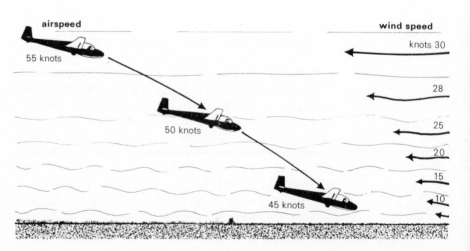

airspeed

55 knots

50 knots

45 knots

wind speed

knots 30

28

25

20

15

10

62 The wind gradient. Friction between the ground and the air slows down the airflow near the ground.

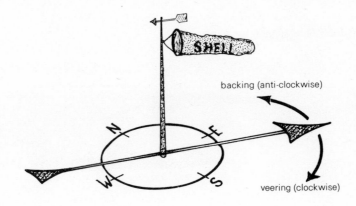

63 Changes in the
wind direction –
veering and backing.

backing (anti-clockwise)

veering (clockwise)

The amount of friction between the air and the ground will also be important and generally the wind gradient will be worst in the lee of rough country and less severe near the sea or to the lee of flat, open country where the surface friction will be low. This effect is shown by the very strong surface winds experienced on the coast where winds of 60–70 m.p.h. are quite common. Inland, only 20 miles away, such winds are rare although the strength of the upper winds is much the same.

In brief, the wind gradient will be serious in a strong wind and particularly in places in the lee of rough ground.

The wind gradient can have a very significant effect on a glider during take off and landing. During a landing for instance, it only takes a few seconds for the glider to descend the final 100 feet or so. One moment it is gliding down against a strong wind and a few seconds later it has lost height and is travelling against a wind which is 10 or 15 knots lighter. This sudden change causes a drop in airspeed, which reduces the lift and results in a much higher rate of sink. Unless the approach has been started with extra speed to allow for this loss, there may be insufficient speed or control to round out properly for a normal landing. There will also be a tendency to undershoot the landing area (Fig. 64).

Because the wind gradient gets more severe close to the ground the glider sinks more once the speed begins to drop off a little, taking it down through the steepening gradient more quickly and causing an even more rapid loss of speed. The effect escalates and in windy weather there is seldom sufficient height or time to regain the lost speed.

By far the majority of heavy landings are due to this cause, for which there is no cure. It is important, therefore, to take the precaution of choosing an

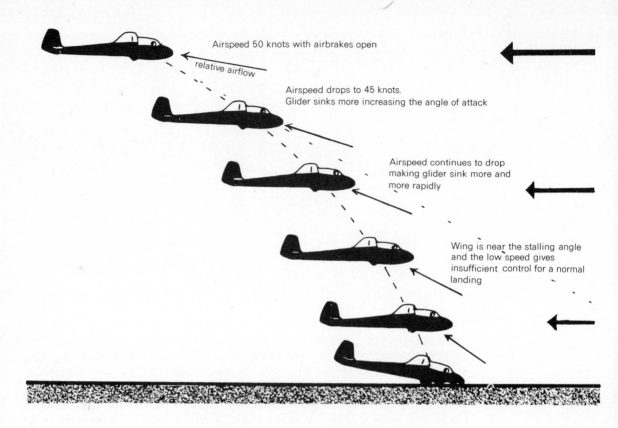

Airspeed 50 knots with airbrakes open

relative airflow

Airspeed drops to 45 knots.
Glider sinks more increasing the angle of attack

Airspeed continues to drop
making glider sink more and
more rapidly

Wing is near the stalling angle
and the low speed gives
insufficient control for a normal
landing

64 The effect of the wind gradient. The increase in the rate of descent when the glider loses speed because of the wind gradient means that at one moment it may be flying against a 30 knot wind at 70–80 feet and only 3 or 4 seconds later it may be flying against a wind of only 15 knots. This causes the sudden loss of airspeed which can leave the glider semi-stalled.

adequate speed for an approach in windy weather. Alternatively, the approach must be steepened progressively during the last 100 feet or so to maintain a safe speed for landing.

The loss of airspeed on the approach causes a loss of lift and therefore a much higher rate of sink. This must be allowed for by aiming the approach further into the field than normal. It feels just as if the glider has flown into sinking air and, in extreme conditions, the glider seems almost to drop out of the air. This effect is often referred to as a 'clutching hand', because it is waiting there all the time for a chance to clutch at and bring down any unwary glider pilot who is foolish enough to make a slow approach or go too far behind the boundary fence.

Some of the worst conditions are to be found on gliding sites at the top of hills. The wind may form a continuous eddy so that the surface wind may even be reversed in some places near the ground. Very high speeds are essential to cater for this kind of wind gradient and the loss of height during an approach can be very severe, sometimes reaching 2000 feet per minute! (See Fig 39.)

The effect of the wind gradient is much more marked if the approach is very steep since the aircraft moves more rapidly from the stronger to the lighter winds. However, in windy weather it is not safe to make a low, flat approach in a glider since sudden unpredictable losses of height can occur in turbulence near the ground. Powered aircraft making shallow approaches are scarcely affected by the gradient but still need a little more speed to give better control in the gusty air.

Gliders with their large wing spans and rather low rate of roll are particularly vulnerable during a low turn into wind. The upper wing may be as much as 30 feet above the level of the lower wing during a well-banked turn and the speed of the airflow meeting the upper wing may be 10 or 15 knots more than that of the lower wing because of the wind gradient. This would cause a serious tendency to over-bank, making it difficult, if not impossible, for even full aileron to be effective in bringing the wings level. This loss of control is nothing to do with stalling and could occur when the glider had quite a high airspeed. In effect the rate of roll becomes too poor to overcome the effect of what the pilot would almost certainly consider was a gust (see Fig. 65).

In windy weather it is wise to keep plenty of extra height in hand until the final turn into wind and then to use plenty of airbrake to lose the height on the final approach. By using plenty of airbrake the glider has a certain amount of stored energy available. If the speed does begin to fall off so that the glider starts to sink too rapidly, the airbrakes can be closed in order to prevent the situation from progressing from bad to worse.

In an extreme case, if the initial approach speed is rather low, a steep wind gradient may cause sufficient loss of speed to leave the aircraft stalled. The only symptom may be the rapid loss of height and the lack of response to the backward movement on the stick as an attempt is made to stop the nose dropping, or to round out for landing. In this case, the nose of the glider will not be high and the stall may occur in an attitude very close to that of normal cruising flight. What has happened is that the glider has lost speed, making it lose lift and sink rapidly. The high rate of sink has made the relative airflow come up towards the wing at a steep angle. A further loss of speed has repeated this process and the airflow has finally reached the stalling angle so that a stall occurs near the ground with no hope of recovery (see 'Never low and slow' on page 123).

This kind of accident used to be very prevalent in the early days of gliding when all the basic training was carried out on open Primary gliders by the solo method. By making ground slides and then progressing to low hops

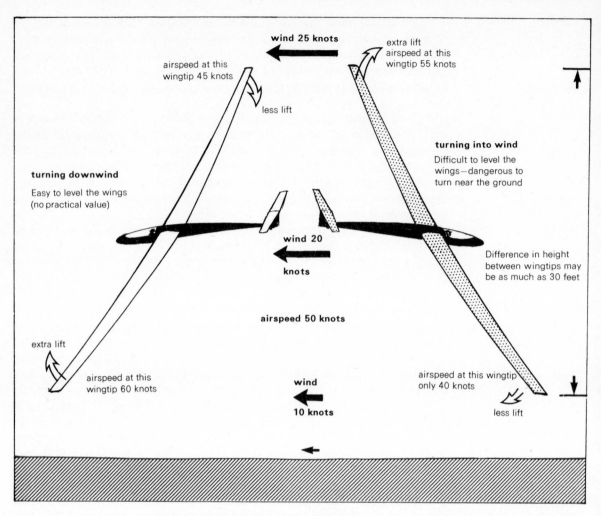

65 The effects of the wind gradient on a low turn. Always complete the final turn into a strong wind with extra height.

and high hops, the pilot taught himself with a few hints and tips from the instructor. Since he would often have had only a few minutes actual flying by the time he started circuits and hill soaring flights in quite windy weather, he had never had any practical experience of stalling. It was not uncommon for a beginner to fly a little too far downwind of the landing area and then to try and get back by 'stretching' the glide. Unless specifically and repeatedly warned against this, most inexperienced pilots would instinctively fly a little too nose high in an attempt to glide further. Once at low speed, even a comparatively mild wind gradient would cause a further loss and the chain of events would then lead to a stall. All the pilot would know was that he had apparently flown into strong sinking air and that the nose had begun to drop inexplicably until he hit the ground. Fortunately, the gliders were very light and flew at low speed so that usually the pilot would scramble out of the wreckage unhurt. They would often be quite convinced that the cause must have been a broken elevator cable because of the sudden loss of control, whereas, as every pupil now knows, the primary symptom of the stall is that the aircraft will not respond to a further backward movement on the stick and drops its nose or wing.

It is very important to realise that because of the effect of the wind gradient, a stall flying into wind at low altitude will take much more height for recovery than one at circuit height. Similarly, a cable break on a wire launch is much more serious in windy weather than at any other time. In both cases, as the nose is lowered to regain speed, the glider is descending steeply through the gradient. Whereas during practice at height only 50–70 feet may be lost in a full stall and recovery, two or three times that height might easily be lost close to the ground. In spite of lowering the nose the speed may, in fact, be decreasing, because of the effect of descending through the steep wind gradient.

Once the speed has dropped below the normal flying speed at low altitude there can be little hope of recovery.

Remember this when you learn to drive the winch or tow car and are launching in windy weather. Give the glider a good clean take off with maximum acceleration until it has reached about 50 feet. This will ensure that, if the cable breaks, the glider has plenty of speed for a safe approach down through the wind gradient again. Above all, do not attempt to provide just enough speed to get the glider off the ground or it will only accelerate very slowly and will be left at a rather low speed for the initial climb.

Many people are rather surprised to learn that when the glider approaches the ground and meets the decreased headwind it does not just glide further and float a greater distance.

This does happen to some extent, but the loss of speed and height on the approach is usually much more serious than any gain in float near the ground. Once the airspeed has fallen much below the normal approach speed, the glider will not penetrate very far against even the lighter surface winds. Furthermore, once the speed is low, the aircraft is at the mercy of any turbulence and the airbrakes cannot be opened quickly without the risk of a heavy landing.

Unfortunately the wind gradient is not constant even for a few seconds because there are always gusts and additional turbulence which vary the actual wind strength. How serious these effects will be again depends on the strength of the wind and the size and shape of any obstructions upwind of the landing area. It is also influenced by the stability of the air at the time.

These additional effects are often much more serious than the gradient itself and it is worthwhile discussing them in detail.

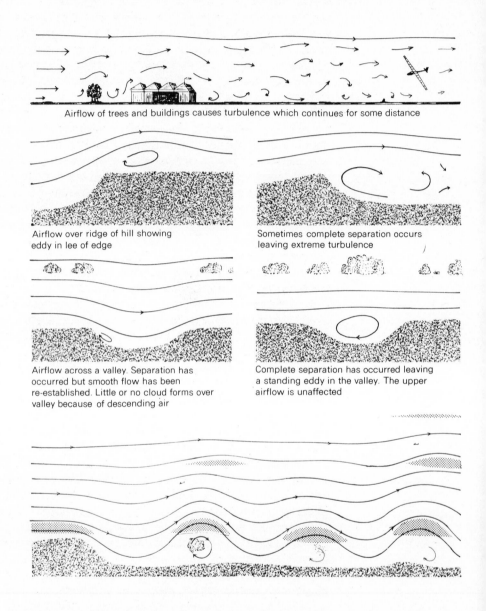

Airflow of trees and buildings causes turbulence which continues for some distance

Airflow over ridge of hill showing
eddy in lee of edge

Sometimes complete separation occurs
leaving extreme turbulence

Airflow across a valley. Separation has
occurred but smooth flow has been
re-established. Little or no cloud forms over
valley because of descending air

Complete separation has occurred leaving
a standing eddy in the valley. The upper
airflow is unaffected

66 When favourable conditions exist, standing, or lee waves form downwind of a ridge of hills or mountains. Violently turbulent rotor flow often occurs below the crest of the wave. Lenticular, or lens-shaped clouds mark the position of the wave.

Surface obstructions The air within two or three times the height of even small obstructions, such as trees or buildings, is seriously disturbed and turned into a mass of unsteady swirls and eddies of various sizes. Depending on their direction and strength, these add to or reduce the effect of the wind gradient so that at one moment it is far more serious and the next perhaps there is hardly any gradient effect at all. While these small fluctuations have very little effect on a Jumbo jet, they can be critical to a glider, and disastrous to a model aircraft coming into land.

The general effect of the wind blowing over a ridge of hills is to give an area of rising air ahead and over the crest of the ridge. In the lee of the hills and near an isolated hill many different variations in the airflow can occur. These may range from the formation of a steady pattern of lee waves as in Fig. 66, to a complete breakdown in the steady flow. These effects usually upset the normal wind gradient for several miles to the lee of the obstruction (often 20–30 miles in the event of a wave system). The pilot should expect extra turbulence in the lee of a line of trees or a wooded area even though it is two or three fields away upwind.

Stability of the air As every glider pilot quickly learns, the stability of the air will vary from day to day if not from hour to hour. It is not possible to soar in thermals unless there are thermals to be soared in! If the air is too stable, the experts will be at home gardening, or 'hangar flying' in the bar at the club.

When the air is unstable, any air which is disturbed and starts to move upwards will tend to continue to move upwards. In stable conditions this movement would be damped out almost immediately.

The effects of the air flowing over obstructions tend to be amplified if the air is unstable and this produces tricky conditions for gliding in strong winds with occasional violent turbulence and the risk of large areas of strong sinking air at unexpected moments.

The effects of changes in airspeed If it were possible to have a perfect, dragless glider, height and speed would be exchangeable with no loss. A given amount of speed could be turned into a definite gain of height as in Fig. 67. In real life, however, there is drag even with the best machines and if, for example, slowing down from 80 knots to 40 knots gives us a gain of height of x feet, accelerating from 40 back to 80 will use up x plus, perhaps, an extra 50 feet. Height energy (potential energy) is being exchanged for speed energy (kinetic energy). The effect of the wind gradient, or any loss of speed due to a sudden change in wind speed, is a loss in total energy possessed by the aircraft. It is therefore bound to cost either height or speed.

There are other causes of changes in airspeed which must be considered if any attempt is being made to analyse a particular situation. Perhaps we have just experienced a case when the airspeed has repeatedly increased each time we have turned into the wind. Since this should not have happened in

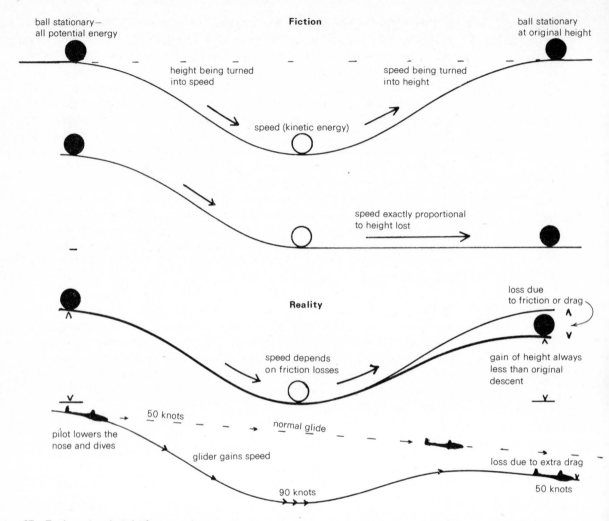

Fiction

ball stationary—
all potential energy

ball stationary
at original height

height being turned
into speed

speed being turned
into height

speed (kinetic energy)

speed exactly proportional
to height lost

Reality

loss due
to friction or drag

speed depends
on friction losses

gain of height always
less than original
descent

pilot lowers the
nose and dives

50 knots

normal glide

glider gains speed

loss due to extra drag

90 knots

50 knots

67 Exchanging height for speed.

a steady wind condition it is interesting to try and understand how else the speed could be increased.

Fig. 68 shows the Yates effect which is often not taken into consideration. As the aircraft flies into a region of rising air there is a definite gain in airspeed, often in the order of 3 or 4 knots. This is only a temporary effect lasting a few seconds and the speed will then settle down again if the glider is allowed to carry on flying steadily. Similarly, a loss of speed occurs whenever sinking air is met. (See Appendix A for explanation.)

If the glider is circling half in and half out of strong lift it may happen that the strong lift coincides with turning into wind each time. In this case there *will* be an increase in speed each time it turns into wind until the glider is properly centred into the thermal.

The effects of thermal activity

Further changes of speed may occur close to, and in, thermals and these may either supplement or reduce this effect. If the thermal has a strong circulating movement (like a dust devil in the desert) there will be a significant change of speed as the aircraft meets such a flow. This would result in either a gain in speed and reduced sink, or a drop in speed, which would cause either a much higher rate of sink, or perhaps even an unexpected stall.

There are some occasions where the horizontal rotation of the air is significant and can be identified. For example, in some bush fires and dust devils (should you ever happen to fly into them) a definite advantage will be gained by turning against the circular flow so that the ground speed is lowered. This results in a lower angle of bank being required for the turn and therefore an increase in efficiency.

The meteorologists and mathematicians assure us that any rotation quickly dies out once the thermal has become detached from the ground. The forces involved are generally quite small and although it might be expected that, like bath water running out down the drain the rotation in the Northern hemisphere should be anti-clockwise, observations have shown that it is

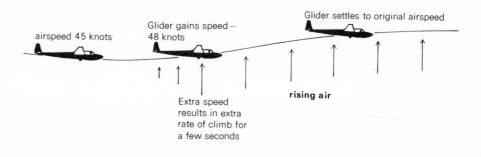

airspeed 45 knots

Glider gains speed — 48 knots

Glider settles to original airspeed

Extra speed results in extra rate of climb for a few seconds

rising air

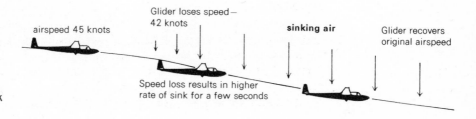

airspeed 45 knots

Glider loses speed — 42 knots

sinking air

Glider recovers original airspeed

Speed loss results in higher rate of sink for a few seconds

68 The result of the Yates effect – speed changes caused by flying into lift and sink (see Appendix A).

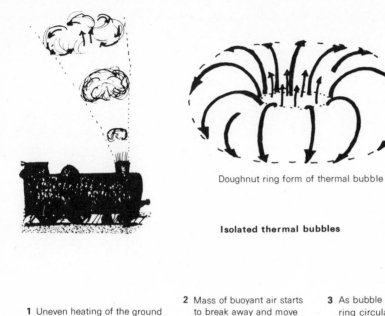

Doughnut ring form of thermal bubble

Atomic bomb

Isolated thermal bubbles

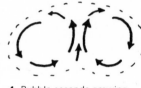

1 Uneven heating of the ground results in a local hot spot

2 Mass of buoyant air starts to break away and move upwards

3 As bubble rises a vortex ring circulation begins

4 Bubble ascends growing steadily as more of the surrounding air is entrained

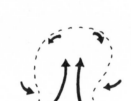

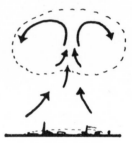

69 The formation of thermal bubbles.

almost pure chance which way a thermal will rotate. The glider pilot can safely ignore the rotation except near the ground, or when the air movement is made visible by smoke or other debris. Any attempt by a beginner to reverse his turn in a thermal will almost certainly result in his losing the lift altogether.

In other types of thermal activity, more common in temperate climates, the thermal bubbles seem to have an internal circulation rather like a smoke ring (see Figs. 69 and 70). The glider may be affected in various ways according to its position in relation to the bubble. It may meet a sudden increase in the wind speed near the cap for a few seconds, giving it a reduced rate of sink or gain of height. Through the centre it would most likely meet strong sinking air (with the resulting loss of speed), and at the base it would suffer

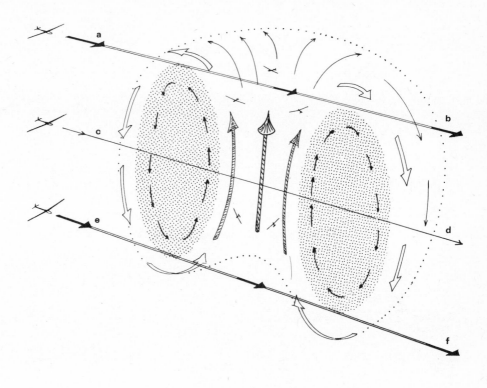

70 A cross-section of a thermal bubble showing the horizontal and vertical movements of the air inside the bubble. Practical experience shows that on many occasions these movements do exist and greatly influence soaring techniques.

a loss of speed and therefore sink before reaching the real lift!

With this type of thermal there will be a region in the base of the bubble where the air is moving inwards horizontally from all directions as in Fig. 71. A glider circling concentrically in this region will be flying with a steady inflow of several knots pushing it inwards towards the centre of the turn. This could be thought of as an infinite number of gusts striking the glider as it turns.

It can be shown that the result of this inflow on a glider banking at an angle of 45° is the gain of an additional rate of climb equivalent to the speed of the inflow. For example, for an inflow of 2 knots the glider would gain a bonus of 2 knots to its rate of climb. Even greater increases may be gained by the use of more bank and these may offset the normal loss of efficiency

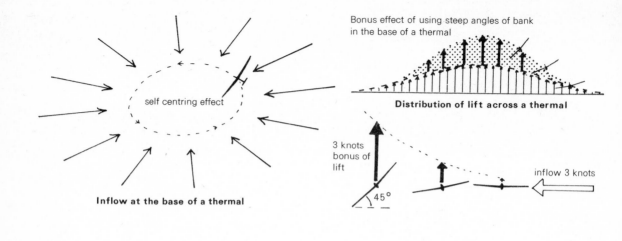

Bonus effect of using steep angles of bank
in the base of a thermal

Distribution of lift across a thermal

self centring effect

Inflow at the base of a thermal

3 knots
bonus of
lift

45°

inflow 3 knots

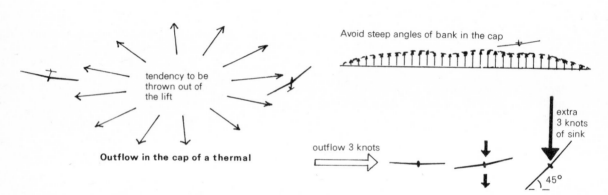

Avoid steep angles of bank in the cap

tendency to be
thrown out of
the lift

Outflow in the cap of a thermal

outflow 3 knots

extra
3 knots
of sink

45°

71 Theoretical effects of turning in the inflow and outflow of a thermal. Inflow increases the effective strength of the lift in the base of an isolated thermal, particularly in well-banked turns.

in the steeper turn. Normally, of course, a very steep turn results in a considerable increase in the rate of sink. However, experience shows that there are many occasions when the best results are obtained by using the steepest possible angle of bank for a few circles. It is usually assumed that the explanation for this is the obvious one that there is a very strong narrow core of lift which is best used by circling very tightly. If this were so, the air in the core of the thermals would be rising so rapidly that a glider would be severely shaken if it flew through this area in straight flight. In practice this seldom happens, which suggests that the core is not as strong or narrow as it might seem and that some of the high rate of climb obtained when circling is being derived from the inflow and can only be tapped by using steeply banked turns.

There are also many occasions when the glider is flying in very weak lift or zero sink but starts to gain height immediately it begins to circle. Sometimes at least this may be the effect of starting to circle in an area of inflow.

In the cap of the thermal the air is flowing outwards radially so that the glider in circling flight is far less efficient than normal. Here a gently banked turn would be most advantageous.

These effects help to give us an appreciation of the complexity of the motions of the air and of the never-ending opportunities for learning more so that we can improve our soaring techniques.

The reader will now understand why pilots so often experience instances of gaining speed when turning into the wind. There are so many possible reasons for its happening that it would be very surprising if it did not occur quite frequently. It very often happens close to a hillside when a glider is hill soaring, and there are several likely reasons for this (Fig. 72). Close to the hillside the glider will be flying out across the wind gradient and also, since the wind is increasing, often into stronger lift. Unless the pilot is very careful the glider may also start to oscillate slightly nose up and down and as the natural frequency of this kind of oscillation is often about 15 to 20 seconds and this is about the same time as it takes for a complete circle, it may easily coincide with facing into wind. This is not easy to rule out as a

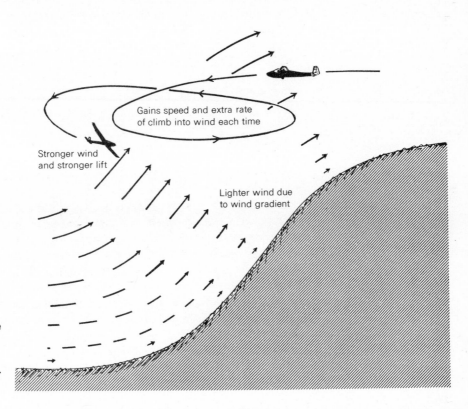

Gains speed and extra rate of climb into wind each time

Stronger wind and stronger lift

Lighter wind due to wind gradient

72 When circling close to a hillside some of the changes in airspeed while circling may be caused by the wind gradient, together with the Yates effect.

cause because, near the hillside, it is very difficult to be sure that the attitude is constant with the horizon ahead at one moment and the hill top ahead a few seconds later.

Away from the ground, the cause is more likely to be poor centring in a thermal so that the glider is moving in and out of the lift with a resultant change in speed. Alternatively, it may be the effect of the inflow and outflow close to the thermal bubble, again most noticeable when the glider is not centred accurately.

Perhaps one significant point is that these changes in speed when turning into wind seldom, if ever, occur except in or near to lift. However windy, a steady turn in non-turbulent air always gives a steady airspeed!

Dynamic soaring No account of the effects of gusts and turbulence would be complete without some comment on dynamic soaring. This is the art of making use of the energy in the gusts and wind gradient. At first sight it all smacks of perpetual motion and of trying to get something for nothing. However *all* soaring is a matter of exploiting the movements of the air, and using the energy in gusts is really a similar procedure.

It has already been explained how, near the ground and when there is a steep wind gradient, descending downwind and climbing into the wind can give the glider extra energy. Since the lift of the wing varies with the square of the speed, even small gains in speed can result in a significant increase in the lift. Simple arithmetic shows that much more is to be gained by an increase in speed of, for example, 5 knots, than is lost by the same decrease of speed. (This is because the lift increases with the square of the speed.)

If the glider cruises at 45 knots and meets a sudden change of wind speed of plus 5 knots, and later minus 5 knots, the variations in lift will be in proportion to $50^2 : 45^2 : 40^2$.

Notice that $50^2 - 45^2 = 475$ whereas $45^2 - 40^2 = 425$.

It should, therefore, be possible to gain more in the gusts, than is lost in the lulls! This would certainly increase the efficiency of the glider and result in a reductions of the rate of sink.

In order to do this the glider must be pulled up slightly as a gust gives an increase in airspeed while still maintaining a reasonably efficient speed during the lulls. In practice, this is very hard and exacting work for a very small gain. Some energy will be gained even without pulling up and the best hope is for the glider to be slightly unstable so that it reacts automatically to the gusts. The principle of pulling up to take more advantage of any increases in airspeed which occur in soaring is generally accepted, since it keeps the glider down to an efficient speed and keeps the radius of turn small besides ensuring that the glider stays in the area of lift longer, if flying into lift is the cause of the increase in airspeed.

Some birds have evolved several ways of using the energy in the wind gradient to save their own energy. However, in order to do this they have to

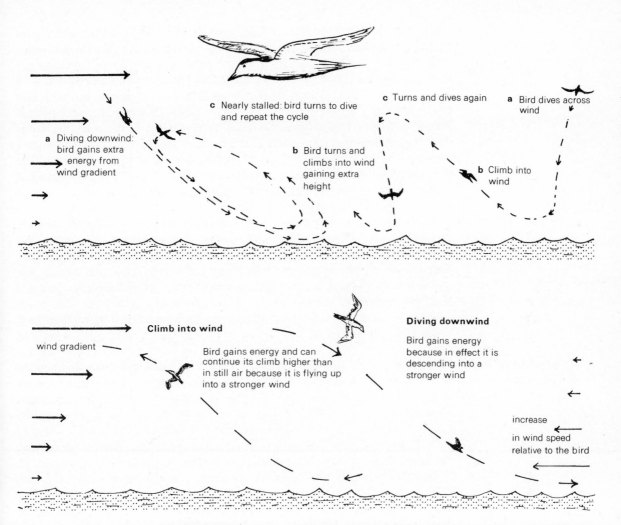

c Nearly stalled: bird turns to dive and repeat the cycle

c Turns and dives again

a Bird dives across wind

a Diving downwind: bird gains extra energy from wind gradient

b Bird turns and climbs into wind gaining extra height

b Climb into wind

Climb into wind

Bird gains energy and can continue its climb higher than in still air because it is flying up into a stronger wind

wind gradient

Diving downwind

Bird gains energy because in effect it is descending into a stronger wind

increase in wind speed relative to the bird

73 Dynamic soaring – strictly for the birds! Climbing into wind or diving downwind in a steep wind gradient the bird (or glider) gains energy compared with normal conditions.

fly very close to the ground, or water, where the gradient is steepest. A glider pilot trying to imitate the birds will find it a difficult and arduous kind of flying with a constant risk of hitting the ground in an unexpected change of wind. The birds always seem to combine dynamic soaring with the use of slope soaring or wave lift and perhaps this is what we should do in our much larger and clumsier flying machines.

Fig. 73 shows two patterns of movement which are efficient ways of using the wind gradient for dynamic soaring.

The top section of the illustration shows the bird diving downwind to gain speed and to take energy out of the gradient until it is very close to the water. It then makes a climbing turn into the wind and climbs up through the gradient, continuing until it is nearly stalled. (By doing this the bird will be able to go on climbing much higher than in still air. The gain of speed due to climbing up into a stronger and stronger wind tends to reduce the normal loss of speed due to climbing.) The bird then makes a further turn and dives down again to repeat the process. If the wind gradient is steep the energy extracted from it by the bird may be sufficient for continuous flight without flapping. Many sea birds use this technique together with a little hill soaring along the sea waves for trans-oceanic flights, apparently soaring for days on end with scarcely any flapping to help them.

In the early days of soaring there were many attempts at dynamic soaring in hill lift, with varying degrees of success. The discovery of thermals and wave lift soon made the gains possible in dynamic soaring so insignificant that almost all attempts were abandoned. However, now that glider performance has reached such a very high level that even the slightest gain is a triumph, perhaps pilots and designers will take a new look at this interesting subject. It would not take much improvement to turn a gliding angle of 1:40 to no loss of height at all!

The behaviour of model aircraft in a wind

The model, like a full-sized aircraft, should be unaffected by a steady wind as it circles round and round. However, anyone who has watched or flown many model aircraft will realise how model behaviour appears to contradict theory.

For example, it is most noticeable that the model will almost always tend to stall as it turns into wind as if in doing so it has gained extra speed with the result that the nose has come up to precipitate the stall.

In order to explain this apparent anomaly it is necessary to plot the path of the model first in still air and then in a wind. Fig. 74 (a) shows the model after it has been disturbed by a bump so that it has begun to oscillate slightly nose up and nose down. Only in absolutely still air and in perfect trim would it glide perfectly smoothly without any phugoid (oscillation) like this.

Fig. 74 (b) shows the same gentle oscillation plotted into wind and downwind in a wind of 15 m.p.h.

Notice how the model scarcely seems to oscillate at all as it flies downwind, whereas into wind the flight path is so foreshortened that the model appears to be stalling quite sharply. If we were to plot the same model when it was slightly over-elevated and stalling gently, it would again appear to be hardly stalling at all flying downwind, whereas into wind the stall would appear sharp and distinctive.

This simple example shows how deceptive the movements of a model can be. In fact much the same impression will be made on the observer of a full-size aircraft or glider in a strong wind. The pilot watching the horizon well ahead would be quite unaware of the apparent difference between the

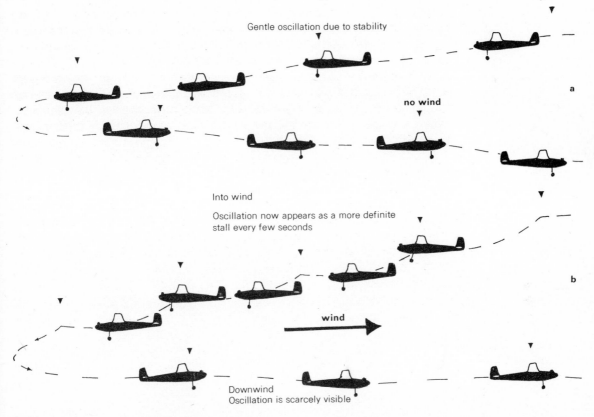

Gentle oscillation due to stability

no wind

a

Into wind

Oscillation now appears as a more definite
stall every few seconds

b

wind

Downwind
Oscillation is scarcely visible

74 Why model aircraft always seem to start stalling as they fly into the wind. Any oscillations appear as a definite stall when the model flies into wind.

flight into and downwind as seen from the ground. The stall will appear sharp to a ground observer when the aircraft is flying into wind, but scarcely noticeable when it is flying downwind.

If the effects of the wind gradient are added to the plot of the model, the loss of height in any stall into wind is increased by the loss of airspeed as the model drops into the lighter winds, and is decreased as the model stalls and loses height flying downwind.

Since the wind speed is such a large proportion of the model's flying speed these effects make it difficult to analyse what is going on by just watching the model in flight unless the wind is very light and the air is smooth.

Models, just like full-sized machines, gain and lose speed as they enter rising and sinking air and either will start a phugoid so that a series of stalls may occur. These will be difficult to detect when the model is flying downwind but will be very obvious if they happen when it is flying into wind.

Thermals tend to stop rotating once they have become detached from the ground and, therefore, the glider pilot will seldom find much evidence of rotation at the height he flies. However, the model flier frequently sees a model swept into a turn by the rotation of a thermal and in some cases being thrown from a well-trimmed circle into a vicious spiral dive.

All these factors tend to make it very difficult to be sure why a model behaves in a certain way. It is not surprising that few modellers understand the real effects of the wind and most of them do not believe, and cannot be convinced, that a steady wind can have no effect on a circling model apart from drifting it away out of sight.

10

Aerotowing

Learning to aerotow	173
Holding the correct position	174
Weaving from side to side	177
The take off	181

Releasing the tow rope	182
Emergencies on tow	183
The wave off	186
The 'I cannot release' signal	189

Learning to aerotow

Aerotowing is probably one of the most difficult things to teach in glider flying but, fortunately, it is very largely a matter of knack. Most solo pilots find it very difficult for the first tow or two, but begin to get things under control by their fourth or fifth attempt. It is largely a matter for them of learning to spot small changes in position before they get too large, and of making prompt corrections. Students who are learning to glide without previous experience will find that until they have learnt to handle the glider fairly competently in the air, the aerotow launch will be a difficult task. In fact, many experienced instructors do not bother to start to teach their students the tow until they are almost up to solo standard. By then it only takes half a dozen launches or less, and it is not so demoralising as starting too early and being unable to manage at all.

Once the pilot has mastered a two-seater glider on aerotow he need have absolutely no worries about being able to manage in a solo machine. Most solo gliders have better control response and far less inertia. This makes them much easier to keep in position. For many years we used to brief pilots very carefully and tow them off in an Olympia, or similar solo machine, without any dual aerotow training. This was standard practice at most clubs in England, and, at Lasham alone, hundreds of pilots made their first aerotows in this way. Of course, this could only be done safely in very smooth conditions with a clear horizon and sometimes we would have to wait for weeks for suitable weather.

Basically, aerotowing is the simplest and most trouble-free way of launching gliders. Unfortunately, unless the glider can soar from most of the launches, it is also expensive. All the glider pilot has to do is keep his glider in a steady position behind the tow plane, and follow it around the sky until they have gained height.

It takes practice to get used to keeping station and spotting any changes before the glider gets seriously out of position. Because the towing speed is above the normal cruising speed of the glider the ailerons are noticeably heavier and stiffer to move, while the elevator in particular becomes much more sensitive. This results in a tendency to over-control badly with the elevator, while often not using positive enough movements with the ailerons.

Holding the correct position

The normal towing position is just above the longitudinal axis of the tug. This axis is a line running through the centre of the fuselage from nose to tail. This keeps the glider out of the wake of the tow plane. The exact position is not critical as long as it stays out of the wake and is not so high that it pulls the tail of the tug up too much. (The glider can also be flown below the slipstream in what is known as the low tow position, but this is used mainly for long distance tows, or tows through very turbulent conditions, such as the rotor of a wave system.)

There are various hints on how to keep the correct position behind the tow plane and spot any change in position up or down. The beginner will need to think consciously of the position all the time and use one of the methods detailed below to keep station. However, as he becomes more and more experienced he learns to relax more on tow and to use a combination of all these methods without thinking about them. The problems of aerotowing are very real at the time, but, within a few flights, like most of the other difficulties in learning to fly, they are soon overcome and forgotten.

If the conditions are clear, it is sufficient to keep the tug sitting in a constant position relative to the horizon (Fig. 75). If it is kept in the correct position, the glider will be well clear of the slipstream and there will be plenty of room to move upwards before the tail of the tug is pulled out of position by the rope. The exact position varies a little with the length of the tow rope and with the climbing angle of the tug. Tugs fitted with engines of 150 h.p. or less, such as the Super Cub and Citabria, will appear to be just below the horizon for an average towing position. More powerful machines will climb more steeply and will need to be positioned a little above the horizon. The instructor will show you the correct position on your first tow.

In poor visibility or in hilly country where there is a false horizon, other methods must be used after the tug and glider have gained a few hundred feet. Once the glider is correctly stationed, it is sufficient to keep the tug in a constant position relative to the nose, or a particular point on the canopy or windscreen. It is helpful for the first few tows to put a vertical China-graph line down the middle of the canopy, with a cross on it to act as a reference point. Once the position of the tug has been found and noted a very small movement on the glider will reposition the mark onto the tug. This results in gradual changes in the actual position of the glider, instead of the usual fault of over-controlling (see Fig. 76). The vertical line will help you to judge when the glider's wings are level with those of the tug.

Another method is to note the look of the tug when it is in the desired

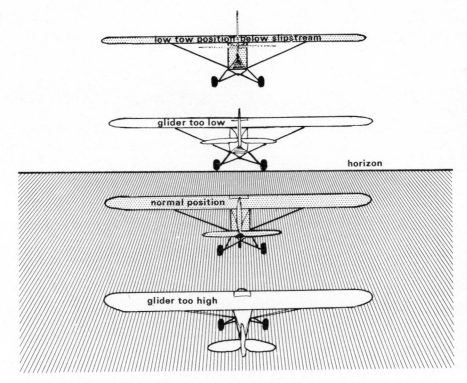

75 Keeping station on aerotow by positioning the tug relative to the horizon.

position on a clear day. The right position can usually be easily recognised by the position of the top of the fin against the top of the cabin of the tug, or the position of the tailplane against the wing or wing struts. With the Super Cub and other tail wheel types the correct view is near enough the same as the view you have of the tow plane as it stands on the ground ahead of you, just before it starts the take off run. If the weather looks hazy, it is always worth reminding yourself of the position by looking at the tug just before take off.

Most aerotows will consist of a steady climb to height, so that a position for climbing is all that is required. A slightly different position would be needed for towing in level flight and for descending on tow. (Descending has special problems because the glider will try to overtake the tug unless the airbrakes are used.)

While learning to aerotow the exact position is not critical but it should give enough room for some up and down movement without upsetting the tug pilot or getting the glider into the slipstream. Experienced pilots usually prefer to fly a little closer to the slipstream than would be wise for a beginner.

When the glider gets too low, the slipstream causes quite a noticeable buffeting and often tips the glider one way or the other. It may be quite difficult, or impossible, to bring the wings level quickly until the glider is

76 Keeping station on
aerotow using a
sighting mark.

a Pilot notes position of tow
plane in relation to
Chinagraph mark on canopy
or other suitable point on the
nose of glider

b Glider has moved up in
relation to tow plane.
Spot is too high

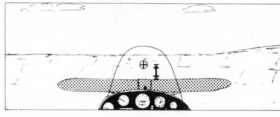

c Pilot moves nose down to
reposition spot onto tow
plane. This requires only a
small movement and so
reduces the tendency for
the pilot to over-control

d Pilot uses controls to
keep the spot in the
correct position and glider
wings level with those of
the tow plane

moved out of the slipstream. The easiest solution is to keep out of the slipstream by keeping slightly above the tug all the time. If you do get too low
and are in difficulties because of the slipstream, move up first and you will
find that you will regain control immediately.

Because of the high towing speed only very small elevator movements will
be needed to make corrections up and down. Each correction needs to
consist of a very small move, or pressure on the stick to start the movement,
followed by a 'check' or countermove, to stop things going too far. Most
beginners over-control badly at first, particularly when they are making
movements up or down.

Movements up or down on tow must be made very gradually. A rapid
movement down will result in the glider accelerating so that it tends to gain
speed and overtake the tug. This creates a bow in the rope which will tighten

up with a bad jerk and which may even break the tow rope. Usually it just gives a glider a bad snatch which will make it surge forwards and upwards so that the rope will become slack again. No attempt should be made to tighten any large amount of slack in the rope, or an even worse snatch will occur. The easiest thing is to stay in the same position, and, as the rope pulls tight, to move the stick forward very slightly to stop the glider zooming up again. Lowering the nose at this moment will also reduce the snatch as the rope re-tightens. This problem can be avoided by keeping station accurately all the time and by making only very gradual movements downwards. At first it may make it easier to try to move up or down in stages of a few feet at a time, instead of moving back to the correct position in one move. This helps to prevent going from one extreme position to the other, a very common fault with beginners.

Moving upwards should also be done gradually and smoothly. If you suddenly find yourself below the tug it is best to hold that position for a few seconds to allow any slack in the rope to come tight again. Otherwise, if you happen to start moving up just as the rope is jerking tight, you will get the extra load caused by pulling up, plus the jerk, and you may easily break the rope. Moving up from a low position always puts an extra load on the rope and should, therefore, always be done gradually.

The knack of keeping position up or down is to spot the beginning of any movement and make a very prompt but tiny correction to stop it before you get badly out of position. Once you are able to do this and to keep a steady position, it is a matter of self-discipline how large an error you are prepared to accept. It is just as easy to hold the ideal position as a position a little too high or too low.

Weaving from side to side

Most students also find it difficult to keep directly behind the tug without swinging violently from side to side. In order to stay in line with the tug the wings of the glider must remain parallel with those of the towing aircraft. If the tug is flying straight and the glider drops its left wing slightly, the glider will be pulled off to the left hand side. Unless the stick and rudder are used together the aileron drag will tend to swing the glider even further as the pilot attempts to bank it back towards the correct position. As the glider swings out to the side the rope is stretched tight so that the pull yaws the nose to the right rather suddenly. This in turn results in a tendency to bank more to the right and exaggerates the banking movement made by the pilot. A few seconds later the glider has swung across to a position even further out on the other side. In fact, each attempt to get to the correct position tends to end in a violent swing over to the other side with the pilot's corrections accentuating the trouble because they are just out of phase all the time.

The easiest solution for the beginner is to stop attempting to get back into line, and instead bring the wings level with those of the tug. This will stop the violent oscillations and allow the rope to pull the glider gradually back into line. If necessary, a very gentle bank can be made to help the movement

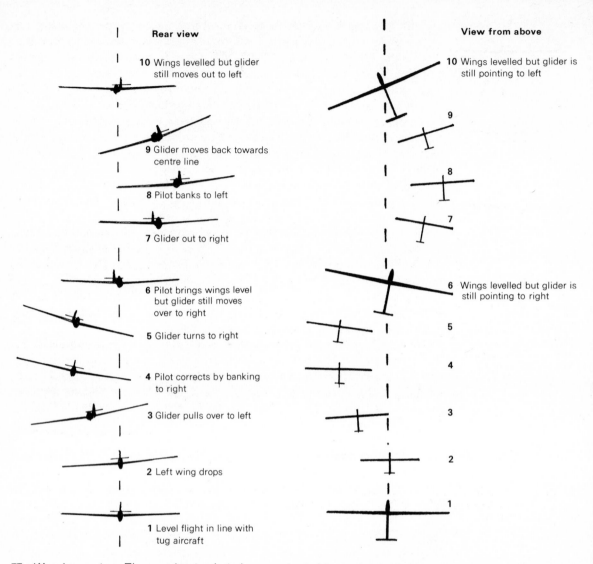

Rear view

10 Wings levelled but glider
   still moves out to left

9 Glider moves back towards
   centre line

8 Pilot banks to left

7 Glider out to right

6 Pilot brings wings level
   but glider still moves
   over to right

5 Glider turns to right

4 Pilot corrects by banking
   to right

3 Glider pulls over to left

2 Left wing drops

1 Level flight in line with
   tug aircraft

View from above

10 Wings levelled but glider is
   still pointing to left

9

8

7

6 Wings levelled but glider is
   still pointing to right

5

4

3

2

1

77 Weaving on tow. The weaving tends to be accentuated by each attempt to get back into position.

back to the middle, but this will always result in a slight overshoot unless a definite counter-correction is made before the glider reaches the central position.

It is worth considering in a little more detail what happens as we attempt to correct this swinging and get back into the centre. Suppose that the glider is out to the left hand side of the tug and a gentle banking turn is made to the right in order to bring the glider back. If the wings are brought level when the glider is almost behind the tug, the glider is then flying straight

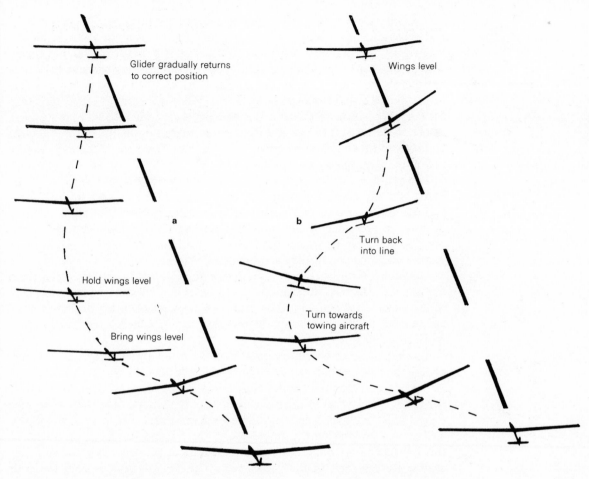

Glider gradually returns to correct position

Wings level

a

b

Turn back into line

Hold wings level

Turn towards towing aircraft

Bring wings level

78 Methods of getting back into position on tow. **a** Do not attempt to get back immediately but instead bring the wings level. Allow the glider to find its own way back into line gradually. **b** A skilled pilot makes a slight S turn back into position, but this requires accurate timing.

but is still pointing to the right. This is bound to result in the glider flying out to the other side instead of keeping station (see Fig. 77).

In order to make the correction from the left hand side to end up directly behind the tug, a gentle S-turn is required. First, a co-ordinated, gentle right hand turn is needed, but this must be changed to a gentle left hand turn to stop the correction and to bring the glider back into line in the correct position. Finally, the wings must be brought level again (Fig. 78). All these manoeuvres need correctly co-ordinated movements of the stick and rudder. Their timing is not easy for the inexperienced pilot and any attempt to get back into line quickly inevitably results in swinging from side to side.

Swinging from side to side can be stopped by bringing the wings level and stabilising the position with the glider out to one side. Just bring the wings level (or parallel with those of the tug if it is turning at the time), correct any error in position vertically, but do not attempt to move back into the middle position. It does no real harm to sit out to one side for a few moments, and, if the wings are level, the glider will start to move back into the correct position on its own. If necessary, a very small banking movement can be made using the stick and rudder movements normally, but this should be followed by a small, momentary banking movement the other way, almost before the tug appears to start to move.

The cause of moving out to one side is almost invariably a small angle of bank, and any attempt to stop this by rudder alone can lead to difficulties and the glider slipping out further in spite of the rudder. The right solution is neat, co-ordinated flying, and attempts to rudder your way back into position will only be successful for very small corrections, and on types of glider which happen to have strong lateral stability.

Inexperienced pilots often forget to use the rudder altogether during their first attempts to keep in position. This results in a constant weaving because of the effects of the aileron drag and is a major problem for beginners who are starting to fly the aerotow before they have reached a reasonable stage with co-ordination.

Another cause of confusion on aerotow is that on many types of training gliders the rudder tends to overbalance unless it is used correctly all the time. For example, if the pilot applies bank to the left but forgets to use the rudder, the glider will yaw off to the right because of the aileron drag even in normal flight. This results in a sideslipping movement to the left, during which the airflow will be striking the fuselage and the fin and rudder at an angle. If this is a fairly large angle the rudder will tend to be blown over to the right, against the pressure of the pilot's feet. The student pilot is very likely to think that this is the instructor riding the controls and, instead of opposing this force, will let the rudder move. The correct thing is to fight the mythical instructor in the back seat and oppose any tendency for the rudder to move itself. In fact, this overbalance has been caused by lack of rudder movement. Similarly, if the student uses much too much rudder the rudder loads change after the initial swing of the nose and the rudder will tend to stay on by itself. In some types of glider a definite force will be needed to recentralise the rudder after this overbalance has occurred.

If the pilot does not co-ordinate the stick and rudder movements correctly during an aerotow so that the glider starts to slip or skid, these changes in rudder load tend to be confusing. The pilot who always uses the controls correctly will never have experienced this difficulty and even quite experienced instructors may not know about it. It causes most students a little trouble when they convert from a motor glider, which does not normally have the problem, onto a glider such as the K7. Unless it is demonstrated on an early flight this effect may remain a mystery and it usually creates the impression that the instructor is riding the controls.

If a nose hook is fitted it should always be used for aerotowing. The rear hook is meant for winch or car towing only, and if it is used for aerotowing it is not so easy to prevent the glider zooming up above the tug and pulling it into the ground. Directional control may also be very marginal and once the glider has swung out to one side it may become difficult to stop it going out further still until releasing becomes the only safe solution.

Some gliders have one hook only fitted in a position which is a compromise between the best position for winching and the extreme front of the fuselage, which would be best for aerotow. This is usually a poor compromise and results both in mediocre winch launches and slightly inadequate directional control during take off on aerotow. However, it is less complicated, saves weight and is less expensive.

The take off The normal pre-take off vital actions are carried out, and the only difference will be in the position of the elevator trim. Since the glider must be kept in position behind the tug at a speed well above the normal flying speed the elevator trim will need to be set a little further forward (nose heavy) for an aerotow. This will avoid the need for a constant forward pressure on the stick to prevent the glider from climbing too high.

The take off should not cause any problems as there is a little more time than with the winch or car launch. If the glider is the type which sits nose down on the front skid at the beginning of the take off run, the ground friction will be very high until the front skid has been lifted clear of the ground. Since the acceleration is rather slow, the stick may be moved well back at the start of the take off run without any risk of the glider zooming up without warning. Once the machine is running on its wheel, the backward movement can be relaxed so that the glider is not pulled off the ground prematurely.

Gliders which have their main wheel well forward of the C of G, so that they rest firmly on their tail, need a forward movement on the stick to lift the tail up into a normal flying attitude before leaving the ground. Obviously, it is important to think which type of glider you are flying if you are changing from one type to the other. However, in both cases the object is the same, namely to get the machine into a flying attitude before leaving the ground.

During the take off run the glider must be kept behind the towing aircraft by steering it with the rudder. Normally the glider leaves the ground first, while the tug is still gaining speed. It should be kept slightly above the tug but it must not be allowed to climb at this stage. As the tug gains more speed, the glider pilot has to prevent the glider from gaining height by making a gradual, progressive forward movement on the stick. If the wings of the glider are kept level, and provided that the take off is directly into the wind, the glider will stay more or less in line with the tug.

A few seconds later the tug will also leave the ground, and, after gaining a little more speed, he will start to nose up slightly into the climb. This is the moment when you must make certain that you do not get left below him as he climbs. You must ease up at the same time and keep him just below the horizon in the correct towing position, or above the horizon if the tug is a very powerful one. If you do not move up with him you will find yourself looking up at the tug and being buffeted about by the slipstream. This is embarrassing while you are still rather close to the ground!

Once you have left the ground and have gained a few hundred feet of height, the rest of the tow is just a matter of keeping station behind the tug. When you see him start to bank into a turn, follow him by applying exactly the same angle of bank and keeping him in the correct vertical position all the time. Concentrate on keeping your wings parallel with his and you will stay in position.

The tug pilot is responsible for keeping a sharp lookout and for avoiding other aircraft during the tow. Until you have mastered the towing and have done one or two solo tows it is probably wise to rely on the tug pilot's lookout and not to try and look around yourself while on tow. Watch the tug all the time and concentrate on holding your position. If the tug disappears from view, even for a moment, you must release at once. This can easily happen if you start looking around you or stare for a few seconds at the instruments.

Releasing the tow rope

The procedure for releasing the rope is different from any other kind of launch. **Never** lower the nose before release. If you do, the glider will accelerate and you may easily fly into the rope end which can smash your canopy (worth £100 or more) or even get wound round the wing. It is also unwise to try and put an extra load on the rope to make it more obvious to the tug pilot that you have released. Firstly, you may overdo the movement and pull his tail up out of control, or, alternatively, you may either break the rope or find that under the extra load it is difficult to release at all. Releasing under extra tension is usually the cause of knots in the end of the tow rope and these, if unnoticed, seriously reduce the strength of the tow rope unless they are cut out and the rope spliced.

Except in emergency, you should get into the normal position and pull the release twice, hard. Only when the rope is *seen* to be released pull the glider *up* into a turn. Do not lower the nose or follow behind the tug after release. Always pull up and off to one side of the tug, clear of the rope end.

The direction of this turn off varies according to the country in which you happen to fly. In England, apart from special competitions, we have the freedom to turn off in either direction. This is ideal because it enables the tug and glider combination to climb in thermals turning in the same direction as the glider above them and for the glider to release and keep turning the same way. An experienced tug pilot can put a beginner right into a thermal and wave him off for his first soaring flight. During competition launching, it is common in this country to make the gliders turn off to the left so that they comply with the rule that all competitors must thermal in a left hand direction within a certain distance of the airfield. The tug pilot must always check to see that the glider has in fact released before starting to descend. Since the glider is, by then, hundreds of yards behind the tug, it makes little or no difference which way the glider turns.

I found it very confusing at Elmira in America and was severely reprimanded for turning off to the left instead of to the right. After many thousands of tows, I found it difficult to remember which way to turn, and guessed wrongly! The Americans for some reason best known to themselves, always turn off to the right.

There is absolutely no risk of collision between the tug and the glider regardless of the way either one turns provided that (a) the glider pilot makes a turn immediately after release, preferably pulling up at the same time, and (b) that the tug pilot checks visually that the glider has released and then *descends*.

On no account should the tug pilot pull straight up into a wing over or peel off. This does create a very real hazard because most tug aircraft are high winged and it is practically impossible for the tug pilot to be sure that he will not turn into his, or some other, glider in the vicinity.

You will not be popular with the tug pilot if you pull the airbrakes open by mistake and go off into a climbing turn with the rope still attached. Always release first, and do not pull away until you have *seen* the rope end free of the glider. Otherwise you will pull the tail of the tug right up and break the rope. This can be dangerous, as the rope may be catapulted forward onto the tug so that it winds round the wings, or even, as happened in one case, round the propeller itself.

If the tug pilot wants you to release he will wag his wings from side to side. This is an order to release immediately and not a signal that you may please yourself whether you obey it or not. In this case you just pull the release twice, hard, and pull up and to the side as soon as you see the rope has gone. As long as you do not just release and follow the tug there is no danger from the rope.

Emergencies on tow

During your first few tows you will not have time to consider such things as what to do if you have a rope break, or what to do if the tug has engine trouble just after take off. Fortunately, both these occurrences are extremely rare, but that makes it even more important to have at least considered them. The ideal is to go up in a motor glider and simulate these situations so that you can see what to do.

There are two distinct emergencies which may occur – the rope breaking, in which case the glider almost always has the normal towing speed, and the wave off, when the towing speed and height will usually be below normal.

The strength of the rope is normally limited to about 1000 lb so that it will break under excessive strain rather than cause structural damage to the glider or tow plane release hooks. During a steady tow the loads are only 50 or 60 lb so that there is ample reserve strength in normal circumstances.

The usual cause of a break is that the rope has become badly worn and frayed at the rings. Aerotow ropes are normally inspected before the start of flying each day and any knots which cannot be untied and any worn pieces must be cut out and properly spliced. A knot reduces the strength of a rope or cable by about half!

If the rope breaks the glider has sufficient speed to be turned off in the same way as the normal release at the top of the launch. This should be done so that the glider is no longer flying directly away from the field. The pilot can then make the decision either to fly back to the gliding site or to make an out landing, whichever he judges to be the safest. On a normal aerotow the glider will be within easy reach of the take off place since the climb is usually a little faster than the normal glide and has a higher rate of climb than the normal rate of sink in the glide. Also, of course, the take off and initial climb has been made against the wind, whereas the glide back will be with the wind. (Fig. 79.) In light winds a downwind landing presents no real

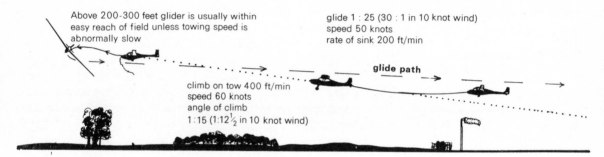

79 In normal circumstances the glider is within easy reach of the field if the rope breaks on aerotow.

problems, and, in stronger winds, the glider would have much more height by the boundary of the field so that a normal, if rather abbreviated, circuit could be made in most cases.

If the rope breaks, do not dither about but pull round immediately through about 90° so that you can assess the situation. (Fig. 80.) If you carry on flying straight ahead for long you will fritter away that valuable speed and get too far from the site to be able to reach it. In winds of less than about 10 knots a downwind landing is easy. If you are certain you can reach the field, turn towards it and start your approach. Do not attempt to be clever and land at the take off point. Instead, use the airbrakes to make a normal approach as if you were going to land in the first one-third of the field, as you come to it. Try to line your glider up so that it is directly downwind, even if this means being a little out of line with the take off direction. You will be travelling over the ground at a rather high speed but do not be tempted to slow down below the normal minimum approach speed. Choose an area which has no

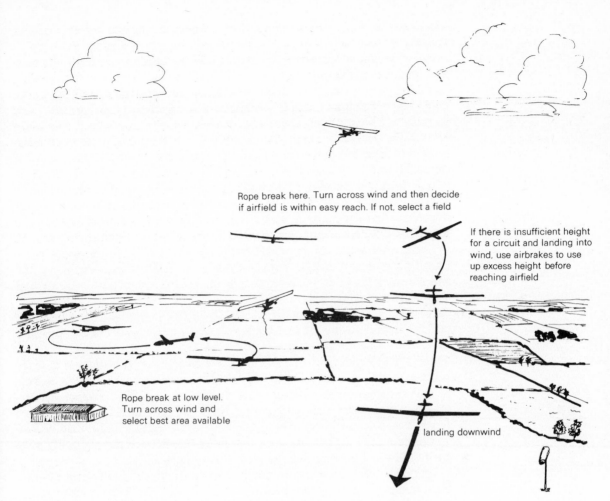

Rope break here. Turn across wind and then decide if airfield is within easy reach. If not, select a field

If there is insufficient height for a circuit and landing into wind, use airbrakes to use up excess height before reaching airfield

Rope break at low level. Turn across wind and select best area available

landing downwind

80 Procedure in the event of a tow rope break on aerotow. A landing downwind is practical except in strong winds but care must be taken to make a low approach over the boundary. Do not attempt to land at the launch point. Land as soon as possible and well clear of all obstructions in case the glider swings badly.

obstructions so that when the glider swings (and it usually will) you cannot hit anything. Make a normal landing, but do not relax. Concentrate on keeping the wings level, *absolutely level*. As the glider slows down after landing, you will probably lose control before you come to a standstill. This is due to the fact that as the glider slows down to the same speed as the wind there is no airflow at all over the wings so that they cannot be kept level with the controls. One wing will inevitably touch the ground and swing the glider round into a ground loop. However, if you have been careful to keep the wings level for as long as possible you will be going very slowly and no damage is likely to be done. The glider must always be inspected carefully after a ground loop as there may be damage to the wing roots or fuselage which is not obvious at a glance.

Never attempt to make a downwind landing back at the take off point. The glider will always float much further than you expect before landing, and it rolls further as well. Keep well clear of any obstructions as the glider may swing either way and you will not be able to prevent it. If you are going to make a downwind landing the decision must be made before you arrive back to the field. It is no good arriving at 300 feet or so and then expecting to be able to get rid of the height at the last moment. You will float out of the airfield if you do.

In most cases the glider will be high enough to fly back, make a circuit, and land at the upwind end of the field. However, if the rope is broken during the first few hundred feet, a field landing will be safer than attempting to get back. With the extra speed of the aerotow this may still leave you with a choice of fields and you must just do the best you can. With the motor glider training it is an easy matter to go and look at the fields at each end of the site and consider them. It is also a simple matter to demonstrate a downwind landing and explain all these points.

Whereas with a rope break it is usual to be able to get back to the take off field, a wave off during the first 500 feet or so is a much more critical situation.

The wave off There are two common reasons for a wave off. (Fig. 81.) Usually it is given because the glider pilot has left the airbrakes closed but not properly locked, so that they have opened themselves during take off. The drag of the airbrakes may prevent the combination from climbing above a few hundred feet and as soon as the tug pilot attempts to turn even this height may be lost. In this case the tug pilot will have no option but to wave the glider off, or to jettison him before they both arrive back on the ground.

The first thing to do if you receive a wave off signal is to release at once, but the second thing is to glance out sideways and check those airbrakes. If they are open, close them quickly, or you will arrive on the ground in a few seconds. Do not attempt to turn round for the airfield unless you have plenty of *height and speed*. If the airbrakes were open the tug would have been struggling to climb at a much lower speed than normal, and after release you will need to gain speed. You will almost certainly have to make an out landing.

If you check the airbrakes after releasing and find them closed, the trouble was probably the tug's engine after all. Again, you will be flying very slowly and you will have little choice but to land ahead in any available open space.

If the tug pilot is alert and checks either in his mirror or by looking back at the glider just after he is airborne, he should be able to see whether the brakes are open. If there is still plenty of room ahead for the glider to land he should jettison it and climb away. The glider will usually land ahead without damage. However, if the trouble is not noticed during the take off or initial climb the chances are that the first indication to either pilot will be the

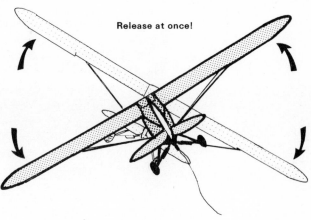

81 The wave off signal given by the tug pilot in an emergency.

Release at once!

apparent lack of climbing power of the tug. The speed will be very slow to pick up and the climb much more sluggish than normal. What happens next depends on the power of the tug and the effectiveness of the airbrakes on the glider. If the tug is powerful the combination will be able to climb away slowly, in which case most tug pilots would try to avoid dropping or waving the glider off until it had at least enough height to reach the airfield. It is usually best for the tug to climb straight ahead and get plenty of height as the combination may lose height if a turn is made. In the meantime the tug pilot can try to draw the glider pilot's attention to the trouble by raising and lowering the flaps, if he has any, or by shaking his fist at him. The glider pilot often carries on happily and then the tug pilot will try to bring him back close to the field and wave him off by rocking the wings of the tug. (The standard signal to release at once.) In spite of this, many pilots continue to be unaware of the cause of the wave off and think that it is engine trouble on the tow plane.

The worst predicament is when the weather is calm and hot and the tug is not powerful enough to make a positive climb against the pull of the glider's brakes. The combination will often get up to about a hundred feet and then will cease to climb at all. Any areas of sink will then cause a loss of height and, almost regardless of the ground below whether it is fields or trees, the tug pilot will have to release to save his own neck and aircraft. Since the glider pilot is unaware that the brakes are open, the landing is usually more of an arrival, with the ground coming up very rapidly as soon as the tow is broken.

Several times when towing I have managed to jettison the glider safely inside the airfield and, on one occasion, I held on until we were just crossing the boundary of a large field and then released so that the glider had no option but to land in a safe area. I have also towed old Olympias and Skylarks around the countryside for what seemed like eternity until we eventually arrived back over the airfield and I could wave them off safely.

I will always remember running through the woods for about a mile to get to a Skylark which had taken off with the brakes unlocked and which had eventually released into the middle of the trees when the tug could not climb. Fortunately, the pilot was unhurt and the glider was not seriously damaged.

This type of incident does not occur if you do your cockpit check thoroughly each time before take off. But because of the possibility of human and mechanical failure it is always worth remembering the following maxim.

If at any time the glider does not seem to be flying normally or does not seem to be climbing properly, whether it is a wire launch or an aerotow, the *first* thing to check is the airbrakes. (Fig. 82.) Look out along the wing and

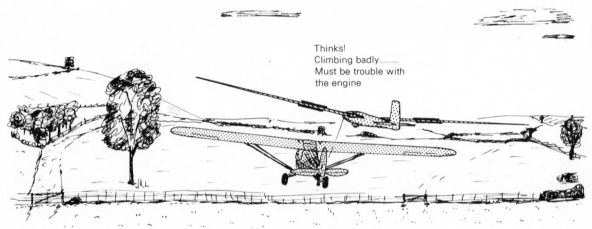

Thinks!
Climbing badly..........
Must be trouble with
the engine

82 Airbrakes open on tow. This is usually caused by careless cockpit drill. If the take off or climb is unusually poor, glance out and check that the airbrakes are closed.

check whether the brakes are open. If you are waved off during an aerotow in ninety-nine cases out of a hundred the trouble will be the airbrakes, not engine trouble on the tug! Tug pilots should also remember this fact. If the take off or climb seems poor, or the tug does not seem to be running at full power, do not assume engine trouble but check the glider and look carefully to see if the brakes are opened. If they are, jettison the glider if there is any risk of not clearing obstructions.

The situation is very similar, but even worse if the tail parachute is un-wittingly opened. Tail parachutes open very gently indeed and it is extremely unlikely that a pilot would know that the chute was out. The drag is much greater than most airbrakes and few tow planes would be powerful enough to climb away. The only hope is that the tug pilot may be able to jettison the glider at the right moment for a safe descent into a field. The most likely cause of the chute deploying itself is poor packing of the chute and its fairing. Special care should be taken to make quite sure that the fairing is securely locked whenever it is fitted.

The 'I cannot release' signal

There is also a procedure to cater for the very unlikely situation when the glider pilot finds himself unable to release the rope from the glider. The main problem is to make the tug pilot understand what is wrong so that he will either release his end of the rope or bring the glider back down to land on tow. This exercise is taught to all pilots in some European countries and involves descending on tow with the glider pilot using the airbrakes in order to prevent the glider from overtaking the tow plane.

In England the 'I cannot release' signal consists of moving well out to the left hand side and attracting attention by yawing and rocking the glider's wings.

With good servicing and the use of the correct release rings at the ends of the rope the only possibility of a hang up at the glider end is the rope becoming tangled in the main wheel or skid during the take off. It is difficult to understand why some countries prefer to make a landing on tow when it would be so easy for the tug pilot to release his end of the rope. Then the only point for the glider pilot to remember is to approach for the landing higher than normal so that there is no risk of rope catching anything on the airfield boundary.

This all sounds rather traumatic until you remember that hang ups are extremely rare, that very, very few tug pilots have ever had an engine failure on tow, and that even fewer glider pilots have managed to break the rope, except in the violent conditions in the rotor of a wave system.

The vital point to remember is that with the wave off you seldom have any reserve of speed or height, whereas with a rope break you will normally have both. On a small site either could lead to tricky situations, and, therefore, it is better to think about them beforehand than to live in the hope that you never have such an occurrence.

These notes are not intended to be a comprehensive treatise on aerotowing but they should help anyone starting to learn to tow. There is more detail in my other book, *Gliding*, for anyone who wants additional information.

11 Advice for Power Pilots Converting to Glider Flying

Handling and the need to
  use the rudder   190
Accurate turns   192
The correct flying speeds   193
Collisions are lethal   193

The approach   194
Landing   194
Planning the circuit   195
Running out of height   196

A very large number of people who learn to glide are already experienced power pilots and their training is just a matter of a conversion from aeroplanes to gliders. Basically, both aircraft are flown in much the same way and have the same controls. However, there are a number of additional pitfalls in gliding which are seldom encountered in powered aircraft. These make it essential to have a thorough grounding and to understand the need to 'play it safe' for the first 20 or 30 hours of gliding.

If you have been used to booking your power flying and being able to drive to the airfield and step into an aircraft straight away, your biggest problem may be learning to accept the idea of always spending at least half a day at a gliding club if you want to fly. During training you can expect to spend much more time helping on the ground than flying because each glider needs to be launched and retrieved after each flight.

Even if you buy your own glider you will still have to depend on the help of other people for each flight and unless you help other pilots you will soon run short of the help you need to get into the air yourself.

This need for co-operation soon discourages the selfish and faint-hearted, with the result that gliding people are a race apart in the flying world. The very nature of gliding also tends to encourage everyone to reach a high standard of piloting ability and technical competence which is seldom found elsewhere among amateur pilots.

Handling and the need to use the rudder

You may feel a little worried about the absence of an engine to get you out of trouble. This probably comes from your experience with practising forced landings in a powered machine. Gliders are far easier to land accurately because of their lower flying speeds and powerful airbrakes.

Compared with a modern light aircraft the handling and effectiveness of the controls will almost certainly come as a shock on your first flight. Because of the large wing span the rate of roll is relatively poor and the stick and rudder *must* be used together for accurate flight. You will probably be astonished to find that you do not know how to use them together and that you have to think hard to remember to use the rudder every time. This is because the rudder is not used in this way on most modern powered aircraft. It is usually used to keep straight on take off and landing and when an engine fails, if you are flying a multi-engined machine. But at all other times it is applied either to overcome the slight swing caused by the extra power used when climbing or to stop the swing in the other direction which occurs when the power is cut and the aircraft is gliding. No rudder is required on most aircraft for straight and level flight at cruising speed, but, as the power setting is changed, a slight swing occurs and the rudder needs to be applied as a correction. An experienced pilot will usually make this rudder correction in time to prevent any appreciable swing of the nose, but unless he is very familiar with the particular aircraft he will make the movement as a correction, rather than make it automatically in anticipation of the swing.

Now, with a glider the co-ordination of the stick and rudder has to be almost instinctive, as any control movement to apply bank or to bring the wings level with ailerons alone will cause a noticeable swing of the nose in the opposite direction to the bank. This swinging is caused by aileron drag and is accentuated by the large wing span and relatively poor directional stability of the glider. On your first few flights you will find the most difficult thing is to prevent the nose snaking from side to side. This will go on until you have learned to use a little rudder *every time* you use the ailerons. Take comfort – every beginner and almost all power pilots, however experienced, find this use of the rudder the most difficult thing to learn. It always takes time to form a habit, and a habit involving the use of our feet is particularly difficult to master.

Do not fall into the trap of thinking that gliders need a large amount of rudder in a turn. Like all other aircraft they need very little rudder once the bank has been applied. All turns are fundamentally just a matter of applying bank and making a backward movement of the stick, but whenever a *glider* is being rolled into and out of a turn the stick and rudder must be co-ordinated and quite large movements of the rudder are needed. The movements required are roughly proportional, i.e. with half the available sideways stick movement, use half the range of rudder movement. It is probably easiest to avoid using very large aileron deflections since there is usually barely enough rudder power to prevent some adverse yaw when full aileron is applied.

Once the glider is in the turn with the required angle of bank the rudder needs to be reduced, leaving just a small amount in the direction of the turn. If it is not reduced a very inefficient, skidding turn will result.

Most pilots are rather surprised to discover that they cannot use the rudder correctly at first, even after it has been demonstrated to them. Do not feel too embarrassed about it as your instructor will expect you to have this problem and will not think you are hopeless. It is only on the oldest types of powered machines that any aileron drag is really noticeable and therefore he will not expect you to have understood the problem before you have flown in a glider.

Accurate turns You will find it necessary to use some aileron deflection to stop the bank from increasing in the turn. This means that you will need the stick slightly to the right in a left hand turn. This is unusual and would generally be bad flying in most other aircraft, but it is perfectly normal in gliders, which require this slightly crossed control position for an accurate turn. Of course, it is not really the fact that the controls are crossed which is dangerous in a light aircraft but the fact that with the controls in these positions the aircraft is slipping or skidding badly. In most gliders the need for a *large* amount of aileron to prevent the bank increasing is a sign of either much too much rudder, or of flying dangerously slowly. From this situation the glider *is* liable to spin. You will find that your sense of feel is inadequate to judge whether you are slipping or skidding in turns until you have a few hours of experience in gliders. With your knowledge of using instruments you will be able to find time to check the slip indicator or the piece of wool on the canopy to tell which rudder is needed to make the turn accurate. If the slip ball is out to the left, for example, you need more left foot forward, or less right rudder to correct it. All you have to do using the wool tuft is to swing the nose of the glider into line with the wool.

Almost all power pilots have a tendency to under-rudder, or to forget the rudder, during the entry to the turns. Then after the bank has been applied they tend to take off too much rudder so that a slipping turn occurs.

There could be various reasons for this. Certainly they are not used to having to hold off the bank with the ailerons during turns and, therefore, it may be that they are loath to use the stick to control the bank and use rudder instead. Another likely cause is that they remember that the stick and rudder must be used together for the entry to the turn and that the amount of rudder must then be reduced for the turn itself. However, if they fail to use enough rudder at the start of the turn and then reduce the rudder by a set amount they inevitably end up with a little opposite rudder and a bad slipping turn. In this case they have reduced a movement which had not been made in the first place, with the result that they are left with a little opposite rudder being held on.

A further possible reason for a badly slipping turn is that the pilot, noticing the unfamiliar feeling of slipping as he applies the bank without enough rudder, tries to stop the aircraft slipping downwards towards the lower wing by applying the rudder. When the machine is already sideslipping slightly in a turn to the left, for example, any right rudder swings the nose up momentarily. This yaws the whole aircraft even further out of line with the airflow, making the sideslip even worse. In spite of attempting to hold the nose up in the turn with the rudder the nose will drop still further after a few seconds, completely ruining the turn.

The best way of overcoming these problems is plenty of practice in turning from one direction to the other. The first essential is to be shown the adverse yaw so that you can recognise the symptoms of having forgotten to use the rudder and understand what is happening. They can be clearly seen by holding the rudder rigidly fixed while looking ahead as the glider is banked from side to side. Next try the same banking movements while using the stick and rudder together in order to stop the swinging of the nose. This will help you to get the two control movements going together nicely.

The important thing to remember is that these movements must *always* go together when the glider is being rolled into or out of a turn, or, for example, when bringing the wings level after the machine has been tipped by a gust or turbulence. Even a small correction using the aileron alone will cause a swing of the nose, and extra drag as the whole aircraft flies sideways for a few seconds.

The correct flying speeds

Contrary to your probable first impressions it is not efficient to fly a glider at the minimum possible speed in straight flight. Every little gust or bump would leave it stalled and it would mean gaining some extra speed before turning. Ideally it should be flown at a speed which will allow it to be put into quite a steep turn immediately any lift is found. With most basic training machines this means flying at a speed of about 10-12 knots above the indicated stalling speed, i.e. about 40-45 knots on most two-seater gliders.

Because of the low flying speed the rate of turn is very high for quite a small angle of bank and the radius of turn is much smaller than you will be accustomed to. However, it is normal practice to use well-banked turns and you will find that this simplifies the circuit planning as well as being more effective for thermal soaring. This is particularly significant when you come to the final turn before landing. Do not start the turn until you are almost opposite the approach line and always use a well-banked turn rather than a gentle, gradual turn. This gives a much cleaner and straighter approach and avoids a gradual, curving approach with the final turn straightening up close to the ground. An angle of bank of 30°-40° is quite normal for all turns and instead of using the indications of the turn needle on the Turn and Slip Indicator to judge how steep to make the turn, as you might in a light aircraft, it is normal to judge the angle of bank visually. The Turn and Slip Indicator on gliders is electrically operated and is calibrated completely differently from those on powered machines. In order to save batteries it is only normally turned on for cloud flying or in very bad visibility. The slip indicator (ball) is, of course, just the same as you have been used to and works all the time.

Collisions are lethal

Do not be too surprised if your gliding instructor keeps reminding you to look around more while you fly. Keeping a really good lookout is even more important in gliders than in powered aircraft and most power pilots do not automatically keep good enough lookout for safety when soaring. Instead of avoiding other gliders you will soon realise that your aim when soaring is usually to join them in order to share their thermal. It becomes a matter of pride to try to out-climb the other fellow and this may mean circling with him only 50–100 yards away. Since collisions are invariably fatal unless you are able to parachute to safety, it is vital to keep a good lookout and to be aware of the position of every glider which is nearby at all times. In reality, lookout is far more important with gliders than flying accurately. It is not unknown for the pilot to be unhurt after spinning into the ground from a bad final turn, although the glider itself is usually a write-off, but you must not expect to get away with a collision. The moral is clear – keep a good lookout *all* the time.

The approach

One fundamental difference between flying gliders and other aircraft is that the flying speed must normally be increased for the approach whereas on all other machines you reduce the speed. Even in calm conditions it is necessary to increase speed by about 10 knots and in strong winds much more speed is needed to ensure a safe and controllable approach. The steep approach makes the wind gradient a serious hazard unless extra speed and height is allowed. Also, the airbrakes raise the stalling speed by several knots as well as increasing the drag enormously. A slightly slow approach may easily, therefore, end up with a heavy, semi-stalled landing and a broken glider. On the other hand a rather fast approach creates no problems except for the extra difficulty in judging how far the glider will float before touchdown. In practice, the additional float can be reduced to a minimum by using plenty of airbrake for the final part of the approach and landing.

Unlike flaps, the airbrakes may be opened or closed at any stage of the approach and landing in order to adjust the glidepath or float. There is virtually no trim change as they are opened, and closing them both reduces the drag and improves the lift so that the glider floats on much further. If there is any tendency to undershoot, the airbrake lever is used rather like a throttle. By pushing it forward and closing the airbrakes the glider accelerates and sinks less. Obviously this effect is limited and depends on the performance of the particular type of glider. For example an old-design glider or a motor glider such as the two-seater Scheibe Falke with rather ineffective airbrakes may have a glide range on the approach between about 20:1 with the airbrakes closed and 8:1 with them fully opened. A modern machine with good airbrakes will have a range of between 30:1 and 6:1 and will therefore require less skill and judgement to land accurately. As with lowering full flap in a light aircraft, opening full airbrake creates a very large amount of extra drag and unless the nose is lowered to compensate, a loss of speed will occur. After several flights you will master the art of using the airbrakes and maintaining the approach speed and you will soon forget your worries about having no engine.

Landing

You will have no difficulty landing a glider but must remember that it has no long undercarriage and that, therefore, you have to be a little closer to the ground than on a light aircraft. Otherwise you will find the glider touching down a little tail first. Try to avoid pumping movements on the stick. This is a bad habit that you may have developed on powered aircraft. It is quite unnecessary (on any aircraft) and it often causes difficulties when the controls are very light, as on some types of glider. The stick should ideally be moved very smoothly backwards during the hold off until the aircraft settles onto the ground.

Planning the circuit   Whereas in a powered aircraft a neat, square circuit is a sign of accurate flying, it means very little in a glider where the amount of height lost depends more on what areas of rising or sinking air are encountered. Since these areas cannot always be predicted, the glider pilot must be prepared to make adjustments to the circuit pattern, either widening it out or cutting off a corner, in order to arrive in a good position for the final turn and approach. In windy or unstable conditions extra height should be kept to allow for flying into areas of strong sinking air which might result in several hundred feet of height being lost unexpectedly. The excess, if any, can then be thrown away on the base leg by using the airbrakes.

If you have all your glider conversion flights in light winds, however experienced you are as a power pilot, you should try to get a few dual flights before soloing on a windy day. Experience all over the world shows that it is safer to do this than to teach yourself. An instructor can help you to avoid the worst pitfalls and may save you from making a fool of yourself. If this is not possible at least get a thorough briefing from an instructor or an experienced glider pilot before you fly in really windy weather for the first time. Even a relatively small increase in the wind speed makes it necessary to bring the base leg and final turn much closer to the landing area and in winds of over 20 knots it is seldom safe to go very far behind the downwind boundary of the field. The effect of a strong wind gradient has to be experienced personally before you will believe it.

If gliders were always launched by aerotow and almost every flight was made in soaring conditions, there would be no need to attempt to soar below 1000 feet and there would always be plenty of height for the circuit. In this situation the flying speed could be increased to the approach speed at about 800 feet and maintained for the whole circuit. Very consistent square circuits can be made using this technique because, at this high speed, the glider flies through most of the areas of sink or lift in a very short time so that they have very little effect. This is the normal practice at many airfields where there is a mixture of gliding and power flying going on at the same time. To avoid confusion all the gliders usually make their circuits on one side of the field and the powered machines on the other.

Where gliders are launched by winch or tow car and where there are no restrictions because of light aircraft the minimum height for attempting to soar may be as low as 500 or 600 feet, providing that the pilots are all trained to understand and obey certain common-sense rules, the most important of which is not to circle at low altitude on or near the downwind boundary.

Every pilot should know the rules applying at the gliding site where he is flying and should ask for an explanation of any which seem illogical or unnecessary. Club rules are usually the result of bitter experience and unless they are understood they are likely to be forgotten, or broken unintentionally, with costly results. *Never* fly from a strange site without asking an instructor or experienced pilot about any special conditions which occur there.

Running out of height

Power pilots are usually aware that they must never attempt to stretch the glide on an approach, and this applies particularly to gliders. In fact extra speed will almost invariably get you further and if you are tending to undershoot you should always close the airbrakes immediately and lower the nose to increase the speed. However, there is another similar trap which catches many pilots unawares.

Flying at the normal cruising speed, the glider takes so much time to pass through an area of sinking air that this can cost an unexpected loss of several hundred feet in surprisingly few seconds. You may also notice that if the glider runs into sinking air it loses speed. This adds to the loss of height and can leave the glider at such a low speed that it will take several hundred feet to regain the extra speed for a safe final turn.

Never allow yourself to be caught flying *low* and *slow*. Cruising speed should always be increased by the time the height is down to 400 or 500 feet. If this is done, even the worst sink can never leave you running out of height and speed together.

You will be surprised by the effect of flying against a wind, particularly if there is a strong wind gradient or you fly into sinking air. In absolutely still air the average training glider has a best gliding angle of about 25:1 and a rate of descent of about 1.75 knots (175 feet per minute). At an approach speed of 50–55 knots the gliding angle is probably about 20:1, but this is reduced to less than 14:1 even by a wind of 15 knots. (The surface wind at this time might be only 10 knots.)

Even a downdraught of less than 2 knots can halve this 14:1 in a few seconds! Sinking air of several times this strength is often found on an unstable day and in the lee of hills. This makes it vital to keep extra height in hand on the final stages of the circuit and to fly well above the normal cruising speed under about 500 feet. Always bear in mind the possibility of an unexpected loss of height and have a plan of action in mind. Keep within easy reach of an alternative landing area and turn in to land on it if it looks as though your height may be marginal to reach the normal one.

With a glider which is fitted with reasonably powerful airbrakes it is a very easy matter to use up a little excess height on the base leg and final approach. This is an ideal situation since you will still have sufficient height if you meet sink on the base leg, yet, if you hit lift, full airbrake together with widening the circuit slightly will still bring you down for an accurate spot landing. Any approach which requires no airbrake at all is extremely marginal since even a slight misjudgement or an unexpected loss of even a few feet of height would leave you crash-landing into the boundary fence.

Appendix A   The Yates Effect

Airspeed fluctua-
tions when flying
into rising and
sinking air

Soaring pilots often ask for an explanation of the increase in airspeed which usually occurs when a glider or powered aircraft flies into lift. This is best explained mathematically by quoting from a short article by Dr A. H. Yates published in *Gliding* in 1951.

'The phenomenon has long been known to glider pilots who, cruising between thermals at a steady airspeed and attitude, suddenly enter a thermal. The immediate response of the glider is an increase in speed to which the glider pilot's ears are very sensitive (he has been trained to judge airspeed by the noise level).

The cause of the forward acceleration of the glider or aeroplane on hitting an upgust is seen if the forces acting on the wing are examined (Fig. 83).

If the aircraft is flying level at speed V, the forces on the wing are lift L, vertically upwards, and drag D, horizontally. If the aircraft now meets an upgust of speed w, then the resultant velocity of the air is V^1 and the angle of incidence is suddenly increased by $\delta a = \dfrac{w}{V}$ approximately.

The forces on the wing are now L^1 and D^1, normal to and parallel to V^1 respectively, and these forces represent a change in drag from
D to $D^1 \cos \delta a - L^1 \sin \delta a$

Now, if the aeroplane is not just about to stall (in which case the upgust would stall it) D^1 and D are almost equal and so are L^1 and L. Also since δa is small

$$\cos \delta a = 1 \text{ approx. and } \sin \delta a = \delta a = \frac{w}{V}$$

Thus, there is a change in drag from

$$D \text{ originally to } D - L.\frac{w}{V}$$

i.e. an accelerating force equal to $\dfrac{w}{V}$ times the aircraft weight. It is this force which increases the speed of the aircraft when it enters the upgust. The fact that a glider is descending and not flying level does not alter the argument.

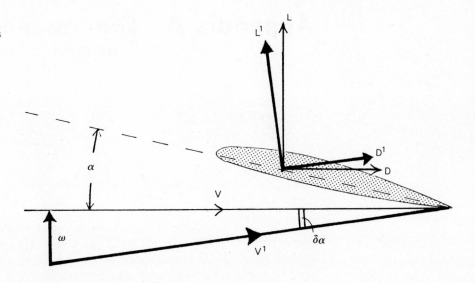

83 The increase in airspeed which occurs when an aircraft flies into rising air.

Appendix B Gliding Awards and Records

Nothing encourages an enthusiastic sportsman so much as keen competition and a sense of pride in personal achievement. This is particularly true of gliding, in which the award of certificates and badges, recognised all over the world, has played a great part in the encouragement of a healthy competitive spirit among both beginners and expert pilots.

Unlike most club or society badges, a gliding badge is an award for actual ability and achievement. It cannot be bought by money or prestige alone, but must be earned by skill, adventure, and, in some cases, endurance.

Gliding is an international sport, and the regulations for world records and the tests for the Silver, Gold and Diamond 'C' badges are laid down by the Federation Aeronautique Internationale, who also control record flights for powered aircraft.

The requirements for the 'A', 'B' and 'C' certificates vary from country to country and are determined by the National Aero Club or the Gliding Association of the country concerned.

In some countries, the 'C' certificate test includes examinations in Principles of Flight, Meteorology, Navigation and Flying Regulations, and is a glider pilot's licence.

British gliding suffers far fewer restrictions and regulations than most of the Continental countries and no licence is required by law. Pilots who have 'C' or Silver 'C' certificates are granted certain concessions if they wish to become private (powered aircraft) pilots and can count some of their gliding experience towards the hours needed for their licence.

The requirements in England for the various certificates are as follows:

'A' Cert. One satisfactory circuit flight solo.

'B' Cert. Two more satisfactory circuit flights during which the pilot demonstrates the ability to make satisfactory turns in both directions.

'C' Cert. A soaring flight during which the glider maintains (or gains) height for at least 5 minutes.

The pilot must also pass a test on the Laws and Rules for Glider Pilots.

BGA Bronze 'C'. This is the minimum qualification for a glider pilot to fly out of gliding range of his base.

He must have 50 solo glider flights (or at least 50 hours PI on powered aircraft and 20 solo glider flights) and 2 solo soaring flights of at least 1 hour after release from aerotow (max. height 2000 feet), or 30 minutes from wire or bungee launches, followed by normal landings as briefed.

In addition, there is a flying test which includes stalling and incipient spins and simulated field landings. The written test includes a general paper on Airmanship, Principles of Flight, and Meteorology, together with the test on the Laws and Rules for Glider Pilots. These requirements are almost identical to those for the German and American Glider Pilot's Licence.

FAI Silver 'C' Duration. A flight of not less than 5 hours.
Height. A flight in which the gain of height registered by the barograph is not less than 1000 metres (3281 feet). Gain of height being the difference between the maximum height recorded and the lowest previous point registered after release.
Distance. A flight of not less than 50 kilometres (31.07 miles) carried out in a straight line.

The loss of height between the release and the place of landing must not exceed 1% of the distance covered.

FAI Gold 'C' Duration. A flight of not less than 5 hours.
Height. A flight in which the gain of height registered by the barograph is not less than 3000 metres (9843 feet).
Distance. A flight of not less than 300 kilometres (186.42 miles) carried out in a straight line, a broken line of not more than 2 legs, a triangle, or an out and return.

Turning points must be declared in writing before take-off.

Diamonds The holder of the Gold 'C' badge is entitled to wear a diamond on the badge for each of the following performances:
Height. A gain of height of 5000 metres (16,405 feet).
Goal flight. An out and return or triangle flight of at least 300 kilometres (186.2 miles).
Distance. A flight of at least 500 kilometres (310.7 miles).

Distance flights may be made in a straight line, a broken line of not more than 2 legs, a triangle or an out and return. Turning points must be declared in writing before take off.

With the FAI badges, any flight may count for Silver, Gold, and Diamond awards; the flights must be made solo and a sealed barograph must be carried on all the flights. (Copies of the full regulations can be obtained from the BGA).

National and International gliding records are divided into two main classes; solo flights and flights made by two or more persons flying together. There is also a separate category of records for women.

In each class there are records for distance, out and return flights, distance to a pre-determined goal, speed over triangular courses and set distances, and absolute and gain of height. Until 1955 there were also duration records but these had become feats of endurance, and because of the danger of the pilots falling asleep at the controls they have been discontinued. In the early days of gliding long duration flights had great publicity value and served some purpose in investigating soaring conditions at night. But flights of over forty hours, nowadays, can have little real value, and serious harm is caused if an accident occurs on such a flight.

Appendix C Conversion Tables

Metres		Feet	Kilo-metres		Miles	Kilo-grammes		Pounds
0.305	1	3.281	1.609	1	0.621	0.454	1	2.205
0.610	2	6.562	3.219	2	1.243	0.907	2	4.409
0.914	3	9.843	4.828	3	1.864	1.361	3	6.614
1.219	4	13.123	6.438	4	2.485	1.814	4	8.818
1.524	5	16.404	8.047	5	3.107	2.268	5	11.023
1.829	6	19.685	9.656	6	3.728	2.722	6	13.228
2.134	7	22.966	11.265	7	4.350	3.175	7	15.432
2.438	8	26.247	12.875	8	4.971	3.629	8	17.687
2.743	9	29.528	14.848	9	5.592	4.082	9	19.842
3.048	10	32.808	16.093	10	6.214	4.536	10	22.046
6.906	20	65.617	32.187	20	12.427	9.072	20	44.092
7.620	25	82.021	40.234	25	15.534	11.340	25	55.116
15.240	50	164.042	80.467	50	31.069	22.680	50	110.231
30.480	100	328.084	160.924	100	62.137	45.359	100	220.462

SPEED CONVERSION SCALE

KNOTS	MPH	KM/H	FT/SEC
10	10	10	10
20	20	20	20
	30	30	30
30		40	40
	40	50	50
40		60	60
	50	70	70
50	60	80	80
		90	90
60	70	100	100
		110	110
70	80	120	120
		130	130
80	90	140	140
	100	150	150
90	110	160	160
		170	170
100	120	180	180
110		190	190
	130	200	200
120	140	210	210
		220	220
130	150	230	230
	160	240	240
140		250	250
150	170	260	
		270	

RATE OF CLIMB CONVERSION SCALE

KNOTS	METRES PER SEC	FT/MIN	FT/SEC	KM/H	MPH
1		100	1 / 2	1 / 2	1
2	1	200	3 / 4	3 / 4	2
3		300	5	5	3
4	2	400	6 / 7	6 / 7	4
5		500	8	8 / 9	5
6	3	600	9	10 / 11	6
7		700	10 / 11	12	7
8	4	800	12	13 / 14	8
9		900	13 / 14	15 / 16	9
			15	17	10
10	5	1000	16	18 / 19	11
11		1100	17	20	12
12	6	1200	18 / 19	21 / 22	13
13		1300	20 / 21	23 / 24	14
14	7	1400	22	25	15
15		1500	23 / 24	26 / 27	16
16	8	1600	25	28 / 29	17 / 18
17		1700	26 / 27	30	19
18	9	1800	28 / 29	31 / 32	20
			30 / 31	33 / 34	21
19	10	1900	32	35	22
		2000	33	36	

CONVERSION FACTORS			
	To convert	**into**	**Multiply by**
Distances			
	Metres	Feet	3.281
	Feet	Metres	0.3048
	Centimetres	Inches	0.394
	Inches	Centimetres	2.540
	Kilometres	Miles	0.6214
	Miles	Kilometres	1.609
	Kilometres	Nautical Miles	0.5396
	Nautical Miles	Kilometres	1.853
	Miles	Nautical Miles	0.869
	Nautical Miles	Miles	1.151
Speeds			
	Kilometres per hour	Miles per hour	0.6214
	Miles per hour	Kilometres per hour	1.609
	Km/h	Knots	0.5396
	Knots	Km/h	1.853
	Metres per second	Feet per second	3.281
	Feet per second	Metres per second	0.3048
	M.p.h.	Knots	0.869
	Knots	M.p.h.	1.151
	Feet per minute	Metres per second	.00508
	Metres per second	Feet per minute	196.85
	Knots	Metres per second	0.515
	Metres per second	Knots	1.944
Areas			
	Square metres	Square feet	10.764
	Square feet	Square metres	0.093
	Square centimetres	Square inches	0.155
	Square inches	Square centimetres	6.451
Weights			
	Kilogrammes	Pounds	2.205
	Pounds	Kilogrammes	0.454
Wing loadings and tyre pressures			
	Kg per square metre	Lb per square foot	0.205
	Lb per square foot	Kg per square metre	4.882
	Lb per square inch	Kg per square centimetre	0.07
	Kg per square centimetre	Lb per square inch	14.3
Weight of Water			

1 Imperial gallon = 4.546 litres = 1.2 US gallons, weighs 10 lb
1 litre = 0.22 Imperial gallons = 0.264 US gallons, weighs 2.2 lb
1 US gallon = 3.8 litres = 0.83 Imperial gallons, weighs 8.3 lb

Index

Page numbers referring to figures are italicised

A 21 glider *83*
Adverse yaw 38, 39, 193
Aerofoils 82, 84; *134*
Aerotowing 35, 101, 114, 128, 173–189; *175, 176, 178, 179, 184, 185, 187, 188*; holding correct position, 174–7; weaving from side to side, 177–81; the take-off, 181–2; releasing the tow rope, 182–3; tow rope break, 183–6; the wave off, 186–8; the 'I cannot release' signal, 189
Age 12–14
Aileron drag 38–40, 177, 180, 191; *39*
Ailerons 23, 35, 38, 43, 73, 84, 85, 140, 142, 145, 157, 174, 191, 192, 193; *14*
Aiming point technique 105–8, 113, 120; *107*
Airbrake gate 100
Airbrake operating lever 23, 36, 89–91, 194
Airbrake spring 99–100, 101
Airbrakes 35, 36, 45–6, 48, 89–101, 194, 196; *81, 83, 84, 90, 97, 104, 188*; use in landing, 57, 58, 66, 67, 70, 71, 103–4, 105, 133–4; sideslipping and, 77; lift spoilers, 78–80; wing, 80–2; trailing edge, 82–3; flaps compared with, 85–6; fuselage, 86; effect of, 89; operating the lever, 89–91; controlling the speed, 91; approach speeds, 91–6, 101; use while teaching landings of, 96–8; controlling the float, 94–5, 98; open at the wrong times, 98–101, 186–8; special advice for beginners on use of, 101; angles of approach and, 111–12, 121–2; open on tow, 186–8

Air sickness 27–8
Airspeed 193; *90, 94, 125, 126, 136, 137, 156, 162, 163, 167, 199*; stalling speed, 78, 79, 83, 85, 86, 87, 95, 138; control by airbrakes of, 89, 91; approach speeds, 96–7, 111–12, 128–9; danger of losing height and, 123–6, 134; relation between angle of attack and, 137; effects of wind on, 147–71 *passim*; ground speed and, 149–50; exchanging height for, 161; Yates effect, 123, 162, 198
Airspeed Indicator (A.S.I.) 23, 37, 49, 92, 133, 140
Alcohol, harmful effect of 19, 20
Altimeter 23, 115, 117
ASK 13 glider *83, 110*
ASW 15 glider 129; *83*
ASW 17 glider *83*
Approach 35–6, 37, 45, 46, 65, 66, 67, 68; *94, 104, 108, 109, 110, 112, 118, 120, 150*; final turn before, 43–4, 48, 95–6, 102; judging the height for, 60, 63; speeds, 91–6, 103, 110, 113, 119, 120, 193; controlling the float and, 98; planning of, 102–34; at other gliding sites, 103, 112; at hill sites, 103, 109, 110, 113; control of, 103–5; aiming point technique, 105–8, 120; 'play it safe' method of, 107, 109–10; undershoot and overshoot, 108, 110–11; angle of, 111–12; influence of launch site, 114; and weather, 114; and type of glider, 114–15; judging position of final turn, 116; and height of circuit, 116–17; height and distance method of positioning for, 117–19; and positioning by the angle,

119–22; joining the circuit planning for a landing, 122–3; never low and slow, 123–6; at integrated power flying and gliding sites, 127–9; preparing to land, 130–1; suggestions for beginners, 131–4; effects of wind on, 155–7; after tow-rope break, 184; by power pilots converting to gliding, 194; *see also* gliding angle, spoiling the; landings, help with the
Autorotation 138, 144

Backing of wind 154; *155*
Balloon flight 149
Ballooning 35, 45, 52, 56, 57, 58, 59, 64, 68, 69, 70–1, 76, 79, 95, 96–7, 101; *62, 97*
Banking 23, 25, 32, 35, 37–8, 39, 41, 157, 165–6, 177–8, 180, 191, 192, 193; *26, 39, 42, 132, 137*
Base leg 35, 48, 49, 50, 89, 91, 95, 103, 118, 120, 121, 123, 132, 133, 196; *47, 151*
BG 135 glider *83*
Big Dipper 26, 28; *28*
Blanik two-seater 83–4
Bocian glider 38
Brake paddles 80–1, 82
British Gliding Association 12, 16, 98, 200
Buffeting 175, 182; from airbrakes, 96; pre-stall, 96, 137, 142, 144

Cable breaks 35, 100, 150, 159; *see* also Tow ropes
Cable release knob 23
Capstan two-seater 99–100
Car launching 35, 114, 127–8, 159, 181, 195
Centre of gravity (C of G) 140, 145; *57, 74, 75*; position of main

wheel in relation to, 56, 73, 75, 181

Cessna aircraft 56

Chair-o-plane 29, 32; *29*

Changing perspective views 60–4; *61, 62*

Cherokee aircraft 56

Chief Flying Instructor 14, 149

Circling 131–2, 148, 150–1, 152; *148, 151*

Circuit 92, 114; *47, 50, 124*; planning the, 35, 46–50, 102, 103, 111, 118, 121, 133, 193, 195–6; judging the height for the, 116–17; angle for positioning final stage of, 119–20; joining circuit pattern for a landing, 122–3; at integrated power flying and gliding sites, 127–8

Cirrus glider 129; *83*

Citabria tug 174

'Clutching hand' effect 109, 113, 156; *113*

Cockpit checks 99, 188

Colds 20

Collisions 193–4

Condor aircraft 56

Confidence 34–5, 51, 52–3

Control column *see* Stick

Controls 23–5, 35, 36

Conversion tables 203

Cross-country flying 58, 112

Cub aircraft 56

Danger areas on gliding site *21*

Day-to-day fitness 19–22

Deafness 17

Disabilities 16–17

Downwind leg 48; *47*

Drogues *see* Tail parachutes

Duration flights 202

Elevator 23, 92, 96, 97, 174, 176; *14*

Elevator trim, trim lever 23, 78, 80, 90, 181; *79*

Eyesight 16, 17, 30–1

Falke Motor Glider 15

Fedération Aeronautique Internationale (FAI) 200, 201

First flights 23–33; nervousness, 14–15; sensations, 11, 25–8; controls, 23–4; changes in 'g' or loading, 28–32; sideslipping, 32–33

Float (before landing) 70, 72, 77, 89, 91, 93, 94–5, 98, 103–4, 110, 111–12, 119, 159; *94, 104*

Flying attitudes 23, 35, 37–8; *24, 106*; aiming point technique and, 105–8

Flying-on landing 54–5, 58; *55*

Fowler flaps 83

Fuselage airbrakes 80, 86

Geometric lock 81–2, 89, 91, 99–100; *81*

Glass fibre machines 82, 84

Glider, parts of *14*; handling on the ground, *18*

Gliding angle 78, 79, 90, 104, 110, *112, 120, 122, 150*; spoiling the, 77–88; sideslipping, 77–8; spoilers, 78–80; wing airbrakes, 80–2; trailing edge airbrakes, 82–3; flaps, 83–6; fuselage airbrakes, 86; tail parachutes or drogues, 86–8; judging angle of approach, 111–12; learning to recognise, 119–22; and wire frame training aid, 121

Gliding awards and records 200–2

Gliding clubs 11–12

Gravity ('g'), changes in, loading of, 28–32, 140; *28, 29*; *see also* Centre of gravity

Great Hucklow club 109

Ground loop 73, 75, 185

Ground run (in landing) 67, 72–6

Ground speed 149–50, 152; *150*

Grunau gliders 110, 115

Handling stage (in learning to glide), 35–6, 37–46

Hay fever 15–16

Health 15–16, 19–21

Hearing 30

Height *61, 62, 90, 124, 125, 126, 132, 162*; judging the, 58, 59–64, 68, 108, 115, 116–17; losing, 77, 89, 101, 111, 121–2, 123–6, 131–2, 134, 157, 159, 196–7; approach speeds and, 92, 93, 95; exchange of speed for, 161

Height and distance method of approach 116, 117–19; *118*

Height and weight (of pilots), 17, 19

Held-off landing, the hold-off 54–9, 65, 67, 70–2, 92, 96, 98, 105, 108;

55, *62, 67*; judging height for 61–4

Hill sites 103, 109, 110, 111, 113, 114, 157; *109, 113*

Holiday Courses 12

Inertia effect 73–5; *74, 75*

Instrument panel 23

Intelligence 15

K6 glider 121; *83*

K7 glider 38, 180

K8 glider 121; *110*

K13 glider 38

Kestrel glider 87; *83*

Knots 9; conversion table for, 203

Landings 35, 36–7, 43, 45; *55, 57 61, 62, 67, 97, 104, 150*; help with the, 54–76: 'flying on' and 'held-off' styles of, 54–9; judging the height, 59–64; learning to, 64–7 the round out, 68–70; the hold off 70–2; the ground run, 72–6; use of airbrakes while teaching, 96–8 planning the, 102–34 (*see also* Approach); preparing to, 130–1 effects of wind on, 149–50, 155–6 after tow-rope break, 184–5; by power pilots converting to gliding 190, 194–5

Lasham Gliding Centre 14, 128, 173

Lateral damping in normal flight *138*

Lateral instability in stalled flight *139*

Launching 35, 127–8, 150, 159; heights, 36, 114, 122; *see also* Aerotowing

Laws and Rules for Glider Pilots 200

Learning to glide 34–53: confidence, 34–5; handling stage, 35–6; planning and judgement, 36–7; advice and help at handling stage, 37–46; circuit planning stage, 46–50; practical problems in gliding instruction, 51–3

Lee waves 161; *160*

Lenticular clouds *160*

Levelling out *see* Round out

Libelle glider 129; *83*

Lift spoilers 78–80, 81, 82, 91; *79, 83*

London Gliding Club, Dunstable 114

Low tow position 174; *175*

Menstrual periods 20–1
Main wheel 74; position in relation to C of G, 56, 72, 73, 75; *57, 74, 75*
Model aircraft, effects of wind on 147, 161, 170–2; *171*
Motor gliders (for training) 11, 35, 65, 73, 119, 128, 183
Mushing 77, 105; *24*

National Gliding Associations/Aero Clubs 12, 200
Nervousness 14–15, 51
Never Exceed Speed (VNE) 80
Nimbus glider 87; *83*
Noise 92
Non-Aerobatic Category 19
Nose skid 54, 55, 72
Nose-wheel type of light aircraft 56–7, 59

Olympia glider 99–100, 173, 187
Overshooting 90, 92, 101, 104, 105, 106, 107, 108, 110–11, 113, 121, 178; *107, 108, 110*

'Pattern' speed 128
Phugoid 170, 171
Pilatus B4 glider 121; *14*
Pitching 23, 37, 135, 146; *24, 136*
Powered flying, power pilots 40; *127*; straight and level flight in, 44, 45; glider pilots converting to, 58–9; integrated gliding and, 127–129; effects of wind on, 157; conversion to glider flying of, 190–6: handling and need to use rudder, 190–1; accurate turns, 192–3; correct flying speeds, 193; collisions are lethal, 193–4; the approach, 194; landing, 194–5; planning the circuit, 195–6; running out of height, 196
Private Pilots' Licence 16

Rhonlercher glider *83*
Rogallo glider 9
Rolling *see* Banking
Round out (or levelling out) 60–1, 63, 66, 67, 68–70, 92, 96, 98, 103, 105, 108; *61, 67, 69*

Rubbing off the speed 72, 73
Rudder 23, 25, 32, 35, 38, 39, 41, 43, 73, 96, 180; *14, 27, 145*; use in spins of, 140, 142, 144–5; and on aerotow, 180, 181; and by power pilots converting to gliding, 190–2; *see also* Stick and rudder co-ordination
Rudder pedals 23, 38

Sailplanes 9
Scheibe Falke two-seater 194
Semi-Acrobatic Category 19
Shock absorption (in landing) 55, 56, 59, 71, 72
Sideslipping 77, 103, 105, 111, 112, 180, 192; *33, 78*; sensations of 32–3
Sideways drift 45, 55, 65, 150–1, 152; *153*
Sigma research glider 88
Skylark glider 187, 188
Slipped disc 15
Snatching 90–1, 142, 144, 177
Soaring 9, 83, 109, 114, 116, 119, 127, 128, 129, 131, 151, 158, 161, 167, 182, 193–4, 198; *169*; dynamic, 168–70
Solo flights 12, 51, 52–3, 157–9
Spins and recoveries 35, 92, 95, 100, 125; *141, 143, 145*; incipient, 138–40, 141, 144, 146; full, 139, 140–2; off steep turns, 142–4; practice, 144–6; *see also* Stalls
Spiral dives 140; *141*
Spring-loaded sealing cap 81–2; *81*
Stalls, stalling 31–2, 35, 77, 92, 93, 95, 96, 125, 135–8, 146, 157; *134, 136, 137, 139, 171*; in a turn, 138; caused by wind gradient, 157–9; of model aircraft, 170–1; *see also* Spins
Stalling speeds 78, 79, 83, 85, 86, 87, 95, 100, 138, 142, 153, 193, 194; *137, 139*
Steering tail wheel 73
Stick (or control column) 23, 25; *14, 26, 28*
Stick and rudder co-ordination 32, 36, 38–9, 43, 44, 45, 65, 66, 73, 75, 177, 180, 190–1; *39, 42*
Straight flight 44–5
Stretching the glide 93; *94*
Super Cub tug 174, 175

T21b glider 110, 114, 115; *83*
Tail draggers 56, 58, 59
Tail skid 55, 56, 73, 74
Tail parachutes (or drogues) 80, 86–8, 101, 188
Take off 61, 76, 155, 181–2
Thermal activity, thermals 43, 44, 114, 122, 129, 131, 152, 154, 161, 163–8, 171–2, 182, 194; *166*
Thermal bubbles 164–5; *164, 165*
Tiger Club 19
Touchdown 56, 57, 58, 71, 72, 73, 86, 98, 103, 104, 105; *67, 104, 150*; *see also* Landings
Tow rope *184, 185*; releasing of, 182–3; breaking of, 183–6; 'I cannot release' signal, 189
Trailing edge airbrakes 82–3; *83*
Tugs *see* Aerotowing
Turbulent rotor flow *160*
Turn and Slip Indicator 193
Turns 41–5; *40, 42, 132, 137, 145, 151, 158*; slipping and skidding in, 44, 96; control movements for, 41–3; final turn before approach, 43–4, 48, 95–6, 102, 103, 105, 111, 113, 114, 115, 116, 117, 119, 120, 121–2, 123, 133; stalling in, 138; spinning off, 142–4, 145; effects of wind on, 157, 166; by power pilots converting to gliding, 192–3
Tutor glider 110, 115

Undercarriage, variation in landing with different types of 56, 59; *57*
Undershooting 93, 101, 103, 106, 108, 109, 110–11, 115, 119, 155; *107, 108, 110*

Variometer 9, 23
Veering of wind 154; *155*
Vital Actions Check 99

Wave off 183, 186–8; *187*
Weather conditions 35, 144; *see also* Wind
Weathercocking effect 73, 74, 75; *74, 75*
Weaving on tow 177–81; *178*
Wheel brake 73, 74
Winch launching 35, 114, 127–8, 150, 159, 181, 195
Wind 49, 56, 57, 58, 114, 115, 119, 147–72; *74, 75, 84, 94, 109, 120,*

148, 150, 151, 153, 154, 155, 156, 158, 167, 169, 171; inertia and weathercocking effects in, 73–5; flaps v. airbrakes and, 85, 86; approach speeds and, 91–2, 93; effect on approach and landing of, 104; 'play it safe' method of approach and, 109–10; positioning by angles and, 120–1; changeability of, 131; flying in steady wind, 148–9; ground speed and airspeed and, 149–50; circling flight in strong wind, 150–1; flying across, 152; effects of variation in, 152–3; wind gradients near the ground, 154–60; surface obstruction, 161; stability in the air, 161; effect of changes in airspeed, 161–3; and of thermal activity, 163–8; dynamic soaring, 168–70; behaviour of model aircraft in, 170–2

Wind gradient 77, 91, 93, 101, 109, 119, 161, 167, 168, 171, 194; *154, 155, 156, 158, 167, 169*; near the ground, 154–60, 168; dynamic soaring and, 168–70

Wing airbrakes 80–2; *81, 83*

Wing flaps 58, 80, 83–6, 91; *83, 84*

Wire frame training aid 121; *122*

Wire launches 35

Women pilots 20–1, 201

Wycombe Air Park, Booker 129

Yates Effect 123, 162, 198; *163, 167, 199*

Yawing 25, 35, 38–41, 43, 140, 177, 180, 189, 192; *27*

Youth training schemes 52